MYTHS AND LEGENDS OF THE MEDIEVAL WORLD

To my wife, Alice

MYTHS AND LEGENDS OF THE MEDIEVAL WORLD

PAUL WATTS

PEN & SWORD
HISTORY
AN IMPRINT OF PEN & SWORD BOOKS LTD.
YORKSHIRE – PHILADELPHIA

First published in Great Britain in 2024 by
PEN AND SWORD HISTORY
An imprint of
Pen & Sword Books Ltd
Yorkshire – Philadelphia

ISBN 978 1 39905 681 6

A CIP catalogue record for this book is available from the British Library.

Typeset in Times New Roman 10.5/13 by
SJmagic DESIGN SERVICES, India.
Printed and bound in the UK by CPI Group (UK) Ltd.

Pen & Sword Books Limited incorporates the imprints of Atlas, Archaeology, Aviation, Discovery, Family History, Fiction, History, Maritime, Military, After the Battle, Military Classics, Politics, Select, Transport, True Crime, Air World, Frontline Publishing, Leo Cooper, Remember When, Seaforth Publishing, The Praetorian Press, Wharncliffe Local History, Wharncliffe Transport, Wharncliffe True Crime and White Owl.

For a complete list of Pen & Sword titles please contact
PEN & SWORD BOOKS LIMITED
George House, Units 12 & 13, Beevor Street, Off Pontefract Road,
Barnsley, South Yorkshire, S71 1HN, England
E-mail: enquiries@pen-and-sword.co.uk
Website: www.pen-and-sword.co.uk

or

PEN AND SWORD BOOKS
1950 Lawrence Rd, Havertown, PA 19083, USA
E-mail: uspen-and-sword@casematepublishers.com
Website: www.penandswordbooks.com

FSC www.fsc.org MIX Paper | Supporting responsible forestry FSC® C013604

Contents

Preface

We live in a world in which science and technology dominates and the future seems more likely to be predicted by AI than oracles. Yet, despite this, some of the most successful books and films of our time tell stories not of a digital future but of a medieval past. Such tales can be re-imaginings of old myths and folktales, like King Arthur or Robin Hood. Others are pure fantasy stories from writers like J.R.R. Tolkien or George R.R. Martin. Yet, even these, as their authors have testified, are inspired by older tales, rooted in our medieval history.

Medieval myths have been re-imagined and re-written many times over the centuries. Each generation has chosen its own way to depict Robin Hood, Camelot, or Lancelot. Such re-tellings adapt the stories to provide renewed relevance for the times. Artistic movements such as Romanticism, the Gothic Revival, and the Pre-Raphaelite brotherhood all chose to look back to the Middle Ages for inspiration. Each added their own twists and embellishments, sometimes making it hard to distinguish between the truly medieval and the Georgian or Victorian.

Our culture continues to be influenced by medievalism even now, drawing on the past to weave new stories, relevant for our day. Why is it that, in an age of fast paced technological change, our distant past continues to inspire and intrigue us? Perhaps there is something in our nature that makes us yearn for a simpler world of chivalric escapism, romanticism, and magic.

However, despite what we might like to believe, the passage of time has done much to obscure our medieval past. The myths and legends we inherited from those times are often filtered through the lens of medievalism. A long artistic tradition or re-imagining and re-inventing has transformed many of these tales. Sometimes that transformation has been so radical that the result would be almost unrecognisable to someone living in medieval times.

This book aims to peel away the layers of medievalism to reveal medieval myths in their original form and context. We all have our own ideas of Robin Hood; of who he was, when he lived and what he did. But what did someone alive in 1430 think? What did Robin Hood mean to them? Who did they think he was? When did they think he lived? What deeds and stories did they associate with him?

To truly appreciate the original story of Robin Hood requires two key things. Firstly, we must focus on the story as it was told at the time, understanding the different tales in circulation, and what medieval writers had to say about him. That much seems obvious.

However, we also require a second crucial ingredient. Originally, the earliest stories of Robin Hood were sung as ballads or seen performed as plays. These performances were witnessed in taverns, at banquets, at fairs or festivals as part of the general entertainment. This is a context we now lack. What was it really like to listen to a Robin Hood ballad at a summer fair in medieval England?

To understand these myths, we need to appreciate how they were experienced and received in the medieval world. A world very different from our own. Ours is a world of modern commerce, scientific progress, urban sprawl, industry, and technology. Their world was a largely rural society, heavily dependent on agriculture, governed by the rhythms of the natural world. A world in which a deep understanding of the seasons for sowing and harvesting was vital for life. A world in which the landscape and the environment often shaped how people lived, rather than the other way around. A world in which knowledge of science was limited and in which education and literacy was restricted to a small minority. Much of what we take for granted today was entirely unknown then.

Medieval society was structured very differently from our own. This, in turn, created a very different culture. Religion was a major part of daily life to a degree often difficult for us to appreciate. And medieval Christianity was quite different from Christianity as it is experienced in the modern world. For most committed modern-day Christians, bible study forms an important part of their faith. In the Middle Ages most Christians couldn't read. Even those who were able to read would need to have been very rich to afford a bible. Religious teaching, therefore, needed to be communicated to people in other ways.

Religious and supernatural experiences featured far more prominently in daily life. We are all familiar with stories concerning the Holy Grail, but we hear them in the context of our world. Ours is a time in which holy relics are widely regarded with skepticism, more fantasy than reality for most of us. Even many modern Christians are dubious about such things. Indeed, Reformation Protestantism explicitly denounced relics as unchristian. However, in the Middle Ages most people believed relics possessed genuine spiritual potency, acting as a conduit through which divine power could, and did, flow. It is hard for us to imagine what this must have felt like. Their world was one in which relics, visions, miracles, prophecies, and superstitious beliefs of all kinds were far more than just abstract concepts. To most people, they were part of an accepted reality; a reality in which the boundaries between the supernatural and material world were far from clear. Think, then, how differently a story about a Holy Grail would have been experienced in such a world.

The Middle Ages covers a long period of history and encompasses a wide variety of different cultures. Different cultures all have their own rich traditions of mythology upon which to draw. If we consider the mythology of Persia, India, or Russia, we immediately encounter very different traditions from those of Western Europe. All are equally rich and all worthy of study. Indeed, each is easily worthy of their own book. To cover them all would be a very significant undertaking. Attempting to cover so many different traditions within a single volume would run the risk of superficiality.

Another consideration is the fact that the Middle Ages technically begins with the collapse of the Roman Empire in 476 AD and runs through to the very end of the fifteenth century. That's an entire millennium! The world at the start of this period was a radically different place from the world by the end. Throughout this period, mythology continued to evolve, new stories were added, old stories were changed, pagan stories gave way to Christian stories.

It makes sense, therefore, to focus mainly (albeit not exclusively) on a particular culture within a more specific timeframe. For this reason, we'll focus our enquiry mainly on the world of the Plantagenets and their Lancastrian and Yorkist cadet branches. The Plantagenet dynasty was founded when Henry II became king of England in 1154. His dynasty would endure for most of the period known as the high and late Middle Ages. Technically, the last true Plantagenet king was Richard II, who died early in 1400. However, he was succeeded by his Lancastrian and Yorkist cousins who continued to rule England until the death Richard III in 1485.

The heart of the Plantagenet realm was undoubtedly the kingdom of England. However, it also encompassed Wales (from the time of Edward I) and significant parts of Ireland. The Plantagenet kings even attempted to extend their reign to Scotland but never succeeded in doing so. So, whilst there was a significant cultural exchange between Scotland and England over the period, Scotland remained outside the Plantagenet orbit.

It is also important to be aware that significant parts of France (most notably Gascony) were ruled by the Plantagenets. This, and the fact that the Plantagenets themselves were originally a French family, led to the evolution of many shared myths and traditions. This was especially true amongst the Plantagenet dynasty's social elite, whose first language remained French for most of the Middle Ages.

More broadly, the Plantagenet kingdom formed part of a Western European culture that shared a common Catholic faith. Many religiously inspired myths and supernatural beliefs were widely shared across Catholic Christendom. This went far beyond the religious teachings found in the Bible. How people regarded saints, angels, demons, miracles, religious visions, prophecies, relics, and the stories associated with them was by no means unique to the Plantagenet realm. These beliefs formed part of a shared pan-Western-European cultural experience.

Our enquiry will concentrate on how mythology was transmitted and understood in medieval times, not on how later writers chose to interpret it. Many other writers have explored the evolution of such things as Arthurian legend through history in great depth. This is an interesting and worthy exercise, as it illustrates how different periods engage with these stories in different ways. Of course, whilst such an approach has its merits, it can make it difficult to focus in any depth on how these stories were understood in any one period. By keeping the discussion of later times to a minimum, we'll be able to focus in much greater depth on the medieval period itself.

Theories concerning the historic 'reality' behind certain myths (e.g., King Arthur or Robin Hood) often form a central theme in other books. This approach tends to adopt a 'detective story' style, setting out the evidence for the existence of characters like King Arthur. Attempting to pin down who such people as Arthur or Robin 'really were' is a well-trodden path. However, in this case our primary focus will be on the stories themselves and the cultural significance they held for people living at the time. The question as to the historic truth behind such tales will be touched on but is necessarily a secondary focus here.

The aim here is to provide the reader with a real sense of what it was like to live in the Middle Ages, actively engaging with its myths, magic, and superstitions. I'll aim to paint a picture of how these stories helped medieval people make sense of their world, conveyed cultural values and, of course, entertained.

The Plantagenet World

What was it like to live in England in Plantagenet times?

The truth is that the world, society, and culture we'd experience would seem very alien. Perhaps the first and most obvious difference between our world and theirs would be landscape itself. The modern world is incredibly urbanised and crowded. England had a population of 57 million in the mid-2020s, around ten times the size of the population in the 1320s. Not only was the country more sparsely populated, it was also more rural. Urban centres occupied only a tiny proportion of the landscape.

Such cities as there were, were far smaller than any modern city. The largest city in England, by a considerable margin, was London, with a population of just over 40,000. That's smaller than most English towns today. But for medieval England, it was enormous, approaching four times the size of any other English city. Aside from London, there were only two other urban centres that could boast populations of more than 10,000 (York and Bristol). Some of the largest modern English cities such as Birmingham and Manchester were insignificant back in the 1320s, not even ranking amongst the thirty largest conurbations.[1]

If you were to visit a typical English village, you'd find that most of the villagers would have no formal education. It would be quite surprising if any of them could read and truly astonishing if there was even a single book in any of their cottages. Education for these common folk involved learning about the seasons, when to plant and when to harvest, how to keep chickens safe from foxes, how to mend fences, how to tend livestock, how to keep warm in bad weather. Most villagers would have spent much of their lives outside, working the land around them from the age of 7. Understanding the land is the only form of education that really mattered.

For most of the Middle Ages, the typical villager would have been a humble villein, on pretty much the lowest rung of the social ladder. Villeins were tied to the land they tended and bound to serve the local lord. They had a duty to help till the lord's land and, in return, they were granted the right to rent their own strips of farmland. But the land they farmed and the cottages they lived in all formed part and parcel of the manorial estate. They were simply the lord's tenants, and literally tied to their village by law. They are not free to leave to find work elsewhere without their lord's permission. Indeed, if he so chose, their lord could even dictate to them whom they should marry. If a woman became a widow, it is likely that the lord would command her to remarry after a time, so that her tenancy remained productive. If she did not choose a husband for herself, her lord might choose one for her.

But not everyone living in the villages were villeins, some were husbandmen. A poorer husbandman might not appear to be any better off than a typical villein but there was one critical difference. The husbandman was a freeman. He was free to marry whoever he chose. He was free to leave the village whenever he chose. He owed the lord no service of labour. Of course, he still rented his home and his land from the same lord but the distinction between his status and that of his villein neighbours was an important one.

Most villages had a parish church either in the village itself or nearby. It may not be a grand building compared to the great churches in cities and towns but, for the villagers, it would have been a most impressive sight. The squat stone towers of rural medieval churches may not seem that impressive today but, in their time, they would often have been one of the most imposing structures in the village.

Inside, such churches might be decorated with impressive carvings and have colourful stained-glass windows. These would truly have been things of wonder for people living their lives in simple cob cottages. The church was the centre of most people's spiritual and supernatural world. Indeed, most medieval folk would attend their local church regularly. The more pious attended more than one day a week and certainly every Sunday. The largest attendances would be at Easter, Christmas, Pentecost, and for the dedication festival of the local church (i.e. on the anniversary of its foundation).[2] On these occasions, the vast majority of people would attend. Here they might hear marvellous stories of miracles, of Christ, Noah, and Abraham, and of the fantastic deeds of saints and martyrs.

However, were you to search any of these little churches for a bible you probably wouldn't find one. You would find liturgical books, that contained extracts from the Bible to be sung or read during services. You would also be likely to find a salter containing the Psalms. You might even find a copy of one of the gospels if you were lucky. A complete bible was a very expensive and rare book. Each one was handmade, taking a skilled scribe over a year to copy. That scribe would be a highly skilled copyist, even if (as might well be the case), he was not even able to read the work he was copying. Whether or not the scribe could read, a year's worth of their skilled labour would still need to be paid for, before you even include the expensive materials used in producing a bible. Copies of the Latin Vulgate Bible would gradually become more common as the Middle Ages wore on. However, they were never widely available until after the invention of the printing press at the end of the Middle Ages.

Everywhere you went in medieval England, the power and importance of the church would have been clearly in evidence. Most of the largest and most spectacular buildings were churches and cathedrals. In most cities, such buildings would dominate the skyline. In some parts of the kingdom, large abbeys owned substantial tracts of land. Here the local villeins and husbandmen were tenants of the abbey rather than any secular lord. Their lord was effectively the local abbot. The largest abbeys in the country, such as at Glastonbury and Westminster, were incredibly wealthy, commanding an annual income of some £2,000-£3,000 in the fourteenth century.[3] This was more than many barons and earls made in a year. The abbots of these prestigious abbeys held considerable power, and were even entitled to a permanent seat in parliament.

If we could travel back to medieval times, we'd be surprised at the number of people we'd meet who had some association or other with the church. Of course, there was the regular clergy; the priesthood that ministered to the public in churches and cathedrals. However, in addition to these there were also the monastic orders (Benedictines, Cluniacs, Cistercians, and Carthusians), Augustinian Canons, military orders (Hospitallers and, before 1308, Templars), and the mendicant orders (itinerant friars who travel the country, preaching).

By the middle of the fourteenth century there were around 1,000 monasteries, nunneries, and friaries in England. If we total up all the clergy, monks, nuns, military orders, friars, religious hermits, and religious scholars living in England, we'd be looking at as many as 30,000 men and women. As many as one in every fifty adult men was a member of the clergy or a religious order.[4]

Located not too far from most villages would have been another large building. This one may not have been fortified like a castle, and it may or may not have been made of stone, but it would have been a grand hall, nonetheless. This was the local manor, usually set apart from the rest of the village, with its own fields. This was the home of the local lord, and everyone farming the surrounding lands would be his tenants. The administration of local village affairs was centred on the manor. Here the lord and his officers administered everything from rent collection to taxes, petty fines, the execution of wills, and even local justice.

Despite its grand appearance and the obvious power wielded by its owner, the local lord or lady of the manor was usually not a member of the nobility. A typical manorial lord would most likely be a gentleman, an esquire, or perhaps even a knight. But, in the overall scheme of things, he would still count as a commoner if he lacked a noble title. Some manorial estates would be run by women. The queen administered her own estates, separate from her husband. But, here again, she and other powerful noblewomen were the exception. A more typical lady of the manor would have been a member of the gentry, not the nobility. You might also be surprised to learn that manorial lords and ladies were also tenants. They were granted the lordship of their lands by their own liege lord – perhaps a local earl or maybe a duke.

It was the nobility, rather than the manorial lords, who were the tenants in chief. Yes, even the nobility were tenants of a sort. But they were tenants in chief because they held the title for their lands directly from the king. The nobility represented a small and highly elite group of families. Throughout England, in the early fourteenth century, there are only around 50-80 dukes, earls, and barons who collectively constituted the secular lords of the land.[5]

There was considerable variation amongst the gentry who sat immediately below the nobility on the social ladder. Some held large tracts of land, acquired considerable wealth, and might even have acquired a knighthood. Such an influential fellow might even have found himself serving a term or two as a member of parliament in the Commons. However, a lowlier member of the gentry would lack a knighthood, live in a humbler manor house, and be unlikely to ever wield any significant political power. Across fourteenth century England, there were around 11,000 esquires and gentlemen of whom only around 1,000 were knights.

Being a member of the gentry might have brought you within the orbit of court circles. Unlike the other inhabitants of the village, most members of the gentry were literate. They, along with their relatives, their clerks, and the local priest, were probably the only people in their locality who could read and write. If they were so inclined, and rich enough, they might even own a small collection of books. However, such books were unlikely to be in English. They were far more likely to be written in French or Latin. Indeed, when mixing with their peers and certainly if they visited court, the ruling classes spoke French rather than English for much of the Middle Ages. Similarly, the manorial inventories, official documents, and letters held in most manors were more likely to be written in French or Latin than English. This only began to change during the fourteenth century, as written vernacular English slowly supplanted Latin and French as the language of choice.

Unlike the villeins and husbandmen in the fields, manorial lords and ladies received a formal education. This might have included attendance at a university if they were a man. If they were a woman, they would often receive an education at a nunnery. Many would study the Trivium (grammar, rhetoric, and logic) and the Quadrivium (arithmetic, music, astronomy, and more advanced logic). University education was heavily influenced by Roman methods, dating back to classical antiquity. It required the study of Latin texts, including classical myths and legends. The study of astrology was interwoven with astronomy and geometry. To the medieval mind, this eclectic mix of geometry, music, astronomy, and astrology were all inter-connected. All working together to create a balanced universal harmony.

This advanced form of education was only available to the social elite and, even then, university level education was only for men. In any one year, only a few hundred people in the entire realm would attend a university.

The local manorial lords would have been served by freemen of a higher class than the local husbandmen and villeins. These people were the yeomanry. Some held important jobs that required them to be literate, such as serving as their lord's principal clerk and accountant. Others held more menial roles, such as looking after the lord's hunting dogs, managing their stables, or serving as a gamekeeper on his lands. Some would simply be employed as messengers and general errand runners. Some might have performed a more military role, helping to recruit and organise the lord's men in times of war.

As the Middle Ages wore on, some of the wealthier members of the yeomanry even became landowners, holding a freehold tenancy, farmed by labourers in their own employ. Others might have been poorer, no wealthier than many of the common husbandmen. It was from the yeoman class that the archers of Crécy and Agincourt were mostly recruited.

Although medieval society appears to have been very ordered and certainly governed by strict hierarchical structures, this did not mean that it was especially law abiding. People travelling on the road would almost always be armed for their own protection, usually with swords if they could afford them. Violent highway robbery and brigandage was a very real threat.

In the towns and cities, brawls and drunken fights were common. Many such incidents passed without any intervention from local law enforcement. Violent crime was an offence but was not taken as seriously as stealing something valuable. If you attacked someone with a sword and wounded them, it would be treated very seriously in our day. However, in medieval Worcester, for example, it was punishable by confiscation of the weapon and a fine of 6 shillings and 8 pence. That's quite a hefty fine (just over a month's wages for a carpenter). However, the same fine applied for selling ale without proper signage.[6]

Violence was more visible and more accepted than in our times. Children, animals, and women were regularly beaten to discipline them. In the absence of death or permanent injury, this was considered perfectly acceptable behaviour. Bear baiting and cock fighting were popular pastimes enjoyed by women as well as men. Indeed, cockfighting was considered a rather fun child's game. Cruel practical jokes resulting in minor physical injuries were generally considered hilarious rather than anti-social. In short, violence was normalised.

This was also a society in which war and armed conflict was common and there were quite a few men walking around carrying battle scars to prove it. The early Middle Ages had been a time of exceptional violence; England had been subjected to savage Viking raids and a Norman invasion that was no less violent. During the eleventh century, Norman knights had an extremely aggressive and bellicose reputation. In addition to seizing the English throne, other Normans invaded and carved out a fiefdom for themselves in southern Italy. Ambitious Normans serving as mercenaries for Byzantium even carved out a small kingdom for themselves in northern Turkey.

The Norman knight of the eleventh century was typically a violent, heavily armed thug, ambitious to forge a personal fiefdom for himself by force of arms. Looting, pillaging, and rape were common practices.

To channel the energies and aspirations of such violent and ambitious men, a culture of chivalry gradually emerged. Chivalry offered a set of codes of behaviour aimed at tempering the more brutal and unrestrained instincts of power-hungry, aggressive, knights. It was a code that made violence respectable but which, at the same time, attempted to channel, regulate, and restrain its more chaotic excesses.

The chivalric code evolved in the twelfth century, during the period when the Plantagenets came to power. Status and respect for a knight increasingly depended on the degree to which his peers felt he lived up to this code. First and foremost, he had to be brave and skilled in war but, crucially, he also had to observe a code of honour. A perfect knight was pious and a staunch defender of the church. He behaved courteously and respectfully towards ladies of rank. He observed his feudal duties both to his king and to his own villeins and tenants. And he always kept his oaths. Or, at least, that was the theory.

There can be no better embodiment of the chivalric ideal than the tournament. However, this seemingly refined and chivalrous affair began life as little more than a violent and often fatal battle practice. Even as late as the thirteenth century, tournaments frequently featured the *behourd* – an early form of jousting. The behourd was essentially a massed melee with few rules, fought by a group of knights either on horseback or foot. Often, participants would divide into two teams or, sometimes, it would just be a free-for-all. The aim was usually to defeat a rival knight in combat and hold him for ransom. However, fights to the death in these mini battles were common. In 1241, eighty knights were killed in a single tournament.[7] Clearly, such carnage in the name of sport had to be reined in.

By the fourteenth century, jousting had acquired many new chivalric rules. The savage behourds of past centuries had become a rarity. After this time tournaments were more refined, civilised affairs. Now knights could joust with capped lances to limit the risk of serious injury or death (although this still happened). Formal tilts between individual knights replaced the brutality of the old free-for-all melees.

Despite such refinements, violence amongst the social elite remained pervasive throughout the later Middle Ages. It simply acquired an increasing number of chivalric rules that allowed it to be presented as civilised and, above all, honourable.

Nevertheless, it is important to remember that the chivalric code was for knights and nobles. Humble villeins and husbandmen were not part of this world. A knight was expected to treat a high-born lady honourably and respectfully, observing chivalric rules in his dealings with her. He was under no such compulsion when it came to low-born women. In times of war, farmers' daughters in enemy lands were often raped for sport without attracting any dishonour at all.

If you spent any time living in medieval society, you'd become painfully aware of the subordinate role played by women. A man, whether father or husband, was master and legal owner of the household. His wife legally owned nothing and was subject to his will and authority. He was free to beat her as often as he pleased. Provided he inflicted no permanent injury, no amount of physical violence was considered excessive.

The medieval world was certainly not an easy time in which to be a woman. You had limited rights and few legal protections. Nevertheless, if a man forced himself on a woman, this was still considered rape in medieval law. However, she first needed to prove it. If the woman concerned became pregnant after being raped, this was taken as conclusive evidence of consent. It was widely accepted that a woman could not become pregnant unless she had enjoyed, and therefore, consented to sex.

The patriarchal nature of medieval society was evident everywhere. All senior political and clerical offices in England were held by men. Even a queen had quite limited official political power. Her role was often confined to playing hostess at social events, pleading with the king for mercy on behalf of criminals, and the patronage of certain charitable and religious causes. Only if her husband was away at war or business, might she get to wield real power as a regent in his absence.

However, despite such limitations, women could and did play an active role in society. Most women living in the village had to work in the fields alongside their menfolk or work full time at spinning and weaving. There was no such thing as a stay-at-home housewife for ordinary people in the Middle Ages. Wealthier women actively managed their households whilst their husbands were away.

A key source of information on life in the late Middle Ages comes from a collection of letters dating back to the fifteenth century known as the Paston letters. The Paston family were gentry who lived in Norfolk and their letters provide us with a uniquely detailed insight into their life and times. The Paston correspondence covers everything from their views on politics, their business interests, leisure pursuits, and domestic lives. Margaret Paston emerges from this collection as a woman with considerable personal agency. Her correspondence shows that she frequently conducted local business transactions. She concluded business negotiations and arranged important contracts on her husband's behalf without consulting him. She wrote to her husband only to inform him of the decisions she had taken. It is quite clear that she had a free hand, and her husband was more than happy to trust her judgement.

Later in the fifteenth century, Queen Margaret of Anjou demonstrated the full practical extent of female power. Her example showed it was perfectly possible for a strong and intelligent woman to command men, even if she lacked any official executive power to do so. She was, of course, vilified as a result but there is no denying the power she came to wield.

Indeed, not everything we might think we know about medieval women is true. Women happily attended and enjoyed watching blood sports like bear baiting or jousting. Wealthier women actively participated in hunting just as frequently as their men. Margaret of Anjou hunted regularly, chasing down deer and shooting them herself.[8]

Women from the nobility and gentry would often receive enough of an education to be able to read and write. Since elite women often needed to manage their household accounts, they were also often numerate. However, they would not have had access to the same advanced university education as their menfolk.

Of course, there were significant limitations to the knowledge of even the best educated members of the social elite.

The true causes of sickness and disease, let alone the cures, were largely unknown. The Black Death of the mid-fourteenth century was viewed very much in apocalyptic terms. Some even feared that no one would survive it given the horrendous death toll.[9] Both its causes and its treatment were a scientific mystery. For many people, all that could be done was to pray for God's mercy or, perhaps, go on pilgrimage to seek the intercession of a saint. Disease was even seen as a test of faith sent by God. It, therefore, seemed obvious that the cure would need to be a spiritual one.

Some cures and treatments were incredulous from our perspective. One physician believed he could predict whether someone would live or die depending on whether there was an even or odd number of letters in their name. Good luck with that in an age where there were no agreed rules for spelling! Some hospitals kept people with different infectious diseases together in the same bed, not understanding that infection could spread between them.

Leeching and bleeding of patients was a common treatment. However, some believed that the ideal time for bleeding patients should be determined by horoscopes and that bleeding them at the wrong time could be harmful. Indeed, the best times for harvesting healing herbs or taking healing remedies was often deemed to depend on astrological conditions.[10]

All that said, people in the Middle Ages did have some rudimentary knowledge of disease. People avoided contact with lepers and those struck down by the Black Death. Indeed, when the Black Death hit, many of the wealthy fled from cities to the relative isolation of their country residences. This shows they at least had an appreciation of the infectious nature of these diseases.

How people think about their world, what they value, and the kind of stories that appeal to them is partly a product of knowledge. What you know about your world, about how things work and why things are as they are, informs your perspective on everything.

Of course, from our perspective, people living in medieval times had quite limited knowledge of the world around them. The causes of many natural phenomena were very poorly understood. Droughts, famines, plague, and other natural disasters could not easily be accounted for in any complete scientific sense. When such events caused hardship and death, how then could you rationalise it?

For many, of course, it could only really be explained as the will of God. Perhaps such disasters were punishment for men's sins? After all, God had punished mankind once before with a great flood. Perhaps it might have been explained in terms imagined to have been scientific, but which today would be regarded as pure superstition. Some of the best educated people in medieval Europe genuinely saw astrology as a science. Natural disasters could perhaps be explained by means of an unfavourable alignment of the stars.

Sometimes when faced with disaster or disease, the only thing many people could think to do was pray, or perhaps cast a protective spell or seek guidance from a horoscope. This may seem like a triumph of faith or superstition over scientific reality. However, in the absence of a scientific explanation, faith is often the only source of hope. This is the medieval world of Plantagenet England, a place and time very different from our own.

The ability to tell myth from history, or superstition from science is understandably difficult in a world where scientific knowledge is limited. Even more so if you happen to have no formal education. The power and ubiquity of the medieval church meant that most people happily accepted tales of miracles, visions, prophecies, and holy relics as unquestioned facts. Having accepted this, it is not hard to imagine how easy it was for people to take other myths and legends equally seriously. Often, the boundary between history and myth, or science and magic, was quite blurred.

Written knowledge and learning were the preserve of the upper echelons of society. These people were usually well educated in such things as classical mythology, Arthurian lore, and the wonderous deeds and miracles of saints.

However, as you may have gathered, transmission of any knowledge in written form was simply not an option for the majority. Most people were, therefore, entirely reliant on ballads, art, plays, rhymes, sermons, and verbal storytelling. That said, the only record we have of medieval myths, legends, and folk belief is what survives in written form. Sometimes, of course, this is a record of older, oral traditions. Nevertheless, we cannot help but wonder how much of the rich medieval oral storytelling tradition is now lost to us. Unfortunately, what survives in the written record is, inevitably, largely a reflection of what the literate elite deemed to be worth recording.

The folklore of the illiterate majority was poorly recorded. Poor commoners may not have been formally educated but mythology was still important to them. For them, their stories were stories shared over a jar of ale, heard preached from a parish pulpit, seen staged in a play, or heard performed in a minstrel's ballad. The earliest tales of Robin Hood were of this sort. We know they were popular with the commonfolk and yet only a few written versions of these stories survive that can be firmly dated to the medieval period. This is almost certainly because the literate elite (especially the clergy) viewed such stories disapprovingly and were, therefore, reluctant to record them.

In exploring medieval mythology it makes sense to start at the beginning. The Plantagenet world inherited a significant number of beliefs and stories from earlier times. These served as a foundation for what came later. Themes from old tales were re-used or served to inspire new stories. Old stories were re-imagined and embellished for a medieval audience. There is no avoiding the powerful influence of the legacy inherited from the old pagan world.

The Legacy of Classical Antiquity

Western Europe had, until the fifth century, been part of the Roman world. Three and a half centuries of Romanisation had brought classical learning and, with it, classical mythology to the Britons.

But classical mythology was not the only legacy from Roman times. Tales and stories from a Celtic past also formed part of the mythological milieu inherited by the Plantagenet realm. In the same manner, the pagan Anglo-Saxons and Vikings brought their own traditions of storytelling with them across the sea to the British Isles in the early Middle Ages. The mythology of the Plantagenet world was, therefore, shaped by a variety of multi-cultural influences. These were blended with new Christian beliefs and re-imagined to create a new, medieval, mythology.

Medieval people looked back to classical antiquity with no small degree of nostalgic admiration. None of the Western medieval kingdoms could compare in terms of longevity, wealth, or power to ancient Rome. Everything about the classical world appeared larger, grander, and more magnificent. Learning about great leaders like Caesar or Alexander the Great formed a key part of the education of the medieval elite. Likewise, stories of Greek heroes like Hercules, Jason, or Achilles were greatly admired in a culture that valued valour and acts of heroism so highly.

During the late eighth century, Charlemagne established an empire that encompassed France, the Low Countries, Switzerland, northern Italy, and much of Germany. Charlemagne, as it turned out, took his duties as emperor very seriously. One area he took a close personal interest in was spiritual wellbeing of his subjects. However, Christianity in Charlemagne's empire had a few problems that needed addressing. The first was that Western Europe did not really use Greek (the lingua-franca of the Eastern Empire). This was a problem because a significant volume of religious writing was only available in Greek.

Another problem was that the Latin works created and copied after the fall of Rome were of a very mixed quality. Most were littered with translation errors. Many used different forms of pidgin Latin that were far from universally readable, or worse, open to confusing misinterpretation.

Charlemagne determined to put this to right. So, in 789 he charged the Western church with implementing a rigorous programme of scholarship known as *correctio*. Religious writings, rulings, and points of doctrine were collated; contradictions and mistranslations corrected; and a more coherent body of up-to-date scholarship created. And, all in grammatically correct classical Latin.

However, this process had an interesting, unintended consequence. These scholars didn't just limit themselves to religious works. They also created new copies of Latin works unrelated to religion. They did this partly to improve and refine their working knowledge of Latin and partly through sheer scholastic curiosity. Thanks to *correctio*, many new Latin copies of works covering classical myths and legends were produced.[1] The movement also cemented Latin's role as the written lingua-franca of Western Europe. Anyone receiving any kind of formal education would study it. And, to learn it, they would study religious works, old Roman texts dealing with grammar and rhetoric and, of course, classical mythology. Thus, the stories medieval scholars became most familiar with were usually the Roman versions of classical myths. This was simply because these texts were more readily available in Latin (as opposed to the more obscure and inaccessible Greek).

The appeal of these stories was twofold. Firstly, they served a very practical function by helping the reader to improve their Latin. Most official documents and records were in Latin, so the ability to read it was a very important skill for anyone wielding economic or political power. Knowledge of classical literature, therefore, identified you as well educated. This was an important way of commanding respect when in the company of the social elite. Henry IV of England, for example, was a keen scholar.[2] He was no doubt impressed by people able to display a sound knowledge of the classical world. Conversely, ignorance of such matters could easily make a bad impression with such a king.

Secondly, these stories became popular because classical mythology harkened back to more glorious times. The Romans and Greeks had built grand monumental stone structures like the Colosseum, the Pantheon, and Hadrian's Wall. Such feats of engineering were beyond most medieval kingdoms. When work began on Old London Bridge in 1176, it was literally the first stone bridge to have been constructed in England since Roman times. Before the fourteenth century, most buildings in English cities were still being built from wood. Imagine how medieval lords would have marvelled at the ancient Romans, capable of building entire cities out of stone.

Aside from their technological achievements, the old Roman Empire also represented the time and place in which Christianity had been born. It had been thanks to the influence of Rome that, in time, Christianity had spread across

Europe. Antiquity, then, was widely regarded as a lost golden age. A time of great civilisations and great deeds. Deeds that men living in medieval times could only dream of achieving. Julius Caesar and Alexander the Great had enjoyed spectacular military success and won glory and honour on a monumental scale. Virtually all medieval rulers greatly desired to emulate their example. It is, therefore, hardly surprising to find that they were hero worshipped and widely studied. For the same reasons, mythical tales concerning the heroic deeds of the Trojan wars, Jason, Hercules, and other Greek heroes were a source of considerable fascination and inspiration for a medieval audience.

The medieval versions of these myths nevertheless differed in several respects from the versions we are most familiar with today. Modern students of the legend of the Troy are most likely to be familiar with it via Homer's *Iliad* and *Odyssey*. These, of course, are the original Greek versions of these tales. However, for the medieval scholar, approaching these stories via Latin rather than Greek, they were far more likely to be familiar with later Roman versions of the story. Three classical works, above all, had a major influence on how classical mythology was viewed in the Middle Ages. The first was Ovid's *Metamorphoses*.

Metamorphoses is a truly epic work, spanning no fewer than fifteen books. It aims to provide a complete panoramic view of classical mythology and history, starting at the very dawn of time and ending with the death of Julius Caesar. Many of the famous tales from classical mythology can be found within it. Creation stories, stories about the gods, and tales of heroes such as Jason, Perseus, Theseus, Icarus, and Hercules are all there. So, just by reading this one work, it is possible to obtain a good basic knowledge of a great many classical myths.

However, Ovid did more than simply compile old stories and re-tell them within a single integrated narrative. He placed his own unique stamp on the re-telling. And this he achieves by weaving these tales together with an over-arching theme of 'Metamorphoses'. Ovid announces this theme in the opening lines of his first book.[3] His stories, therefore, feature mystical transformations throughout. Humans are transformed into animals, objects, or even stars. Gods adopt different forms to seduce mortal lovers, creatures change genders, and objects change colour. Sometimes the change comes violently, other times tragically. His work features violence, passion, comedy, and tragedy. Ovid's bizarre tales of mystical transformations have been popular for centuries and clearly held a strong appeal for the medieval mind.

The second major classical contribution to medieval mythology came from Virgil's *Aeneid*. Originally produced as a piece of Augustan propaganda, it was aimed at glorifying Rome's mythical connection with Troy. It focuses on the Trojan Prince Aeneas, no more than a minor character in Homer's stories, and is set in the immediate aftermath of the war.

Virgil tells us how Aeneas flees the ruin of Troy, wandering the seas, looking for a new land for Trojan refugees to settle. Initially, he comes to Carthage and has a passionate love affair with Dido, the city's exotic queen. However, it is not the will of the gods for the Trojans to find a home in Carthage. And so, Aeneas departs much to the despair of Dido, who becomes so distraught that she kills herself. Aeneas then travels to Italy where he seeks to marry Lavinia, the daughter of a local king, to secure his dynasty and find a permanent home for his people. Unfortunately, a rival local lord, Turnus, also seeks Lavinia's hand, resulting in war. Finally, Aeneas triumphs and successfully founds his dynasty. It is a dynasty destined for greatness since his descendants, Romulus, and Remus, are the founders of Rome.

It is the *Aeneid* that serves as the inspiration for an astonishing claim made in the ninth-century British work *Historia Brittonum*, attributed to the Welsh monk, Nennius. According to *Historia*, in ancient times, Britain itself had been founded by a descendant of Aeneas (a Roman consul by the name of Brutus). This demonstrated a prestigious connection between Britain and Rome and, through Aeneas, with fabled Troy. In fact, *Historia* goes even further, claiming that Aeneas himself had ultimately descended from Noah![4]

Historia reflects an intriguing example of an early medieval attempt to demonstrate a connection with a grander Roman and Trojan past. It also seeks to construct a biblical heritage for the Britons. Association with Rome and legendary Troy demonstrates an illustrious and ancient lineage and offers an important form of cultural validation. We see the same phenomena in the dynastic claims of early Anglo-Saxon kings. However, these pagan kings asserted their legitimacy by claiming descent from the god Woden.[5]

The third work we need to consider is less well-known in modern times. This is the epic story of the *Thebaid* by Statius. It would serve as an inspiration for several important medieval writers, including Dante and Chaucer.[6] The *Thebaid* is a story of mythical Thebes. It opens just after the tragic disgrace and exile of the old king, Oedipus. In his place, the rule of Thebes passes to his two sons Eteocles and Polynices. In the initial instance, the two brothers agree to share the throne between them. Of course, such a precarious arrangement doesn't last. The two fall out and Polynices is exiled but, undeterred, draws together an alliance of seven warlords to overthrow his brother and reclaim his birth right. This is the famous 'seven against Thebes'. The ensuing war ends in tragedy (as Greek stories often do) when the two brothers slay each other in single combat.

After the war, Creon becomes king of Thebes and, infamously, refuses to allow the wives of the invading army to bury their dead husbands. As a result, the women go to Athens and ask King Theseus (of Theseus and the minotaur fame) for aid. Theseus then overthrows Creon, which opens the way for the dead to finally be laid to rest.

Whilst Latin readers had increased access to these old stories after *correctio*, they, nevertheless, remained inaccessible to most people. The Latin literate section of society was limited to the scholastic members of the clergy, the nobility, and some members of the affluent gentry. No versions of these stories were available in living languages such as French, let alone English, before the late twelfth century.

Classical mythology, therefore, remained the preserve of a small elite during the pre-Plantagenet period of the Middle Ages. Outside of this elite there was likely to have been some awareness of these stories, but it would have been second or third hand. Classical mythology, as inherited from Rome, had no strong tradition of oral transmission since it had always been primarily transmitted through the written word. So, any knowledge people had of these stories, outside of the educated elite, was likely to have been patchy and superficial.

This raises the question of the extent to which many people were able to make distinctions between myth and history. If you had heard second hand stories of the deeds of Alexander and of Aeneas, would you necessarily have seen one as any more or less historic than the other? For poorly educated people living in the Middle Ages (i.e., the great majority), drawing such a distinction must have been difficult.

So how did people interpret these myths and stories?

Some of the best educated people undoubtedly regarded these myths in the same way as many of us view them today. That is to say that they were seen precisely as mythical stories, possibly containing some historic truth but potentially no more than myth. Many felt these tales reflected a certain truth from the ancient past, that the Trojan wars were a genuine historic event and that figures like Aeneas, Jason, and Hercules were as real as Alexander or Caesar. The specific details of some of these tales may have been regarded as something akin to historic fiction but based on genuine history none the less.

And how would you have explained the presence of fabulous creatures such as harpies and dragons in these tales? Most may have regarded them as being as mythical as the stories themselves. However, others may well have felt such creatures might still possibly exist, somewhere in the remote corners of the world.

One problematic aspect of classical mythology for a medieval audience was, of course, the classical gods. The medieval world was a Christian world. There was only one true god, and all other gods were regarded as unquestionably false. Who then was Zeus? Naturally, if you regarded these tales as pure myth, then Zeus was easily explained – he too was nothing but a myth. Many explained the presence of gods in these stories as misguided pagan embellishments. Others saw them as nothing more than powerful supernatural beings or, perhaps, poorly remembered ancient kings and queens. Different people had different explanations for the appearance of these beings in ancient stories. However, one thing was certain. Zeus, Apollo, Hera, and Athena were not real gods and goddesses – except in the minds of misguided pagans.

Chaucer, despite drawing literary inspiration from Statius, viewed the pagan gods quite negatively. They were a source of ignorance and ill counsel, leading men astray with deception and falsehood. They were, for Chaucer and probably for many others in the Middle Ages, a source of ignorance worshipped out of fear.[7] They were, after all, for the medieval writer, the embodiment of false belief.

Tales of the Druid Bard

When the Romans finally abandoned Britain in the early fifth century, it had been part of the Roman world for three-and-a-half centuries. During that time, native Britons had absorbed much from Rome, so by the time the Romans left, they had bestowed a legacy of classical culture and a Christian faith. However, Romanisation and Christian conversion never wholly supplanted native Celtic traditions.

In the few centuries prior to the dawn of the Middle Ages, Celtic mythology had evolved in Britain alongside Christianity and Romanisation. And, in post-Roman times, it continued to develop. Less reliant on a written literary tradition, it largely depended on oral transmission. In post-Roman Britain, this was primarily done by bards and poets. These men were employed by Romano-British chiefs and petty kings to sing their praises, record their deeds, and re-tell the stories of their people. In doing so, the bards helped keep the old Celtic traditions alive.

But, when we talk about 'Celtic' culture and mythology, what do we mean? We should start by saying that whilst Celtic Europe shared some traditions and beliefs it would be wrong to see it as some all-embracing monoculture. The Irish Celts were not the same as British Celts or the Celts of Gaul. They shared many common cultural traits, but these were supplemented by their own local traditions and beliefs. The Celtic legacy inherited by the Plantagenet world was, therefore, primarily (but by no means exclusively) native British rather than Irish or Scots. But what exactly was 'native British'?

Not long after Roman withdrawal, Britain experienced significant waves of immigration from northern Germany and the Low Countries. These peoples were Angles, Saxons, and Jutes, who brought with them their own distinctive Germanic culture and traditions. In time, they were followed by Scandinavian settlers (who we, rather simplistically, label as 'Vikings'). Successive waves of invaders arrived from the east, gradually forcing the indigenous Brittonic culture further and further west.

Within two centuries of Roman departure, what remained of Celtic Britain was largely limited to Wales, Cornwall, north-west England, and south-west Scotland (excluding the western Scottish Islands and coastal areas, which were increasingly settled by Gaelic immigrants from Ireland).

As the Middle Ages wore on Celtic Britain south of the Scots boarder became increasingly synonymous with Wales. Native Brittonic languages (of which Welsh is one) died out elsewhere in England. Brittonic speakers persisted in the far south-west (Cornwall), albeit as an ever-dwindling minority up to modern times. Brittonic language in north-west England (Cumbria) endured until around the twelfth century before finally dying out. Much of the mythology of these peoples survived into the high Middle Ages as part of Welsh tradition and it is in this context that we tend to regard it today. However, certainly for the first few centuries after Roman departure, it should be seen as native British, rather than purely Welsh, mythology.

For a long time, these old British myths and stories were primarily transmitted orally by bards and poets. However, they began to be recorded in written Middle Welsh as the Middle Ages wore on. By the thirteenth and fourteenth centuries, compilations and collections of old stories and myths from the preceding centuries became available. Some of these may have been the first attempts at recording old, oral, story-telling traditions in writing. Most were likely adapted and modified to suit the times, introducing new themes and elements from other traditions.

One significant collection produced at this time is a collection of old Welsh/British myths and stories compiled between the eleventh and fourteenth centuries which we now call the *Mabinogion*. The *Mabinogion* was published in its modern form during the nineteenth century, combining two separate medieval manuscripts. These were the *White Book of Rhydderch* and *The Red Book of Hergest*, both of which date to the fourteenth century.[1]

Another important source is the *Triads of the Island of Britain* – which is something of a catalogue of old mythical characters and places. These read somewhat like lists of such things as the 'top ten movies of the year' you might see on social media in our day. However, these lists deal with top threes (hence triads). Examples include 'Three Fortunate Princes of Britain', the 'Three Splendid Maidens of Arthur's Court' and the 'Three Powerful Swineherds of the Island of Britain'. The latter of these was deemed worthy of a particularly lengthy write up! The earliest surviving written example of a triad can be dated to the latter part of the thirteenth century.[2]

Another important work appearing in the fourteenth century was the *Book of Taliesin*, a collection of poems from the most famous bard of post-Roman Britain. Before we look at this in more depth it is also worth mentioning the

Ystoria Taliesin – a mythical account of the bard's life. *Ystoria* was not collated together in its final form until the sixteenth century but is, at least in part, based on earlier myths and stories.

In these old Brittonic stories we find the first early references to King Arthur and Merlin. We also find many themes, concepts, and ideas that had significant influences over the development of mythology during the Plantagenet period.

A key mythical figure from this period is the famous bard Taliesin. I would be surprised if you have not heard the name. Many people know the name and are at least aware that he was a famous bard. However, when it comes down to it many people sadly know little else about him.

So, who exactly was Taliesin? The question sounds a simple one, but it is perhaps one of the most complex and difficult questions to adequately answer in British literature. In truth, it is a question that has a very simple answer and a very complicated answer (which is a very Taliesin-like statement in itself). Let's start with the relatively simple answer.

Taliesin was a bard and poet who lived in the late sixth century. However, only a small number of compositions contained in the *Book of Taliesin* are thought to have their roots in his original work. Taliesin was originally employed as court poet, primarily but not exclusively, within the northern British kingdom of Rheged (which was, broadly speaking, Cumbria plus 'bits' of south-western Scotland, western Yorkshire, and perhaps Lancashire). Most of this work relates to Urien, King of Rheged, but he also appears to have written for Welsh patrons such as Cynan Garwyn of Powys. Although he writes mostly of Rheged, he explicitly states he is not a man of Rheged. Most likely Taliesin was Welsh.

Today we can only really appreciate Taliesin's writing as poetry. However, in his own lifetime, his poems would have been performed publicly as songs with accompanying music. In addition to being a highly respected poet, Taliesin was also an accomplished musician and performer – a bard. Not just any bard but clearly regarded as one of the most talented of his age.

Now, given the fact that we know he was living and working in the late sixth century it would not be unreasonable to guess that he probably died sometime between the end of the sixth century and the mid-seventh – except that he appears to have carried on writing.

The *Book of Taliesin* is a complete collection of work attributed to him. Some of these works do appear to be versions of genuine late-sixth-century compositions. However, many of the poems in the book are certainly of later composition. The collection spans seven centuries of work, right up until the time the book was compiled. Even in the case of work thought to be sixth-century, there is some debate over whether this really was the work of one poet or three. This, as you may have guessed, is where the question 'who was Taliesin?' starts to become complicated.

Taliesin became so famous and so respected that, even after his presumed death, later anonymous bards continued to write as 'Taliesin'. Over time a large body of work built up revealing a Taliesin who was not just a bard but also a sage, a seer, a mystic, a shapeshifter, and a druid. His poems encompass old British myths, enigmatic prophecies, and even claimed an ancient mystical insight into the nature of creation itself. Christian devotional stories sit happily alongside old pagan stories. Some of his work even strays into stories from the classical world or uses pidgin Latin to recall a bygone Roman age. At least one of his poems is heavily influenced by Irish mythology. However, despite clear classical, Christian, and occasional Irish influences, his work remains primarily the product of native Brittonic mythology.

What we have, therefore, are a few works from the original Taliesin mixed in with the work of an unknown number of anonymous successors and imitators. It spans a British/Welsh mythological world that evolved over the period between the fall of Rome and the early fourteenth century. That is a very long period and, potentially, represents a significant number of different writers. However, the resulting Taliesin gestalt persona strives to maintain the semblance of a consistent voice and identity. Unless, of course, we choose to believe that there was just one Taliesin; a long-lived druid, whose work spanned seven centuries! Clearly by the high Middle Ages, Taliesin had acquired a legendary reputation. The *Triads* list Taliesin, alongside Myrddin (Merlin), as being amongst the Three Skilful Bards of King Arthur's court.[3]

Setting aside Taliesin's actual historic identity, several myths surrounding his origins sprang up during the Middle Ages. The best-known of these is reported in the *Ystoria Taliesin*. It supplies us with a supernatural explanation for his genesis that is clearly more pagan than Christian.

In this story, Taliesin begins life as a mere servant called Gwion Bach. His mistress is the lady Ceridwan, a powerful noblewoman and sorceress from the time of King Arthur. Ceridwan, we are told, had a problem – her son was painfully ugly. To provide the hapless lad with a chance in life, his mother set about brewing a potent magical potion. The brew could not hope to improve the boy's looks, but it could grant him the gift of poetic inspiration to compensate. Poetic inspiration of this sort would also grant a profound mystical insight into the nature of things. This power had a special name in British mythology – the *awen*. Such powerful magic took Ceridwan an entire year to prepare in her enchanted cauldron. However, just as the brew was ready, disaster struck! Her servant, Gwion, stole the draught before her son could drink it.

Gaining wisdom, Gwion realised that Ceridwan would be very angry when she discovered what he'd done and so he fled. Ceridwan pursued him and the two engaged in a shapeshifting contest as one tried to evade the other. Eventually, Gwion was transformed into a grain of corn and Ceridwan, now a black hen, ate him. But this was not the end of Gwion. Ceridwan became pregnant and, although aware that the child would be Gwion re-incarnated, she could not bring herself to slay him. The re-incarnated Gwion was thus gifted with the *awen* granted by the power of the cauldron. It would be this child who would grow to become Taliesin.[4]

Of course, even this story raises more questions than answers. Some of Taliesin's own poetry contains hints of this story. This suggests that although *Ystoria Taliesin* was compiled in the sixteenth century it probably reflects, at least in part, earlier medieval stories. However, Taliesin himself also provides us with his own (different) explanation of his supernatural creation. Through his poetic verse, he claims to have been conjured into existence from natural elements such as fruits, flowers, and trees. He goes on to claim that he was conjured into existence by the sorcerer Gwydion … and by a king … and by the wisdom of ancient sages.[5]

The myths surrounding Taliesin's origins appear enigmatic and obscure, even contradictory. But perhaps this is the point. For with Taliesin, one cannot help but get the impression that asking the question is more important than the answer itself. If we are to truly understand the bard, perhaps we are better advised to approach him by exploring the concepts and ideas he wrote about.

One particularly important concept present in Taliesin's writing is a force that Taliesin refers to as the *awen*. The *awen* might be translated as 'inspiration', something akin to what we might understand as a poet's muse. At one level, this is precisely what the *awen* represents. However, it is also so much more. The *awen* is a powerful and transformative energy. Not only does it grant a bard the creative inspiration to write great songs, it also allows him to transcend the mundane material world. The *awen* grants insight into ancient wisdom concerning the nature of creation. For Taliesin, the *awen* enabled him to perceive things that are, things that were and things that have yet to be. Thus, in his prophecy poems, Taliesin does not say 'I foresee' or 'I predict', he says that it is the *awen* that predicts. Taliesin himself becomes a vessel through which the *awen* channels. The *awen* also enabled Taliesin to transcend states of existence and adopt different forms. It is not clear whether this supernatural gift of shapeshifting was intended to be interpreted as a literal or metaphysical transformation. So, in answer to the question 'who was Taliesin?' we get the answer:

> 'I have been a drop in a shower;
> I have been a sword in the grasp of the hand
> I have been a shield in battle.
> I have been a string in a harp,
> Disguised for nine years.
> in water, in foam.
>
> Taliesin, *The Battle of the Trees*[6]

It is through the force of the *awen* that Taliesin claims to be able to craft prophecies. For the most part these visions foretell a future in which old British heroes will arise to drive 'the foreigners' from Britain. These foreigners are, for the most part, the Angles and Saxons. However, in later poems they refer to the early Normans and Plantagenet kings who had supplanted the Anglo-Saxons as the primary threat to the British Celtic world.

As to which heroes will arise to save the Britons, prophecies vary. In some, they refer to an enigmatic mythical figure known as 'The Leaper' (a reincarnation of some ancient, lost, British warlord). Sometimes they refer to specific sixth/seventh century warlords such as Cadwallon of Gwynedd who briefly conquered and occupied (or liberated, depending on your perspective) Northumbria in the mid-seventh century.[7]

In the prophecy known as the 'Great Prophecy of Britain' there is a reference to another sage and seer whom Taliesin calls 'Myrddin'. This is significant because this poem is thought to be dated to the early tenth century, and because 'Myrddin' is an early form of the name 'Merlin'. The first written record of Myrddin, however, dates to the ninth-century *Annales Cambriae*, the annals of Wales.[8] However, the *Annales* only briefly records that Myrddin went mad after the Battle of Armterit in southern Scotland. Taliesin's 'Great Prophecy' is probably the earliest reference to Merlin aside from the *Annales*. In it, Taliesin tells us that Merlin predicted that a Saxon leader known as the 'Overlord' would meet with the Britons on the upper river Wye and there give battle.

Later in the Middle Ages, Taliesin and Merlin become more closely associated. They are sometimes portrayed as contemporary seers and sages with similar supernatural powers, such as in Geoffrey of Monmouth's Life of Merlin. Sometimes Taliesin, like Merlin, is associated with Arthur's court. Occasionally, Taliesin and Merlin are even presented as different manifestations of the same person.

Arthur himself is briefly mentioned in several of Taliesin's poems and in one, the cryptic 'Spoils of Annwfn', he claims to have voyaged to the mysterious realm of Annwfn with Arthur. Annwfn (pronounced Annovan) is the Otherworld of British mythology from this period. In some ways, it is like the fairy realms of Irish mythology. It is a domain that overlaps with our world. As a result, mortals can find themselves wandering into Annwfn unwittingly and, by the same token, supernatural beings from the Otherworld can cross into ours.

In the story of 'Pwyll Prince of Dyfedd', which appears in the *Mabinogion*, the prince goes hunting and encounters a strange pack of shining white hounds. He chases them off only to discover they belong to Arawn, King of Annwfn. These hounds represent an early depiction of the Cŵn Annwn, the Welsh version of the Wild Hunt and Arawn is the hunt's master. Arawn takes offense at having his hounds chased and, to make amends, Pwyll agrees to swap bodies with the otherworldly king. For a year, the two exchange bodies and, at the end of this time, Pwyll must defeat Arawn's otherworld rival Hafgan before returning to our world.[9]

In Taliesin's 'Tale of Annwfn', the bard claims he travelled to the otherworld with Arthur and three ships full of men. He says they were the first mortals to make this voyage since Pwyll. There, they visit several mysterious castles (or perhaps they are just one castle with different names). This place is variously referred to as the Castle of the Otherworld Beings, the Castle of Feasting, the Freezing Castle, the Glass Castle, the Castle of Obstacles, the Castle of the Protector, and finally the Foursquare Castle. The voyage, we are informed, was destined for ill fortune and, from the three ships that set out only seven men returned.[10]

In another of Taliesin's enigmatic poems, 'The Battle of Trees', he describes a supernatural conflict between the Britons and a mysterious enemy. The poem is so named because it describes how the sorcerer Gwydion conjurers an army of trees to save the Britons. The identity of the enemy is obscure (typically for Taliesin) but, a sixteenth-century Welsh document (*Peniarth* MS 98B) suggests the enemy is Arawn's army. The host has been sent to punish the Britons for stealing a dog, a lapwing, and a roebuck from Annwfn. Taliesin conjurers some truly hellish images of the otherworldly enemy, describing a scaled monster with a hundred heads, a black clawed toad, and a crested serpent. These beasts appear capable of consuming the souls of men as one has a multitude of souls, trapped within its throat.[11]

Concepts such as the *awen* and Annwfn are clearly pagan rather than Christian. However, it would be wrong to view Taliesin as a pagan. Ten of the sixty-one poems contained within the *Book of Taliesin* overtly deal with Christian devotional themes. Even the earliest poems contain clear Christian references. And, for all the supernatural pagan themes that run through 'The Battle of the Trees', it ends with an image of the second coming of Christ.

Taliesin may cling to pagan British mythology and superstition, but he interprets these through the lens of an essentially Christian cosmology. This naturally leads to some tension in his writing, which is particularly in evidence when the world experienced through the wisdom of the *awen* and the world defined by church scholarship clash.

Taliesin believed his *awen* gave him insight that the bookish church scholars could not hope to access through study alone. And, on more than one occasion, this belief manifests as scepticism directed at the scholastic approach to knowledge. In the 'Spoils of Annwfn', Taliesin openly pours scorn on stuffy church scholars whom he describes as small men.[12] And yet, the same poem contains overtly Christian references and ends with the stated belief that Christ will reward him on Judgement Day.

So, whilst Taliesin clearly shares the same Christian faith as the bookish monks, he has a very different view as to how a Christian faith should be experienced. For him, the wisdom obtained from ecstatic visions granted by the *awen* transcend the knowledge to be gained from book learning. In effect, he espouses a form of Christianity experienced in a pagan way. In the poem known as 'Young Taliesin's Works' he taunts scholarly monks claiming that wisdom granted by the *awen* cannot be found in their books. For all their learning and scholarship, the bookish monks cannot hope to explain the mysteries of nature revealed by the *awen*.[13]

So, what does all this tell us about Taliesin? The mystical accounts of his origins and the supernatural concepts about which he writes draw on pagan traditions. To what extent, then, can we read him as providing us with a window on the pagan world of the Celtic Britons? In his poems he claims, amongst other things, to have been a druid. Some have interpreted Taliesin as providing us with insight into what it meant to be a druid.

Can we reasonably draw a direct connection between Taliesin and ancient druidic beliefs? In answering this question, we face an obvious problem. Since the religion of the pre-Roman druids was transmitted by oral tradition, we have few written records of druidic practice or belief. All we have are a few Roman accounts. Given that these are a) limited in their scope and b) hostile and biased, we don't have much to go on.

What we do know, however, is that the Romans engaged in a systematic campaign to eradicate the druid religion during the first century. This was largely achieved by killing all living druids. It was a typically ruthless Roman solution to the problem. Killing all the priests of a religion that relied on oral transmission clearly prevented detailed religious knowledge being passed to later generations. By the time the very first Taliesin poems could possibly have been written, Britain had been Christian for around two-and-a-half centuries and the druids had been gone for five. It is also the case that whilst a medieval Taliesin claimed to be a druid, he never mentions performing the priestly rites of a pagan religion. Neither does he worship any pagan gods.

Whatever else Taliesin was, he was not a druid in the same sense as a true pre-Roman druid. Nevertheless, his engagement with such concepts as the *awen* and Annwfn and his prophetic visions, clearly owe more to a pagan past than Christian orthodoxy. Some of the themes, and beliefs he draws on, probably do date back to the old pagan world of pre-Roman Britain. Taliesin, therefore, remains something of an enigma, neither clearly of one world nor the other. We could see Taliesin as the last bard of the Romano-British world, or the first bard of medieval Wales. We could see him as the last druid of the old pagan world, or an early religious mystic of the medieval Christian one. Who was Taliesin? In his writing, we can find reflections of all these worlds.

The Mead Hall of Beowulf

When the Romans left Britain to its fate in around 410 AD, the Romano-British culture they left behind was in decline but largely intact. But, within two centuries, the native Britons would find themselves overrun by a new wave of settlers. The newcomers arrived in the east and quickly spread out to occupy most of what is now England. They brought with them strange foreign customs, spoke alien Germanic languages, and worshipped unfamiliar pagan gods.

The civilised Christian world of the late Roman Empire was finally gone. The age of pagan Anglo-Saxon England had dawned. However, it was an age that was not destined to last long. In 597 missionaries arrived in England, sent by Pope Gregory the Great, to set about the task of converting the Anglo-Saxons to Christianity. During the seventh century, the old Germanic pagan beliefs were gradually replaced by a new Christian faith. The last significant stage in this process came with the Christianisation of the Isle of Wight in 686 AD.[1] By the end of the seventh century Anglo-Saxon England had fully converted to Christianity.

When the Angles, Saxons, and Jutes first arrived in England, the myths, and stories they brought with them were communicated orally by bards and story tellers. In this respect they communicated their mythology in a similar manner to their British neighbours in the west. These story tellers were known as *scops* and, rather like Taliesin, they were often attached to the courts of leading chieftains or kings.

Unfortunately for us, this early period of Anglo-Saxon history is poorly documented, to say the least. We lack written examples of stories from this period or, even, contemporary written accounts of the *scops* and their role in society. For written evidence, we need to look to later Christian times. Writers like the Venerable Bede tell us something about earlier Anglo-Saxon times, but Bede was a Christian monk who wrote in the early eighth century, at a time when the old pagan Anglo-Saxon world had passed.

Pagan Anglo-Saxon mythology arose from a very different culture than that of the British Celts. Like the pagan pre-Roman Britons, the Anglo-Saxons were polytheistic, and their myths and stories were transmitted orally, but there the similarity ends. Anglo-Saxon paganism belonged to a Germanic/Scandinavian tradition, a close relation to Norse/Viking mythology. Exactly how similar (or different) pagan Anglo-Saxon and Norse beliefs were from each other is impossible to tell due to the paucity of evidence. However, there is no doubting there were many similarities. Perhaps the most obvious illustration of this lies in the gods and goddesses venerated by the two cultures. Both accepted a pantheon of deities which included several gods and goddesses with similar names and powers:

Anglo-Saxon God	Norse equivalent
Woden	Odin
Tiw	Tyr
Thunor	Thor
Frig	Frigg
Ingvi	Yngvi-Freyr

It is likely that at least some of these gods pre-date the medieval period by several centuries. Tacitus, writing in the first century AD, tells us that German tribes of that time venerated Mercury, Hercules, and Mars. Typically for a Roman writer, he uses Roman names to describe them. However, he was probably referring to early Germanic versions of Woden, Thunor, and Tiw.[2] No doubt detailed stories and beliefs pertaining to these gods varied to at least some extent when comparing Norse with Anglo-Saxon. How different or how similar exactly are questions we cannot easily answer.

It may be helpful here to consider the comparison between ancient Greek and Roman gods as both also arose from shared cultural traditions. Fortunately, in this case, the similarities and differences are well documented. Here, both Jupiter and Zeus are alpha male gods, heads of their respective celestial households. Both share an association with lightning and eagles. Both dwell in a celestial realm in the sky. They are often thought of as one and the same (or that one is a variation on the other). To a degree, this is true but there are also differences. In their stories, Zeus interacts with humanity more than Jupiter. Jupiter has the power to determine fate (Zeus does not). They also have different familial relationships and so on. At the detailed level, and in terms of specific stories, the two have many (often small) differences. By the same token, it is quite likely that Woden and Odin share several similarities and differences of this sort.

Norse mythology is documented in greater detail and more completeness than Anglo-Saxon. This is partly a result of the fact that Norse paganism persisted for longer, enduring into a period where literary records were becoming more commonplace. We are also fortunate to still possess a copy of two key medieval works – the *Prose Edda* and *Poetic Edda*. Much of what we know of pagan Norse mythology today comes from these two sources.

Some have attempted to use Norse tales to 'reconstruct' Anglo-Saxon myths – using stories about Odin to create a more in-depth view of Woden. At one level, this is not an unreasonable exercise but, if we consider the examples of Jupiter and Zeus, it is easy to see how it can be fraught with pitfalls.

The Old English epic poem, *Beowulf*, is the only significant work of Anglo-Saxon mythology that survives. However, like the writings of the Bede, it is a post-pagan work, from much later Christian times. The earliest written copy is a manuscript from the late tenth/early eleventh century. Its writer is clearly a Christian and, although it is probably based on earlier written and/or oral versions of the story, we cannot be certain of this.

Despite being written in Old English, the story of Beowulf is not actually set in England. The characters and the events of the story are set in Denmark and Gotland in Sweden. So, you might ask, is it really an Anglo-Saxon story, or is it a Norse story? In fact, its existence shows the extent to which the cultural differences between pagan Anglo-Saxon and Norse were extremely blurred. The Beowulf story is believed to have connections with the Angles of East Anglia.[3] It may well have been a story popular with the people responsible for the Sutton Hoo burial site (in use from the late sixth through to the early seventh century).

But why would Angles in Suffolk be interested in Scandinavian stories? As it turns out, the Angles had close cultural ties with Scandinavia. The Sutton Hoo burial site contains several items that are distinctly Scandinavian – showing that trade with Scandinavia was well established long before the Viking Age.[4] The Angles themselves originally migrated to Britain from what is now southern Denmark. The fact that Beowulf is such a mix of Anglo-Saxon and Norse isn't that surprising given the closely shared heritage of the two peoples.

Despite being a story that is set in pagan times, the author of *Beowulf* is a Christian. Like Taliesin, he is partly detached from the old pagan world about which he writes, but not so detached that he does not value its stories and cultural traditions. Some academics (notably J.R.R. Tolkien) have argued that this suggests an author writing not long after the pagan age, during the eighth century. Others feel it was written much later and that it is possible that the surviving tenth-century manuscript is the original version.

The story itself focuses on the hero Beowulf, a famous warrior amongst the Geats (inhabitants of Gotland in southern Sweden). He comes to the aid of Hrothgar, King of Denmark, whose hall is being attacked by a monstrous beast called Grendel, a savage creature who lurks in a dark cave, driven mad by the sound of singing and merriment from Hrothgar's hall. The monster possesses superhuman strength, capable of ripping Hrothgar's warriors apart with his bare hands, before devouring them. Grendel is often depicted as ogre or troll-like but, his physical description is not elaborated on in the epic. We are, however, informed that he is a grotesque monstrosity descended from the biblical Cain.

This overt biblical reference is typical of the Christian lens through which the story is told. Despite being set at a time when Anglo-Saxons, Danes, and Geats were all pagan, it has been adapted to fit in with a Christian worldview. The author is aware that the people he was writing about were pagans and, explicitly, makes the point that they were ignorant of God. Indeed, we are informed that it is because of their ignorance of God that their own pagan prayers are to no avail.[5]

Beowulf demonstrates his prowess in combat by fighting Grendel on the monster's own terms – using only his bare hands. Sure enough, after a fierce fight, Beowulf triumphs. However, the defeat of Grendel is just the first of three great trials he must face. Grendel, as it turns out, has a mother. It soon transpires that the mother is every bit as savage and monstrous as the son and, when she learns of her son's fate, she is keen for revenge. Beowulf, again, comes to the king's aid and eventually hunts her down to an underwater lair. To reach his foe, Beowulf must battle his way past sea monsters before he finally locates her underwater grotto. There, a fierce fight ensues and, eventually, he slays her with a giant's sword. Beowulf returns triumphant to Hrothgar's halls with a sword hilt and Grendel's head to prove he has completed his quest.

There follows a passing of years, during which time Beowulf becomes king of his people. The final challenge arrives many years later. This time, the trouble begins when one of Beowulf's subjects steals from a ferocious fire-breathing dragon's hoard, incurring its wrath. The old hero must set out on one final quest to save his people from the dragon. In the end, only one loyal companion is brave enough to accompany him to the dragon's lair. Then, in a final desperate battle Beowulf slays the dragon. However, he is mortally wounded in the process. The story ends with the great hero-king being ceremonially cremated on a funeral pyre before being interred in a long barrow. It is a fittingly honourable send off for a great hero and king.

One of the characters mentioned briefly in the *Beowulf* epic is the intriguing figure of the renown smith, Wayland. In *Beowulf* it is Wayland who crafts the hero's armour.[6] Aside from his appearance in *Beowulf*, he is also mentioned in the Anglo-Saxon poem *Deor* (from the tenth century). He was also linked to a long barrow in Berkshire, known as 'Wayland's Smithy' from as early as the tenth century.[7]

However, the earliest Anglo-Saxon attestable reference to Wayland is not to be found in literature but in art. *The Frank's Casket* famously depicts Wayland Smith alongside an image of the *Adoration of the Magi* and can be dated to Northumbria in the early eighth century. As with other figures from Anglo-

Saxon mythology, we also find him (or versions of him) appearing more widely within Germanic and Norse mythology. His appearance alongside a biblical scene on this early casket further illustrates the blending of pagan and Christian motifs that were a feature of this period.

It is from Norse mythology that we get the most complete version of the Wayland Smith story. As far as we can tell, the Norse version of the myth matched reasonably well with the fragmentary knowledge we possess of the Anglo-Saxon version. Wayland was, as we might expect, an incredibly talented smith. He was also, according to the Scandinavian version of his tale, an elf.[8] Wayland's ability to craft magnificent items, some of which have magical powers, are a product of his otherworldly, elfish identity. Wayland's skill was so highly regarded that King Nithad (to use his old English name) has Wayland taken captive so that the smith can forge fantastic items for him. To prevent Wayland's escape, the king has him hamstrung and imprisoned upon an island. Wayland bides his time and, when the opportunity arises, takes terrible revenge on his captor. He kills the king's sons and rapes the king's daughter before making good his escape using magic to fly away.

Wayland is no king but a smith, capable of making magnificent items. He is not a leader, or even a warrior, but he nevertheless commands significant cultural status – his skills being greatly prized. In tribal societies such as early Anglo-Saxon England or pagan Scandinavia, the blacksmith would have been the prime source of advanced technology. Wayland, as a master smith, held a cultural significance for these people, not unlike that which a tech-guru commands in our own time.

These early tales of Beowulf and Wayland come from a time of petty chieftains and kings. Tribal loyalties and the personal strength and charisma of the ruler are key social values. A king (such as Beowulf) needed to be a charismatic warrior-king to earn the respect and loyalty of his subjects. However, the age of Beowulf and Wayland was not destined to last. By the dawn of the eighth century, the Anglo-Saxon kingdoms were no longer pagan. Within a century, Christianity was very well established, and the old pagan myths were no more than a nostalgic memory.

In the last decade of this century, foreign sea-raiders attacked and plundered a small, peaceful, religious community on England's eastern coast. The shocking deed is recorded in the *Anglo-Saxon Chronicles* for 793: 'the harrowing inroads of heathen men made lamentable havoc in the church of God in Holy-island [Lindesfarne], by rapine and slaughter'.[9] The raiders were Vikings and the infamous events of 793 heralded the dawn of the Viking age. Unlike the Christian Anglo-Saxons, the Vikings still retained their old pagan ways. Their warlike culture and their heathen beliefs made them the terror of Northern Europe for the next two centuries.

Skalds of the North

In England, the Viking raids eventually escalated into a full-scale invasion, followed by immigration and settlement. In 865, large parts of eastern England were overrun by Norse invaders. This time the invaders stayed, establishing what became known as the Danelaw. The Danelaw encompassed East Anglia and large tracts of eastern and northern England. It would endure for nearly a century, during which time Norse culture, mythology, and social values would make a lasting impact on what was to become known as England. The Danelaw endured until 954, when it was finally conquered by the Christian Anglo-Saxons and Norse settlers who, like the Anglo-Saxons before them, converted to Christianity. Nevertheless, some Viking customs and stories endured. Half a century later, the archbishop of York complained about pagan Viking 'nonsense' and 'sorcery' still being practiced at New Year in York.[1]

The myths and stories the Vikings brought with them were transmitted purely through oral tradition, just as they were in earlier British and Anglo-Saxon societies. In the case of Norse culture, the key storytellers were known as *skalds*. Like the *scops* and bards, they were skilled poets and musicians.

Only a very limited amount of written pagan material survives from the Viking age. Mainly, this takes the form of runic inscriptions carved into stone, wood, or metal objects. However, none of these constitute particularly detailed records of myths or Norse cosmology. Typically, all that survives are short phrases or inscriptions. These might be something as simple as someone's name being written on an object. Often, they were used to inscribe a spell or charm on an object or to write a commemorative inscription on a memorial.[2] It may be that more extensive written material once existed on material such as leather that has long since perished. Alternatively, it may be that runic writing was only used in a very limited way and that knowledge of stories and myths relied primarily on oral transmission by the skalds.

It is thanks mainly to the efforts of medieval Icelandic writers that a significant collection of Old Norse myths and legends have survived. These were collated together centuries after the Viking age had ended. Two key works, both originating in thirteenth century Iceland, provide us with most of what we know of pagan Norse mythology. These are known today as the *Poetic Edda* and the *Prose Edda.*

The author(s) of the *Poetic Edda* are unknown. However, the person responsible for the *Prose Edda* was a remarkable individual by the name of Snorri Sturluson, an ambitious Icelandic nobleman. By his time, the old pagan Viking age had long passed – no more than a distant memory. Despite this, the old stories and poetic techniques of the skalds were a source of nostalgic fascination for Snorri. Determined to preserve a fast-disappearing heritage, he set about collecting and recording old Norse stories.

Sturluson, like Taliesin and the anonymous author of *Beowulf,* was a Christian. As a result, he also interpreted old pagan stories within the context of a Christian cosmology. However, he took a slightly different approach. He begins his work with a Prologue in which he explains that the old Norse gods, such as Odin and Thor were not really gods but men. They came to Scandinavia from Troy and their knowledge and skill so far exceeded the local culture that they appeared to be gods.[3] With this explanation safely out of the way and his Christian duty done, Sturluson then proceeds to simply recount the old pagan myths. These are presented as pagan folk stories, largely untroubled by any but the most fleeting Christian references.

Of course, these old stories are written down as they were remembered some two-and-a-half centuries after the pagan age ended. Some may have been based on older written versions, now lost. Many were probably based on what remained of skaldic oral tradition in Iceland at the time. *Prose Edda* is a record of what survived in a time when the old skaldic traditions were vanishing.

The *Poetic Edda* consists of a compilation of works. Much of its contents can be found in a manuscript known as the *Codex Regius*, which dates to 1270.[4] However, its contents are earlier and its two oldest poems probably date to before 900 AD. The *Prose Edda*'s history is better known but we know that it was not really known in England until after the Middle Ages. We can only guess as to how well-known or widespread the stories the *Edda*s contained were in the Danelaw. However, variations of at least some of these myths must have been present in early medieval English culture. Whether through the Danelaw or as older pagan Anglo-Saxon versions, many of these stories were absorbed into the English mythological milieu.

Reading these old Norse myths, one cannot fail to note the violence inherent in many of them. People and gods take offence and resort to violence almost casually. Although the violence is often fatal it is accepted as a normal part of life. Escalation is avoided by paying compensation to the relatives of the slain. It is this and this alone that prevents violent tit-for-tat feuds developing. Of course, this reflects the nature of old Norse society, a society of warriors and raiders.

This was a society in which violence was common and in which human sacrifice occasionally played a role in religious ritual. Their pagan religion was raw, often crude, and sometimes the differing stories offer apparent contradictions.

The gods of the old pagan world were known as the Aesir. These deities governed the universe from their home in Asgard. Odin is identified as chief amongst the Aesir and lord of the divine hold of Asgard. He is a god of wisdom, a power he craved so much that he sacrificed his own eye to be able to drink from the well of wisdom. He also willingly hung himself to gain knowledge of the runes, earning himself the epithet of the 'Hanged God'.[5] Since Odin is the god of wisdom, he is also associated with the poets and *skalds* who served as an important source of folk wisdom in Norse society. He acquired the gift of poetic inspiration by stealing a magical mead, originally crafted by dwarves. This drink he portions out to those destined to become a talented skald.

Odin is the All-Father, the ultimate judge of both gods and men. In times of war, he sends out his servants, the Valkyries, to determine who lives and who dies. Those who die in war are rewarded with an afterlife in either Valhalla or Folkvanger. Valhalla is a paradise of heavy drinking, banter, and fighting. There they are destined to remain until the time of Ragnarök, the cataclysmic end of days of Norse mythology. At this time, the warriors of Valhalla will issue forth to fight at Odin's side in one last, glorious, battle.

Aside from Odin, the most prominent of the Norse gods was Thor. Thor was renowned for his strength and for his possession of three potent items: a magical hammer, a set of iron gloves that enabled him to wield it, and a belt that doubled his strength. He is a strong and fierce warrior but down to earth and accessible in a way that Odin was not. The Romans equated Thor to a figure rather like the Hercules of classical mythology. In most old Norse tales, in which Thor appears, he acts rather like Hercules – a heroic figure of superhuman strength, winning impossible challenges and contending with powerful enemies. There are more Norse tales relating to the deeds of Thor than any of their other gods. He is, of course, the god of thunder. However, he was strongly associated with agriculture and seafaring, which made him popular with farmers and sailors. In pagan times he was probably the most widely venerated of the Norse gods.

A third major figure of the Aesir is the god Tyr. He is the most courageous warrior amongst the gods and the *Prose Edda* tells us he was the god most likely to be invoked by men of action during a battle.[6] He famously loses his right hand, whilst tethering the fearful Fenris wolf. It is an act of courage and sacrifice that no other god was prepared to make. The Romans regarded Tyr as having clear parallels with their war god, Mars.

Another god, important enough to be mentioned third, after Thor and Odin, in the *Prose Edda*'s list of gods, is Baldr. Baldr is Odin's second son and, we are told, he is wise, merciful, and beautiful. He appears bathed in radiant light and is, in many respects, a god of peace and tranquillity. However, the *Prose Edda* casually mentions (with a typical hint of Viking humour) that, for whatever reason, none of the decisions he makes are ever effective.

Perhaps the most intriguing of the Aesir is Loki. As far as we can tell Loki was not worshipped or prayed to. He nevertheless features prominently in many important myths. He is described as evil, self-serving, deceitful, and unreliable. His tricks often lead to misfortune, and he happily betrays his fellow Aesir to get himself out of a tight spot.

However, Loki's cunning sometimes comes in handy and occasionally he provides a valuable service for his fellow Aesir. The *Prose Edda* sums up Loki's dichotomous nature with a typically direct Norse statement: 'He constantly places the gods in difficulties and often solves their problems with guile.'[7]

In the end Loki's downfall is that he, almost inevitably, goes too far. A cruel trick leads to the death of the beloved Baldr. Loki goes further by wilfully sabotaging the attempts of the Aesir to rescue Baldr from the land of the dead. It is this last spiteful act that leads to him being bound until Ragnarök as punishment.

Loki acts as a chaotic figure in Norse mythology, a force for disruption and a threat to the universe. Indeed, he is prophesied to play a leading role on the side of the chaotic forces unleashed at Ragnarök. One of Loki's most dangerous acts is that he sires three monstrous children with the ogress Angrboda. The fearsome Fenris wolf is one; a terrible and powerful beast, tethered until such time as he breaks free at Ragnarök. Another is the enormous, venomous, Midgard serpent. This creature was thrown into the outer seas by Odin but grew so large that it eventually encircled the entire outer ocean of the world. At Ragnarök, we are told, the serpent will return from its exile to do battle with Thor.

Loki's final monstrous offspring was Hel. She is described as half black and half white and of a gloomy and cruel disposition. Odin cast Hel down into Nifelheim, the cold land of the dead. Hel was granted dominion over those who die of old age or disease and her realm is an altogether dismal place. Nifelheim is not a hell in the Christian sense, probably more of a purgatory. We are told that it is a grim and cold place. Hel's servants (named Lazy and Slothful) hardly inspire great enthusiasm for spending the afterlife in her company. In a similar vein her dish is called Hunger, her knife is Famine, and her bed is called Sick Bed. It is from the name of this ancient Norse/Germanic goddess that we derive the modern English word *Hell*, German *Hölle*, Danish *Helvede*, and the Swedish and Norwegian *Helvete.*

The afterlife in Norse mythology is not as simple as it first appears. Before the world ends, half of those who die glorious deaths in battle belong to Odin and are sent to Valhalla. However, the other half belong to the goddess Freyja and reside with her in the halls of Folkvanger. What happens to everyone else, is not necessarily consistently portrayed. The *Prose Edda* tells us that all those who are righteous will live with Odin in the hall of Gimle (also called Vingolf).[8] However, it also says that those who die of old age or disease are consigned to Hel's Nifelheim.[9]

However, after Ragnarök, this all changes. Good men and women will be rewarded with an afterlife in one of the heavens that provides refuge after this time. The *Prose Edda* mentions a number of these places; Gimle (for the best and most worthy of us), the hall of Brimir (for those who enjoyed drinking in life), and Sindri (reserved for the good and the virtuous). Oath breakers and murderers, however, find themselves consigned to a true hell in the hall of Nastrandir – a hall of serpents and poison. The most evil and corrupt will find themselves in a place of eternal torment, called Hvergelmir.

The Norse concept of the universe centres on a sacred ash tree, called Yggdrasil. This great tree links together the heavens, the material world, and the underworld. The Vikings believed it was the spiritual heart of the universe and that everything and everyone was connected to it. The upper part of the tree is where we find the heavens and gods' home at Asgard. This is connected to the material world below (Midgard) via a fantastic rainbow bridge called Bifrost. Midgard is enclosed by a wall that separates it from a perilous outer region called Utgard, the home of Frost Giants, and beyond that is the vast outer seas. The outer sea is itself enclosed by the immense horror that is the Midgard serpent. Below this is the underworld, seething with many serpents and guarded by a great hound, Garm. Through the underworld, it is possible to enter Nifelheim, the realm of the dead.

The Aesir hold court near one of the tree's roots, a place called the Well of Urd (the Well of Fate). It is in this place that the three enigmatic Norns, named *Fate, Becoming* and *Obligation* dwell. The Norns are potent supernatural beings and, we are told, that 'these maidens shape men's lives'.[10] In effect they possess the power to see a man's fate, the knowledge of which they pass on to the gods at the time of his birth.

Sacred trees appear in other myths. The tree holding the forbidden fruit in the Garden of Eden is an example. Sacred trees also feature in other ancient Middle Eastern traditions. Whether or not any of these traditions influenced the formation of the Scandinavian/Germanic Yggdrasil myth is very uncertain. However, the Viking concept of Yggdrasil is undeniably unique in many respects.

Aside from the gods, Norse mythology is populated by several supernatural beings. The Norns are an example of this, but it is the frost giants that feature most prominently in the stories. These ancient beings existed before the world began. Creation, as we know it today, was fashioned by Odin from the body of Ymir, the most ancient and greatest of giants. The giants vary in size in the tales, and many are clearly portrayed as truly immense. Indeed, in one story Thor enters the thumb of a giant's glove believing it to be a hut! Some, however, marry gods and must therefore, presumably, have been not that much larger than a large man. Mostly the frost giants are portrayed as dangerous and a potential force for chaos. Often, they serve as adversaries to individual gods such as Thor in the stories. However, they sometimes trade with the gods, cooperate with them, and even intermarry with them. Ultimately, however, they are destined to fight on the side of chaos at Ragnarök.

Another strange race of creatures that feature in these early Norse tales is the dwarves (*dvergar*). These beings began their existence as maggots feasting within the flesh of the dead giant Ymir. However, they evolved to assume the likeness of men, save that they dwell underground. Some live in earth and others in rocks. There is little in these early stories to suggest that they are necessarily shorter or smaller than men. Neither is their physical description elaborated on in any detail. They clearly possess supernatural powers, such as shape-changing magic and, for this reason, could potentially assume any form. However, their greatest talent appears to be their skill for fashioning marvellous magical items such as weapons and rings. Some of the dwarves named in the *Prose Edda* have familiar sounding names: Gandalf, Durin, Dain, Thorin, Nori, Gloin, and so on.[11] These names clearly struck a chord with Professor Tolkien as he studied the *Prose Edda* during his time at Oxford University.

Elves also feature in the earliest stories. The *Eddas* tell us there are two races of elves. The light elves dwell in the heavens in a place called Alfheim (literally 'Elf World'). The light elves are more beautiful than the sun and, in addition to their own world, they also dwell in a distant heavenly realm called Vidblain ('Wide Blue'). The *Eddas* inform us that the light elves are the only beings currently residing in this distant paradise. The dark elves, by contrast, are black as pitch and dwell deep underground in a world called Svartalfheim ('Dark Elf World'). Rather like the dwarves, the elves appear capable of making magical items. In order to restrain the fearsome Fenris wolf, Odin sends Skirnir to Svartalfheim to get the dwarves to make a fetter so powerful that the wolf cannot break free of it. It is in this way we learn that dwarves also dwell in Svartalfheim. Or perhaps dwarves and dark elves were one and the same in these earliest Norse myths.

A particularly famous Norse/Germanic myth is the tale of Sigurd (known in German mythology as Siegfried). This tale appears in Norse mythology in the *Eddas* and in German mythology in another thirteenth-century work called the *Nibelungenlied.* It is very likely that a version of this tale was also known in the pagan Anglo-Saxon world. In the Norse version, the story begins when Loki is tasked by Odin with obtaining gold to pay off a debt owed to a sorcerer named Hreidmar. Loki travels to Svartalfheim and captures the dwarf Andvari.

He forces the dwarf to pay a ransom in gold to buy his freedom. The dwarf offers to pay with everything he owns, except for his prized gold ring. He begs Loki to be allowed to keep the ring, since he could use its powers to make more wealth. Loki refuses his pleas and moves to take the ring anyway.

Andvari reluctantly surrenders the ring but curses it so that it brings death to anyone who owns it. Loki is not bothered by this since he intends to use it to pay a debt rather than possess it for himself. Of course, Loki being Loki, neglects to forewarn Hreidmar of the curse when making the agreed payment. Somewhat cruelly, he only chooses to mention it after the hapless Hreidmar has already accepted the ring.

The story then traces the tragic history of the ring, Andvaranaut (Andvari's gift), as it passes hands from one doomed owner to the next. In time it finds its way into the possession of the dragon Fafnir who is famously slain by the heroic warrior Sigurd. Of course, in slaying Fafnir, Sigurd fulfils the curse that possessing the ring brought down on the dragon. But by taking the ring Sigurd is himself cursed.

Sigurd marries Gudrun, the daughter of King Gjuki, and swears an oath of brotherhood with her two brothers Gunnar and Hogi. He is soon called upon to fulfil his oath when it transpires that Gunnar wishes to marry the Valkyrie Brynhild. As one might expect, courting a Valkyrie has its pitfalls. Brynhild lives on a remote mountaintop, and her hall is surrounded by a magical fire. As if that wasn't a problem enough, she has sworn to only marry a man who is brave enough to ride through the fire. Sigurd, Gunnar, and Hogi set off for the mountain intending to help Gunnar win his bride. However, when they get there the only horse willing to pass through the flame is Sigurd's. It is Sigurd then who passes through the fire. In order to keep his oath to aid Gunnar, Sigurd changes his shape to appear like his friend. In this way, Brynhild was deceived into marrying Gunnar. Sigurd, in Gunnar's form, gives Brynhild Andvaranaut as a wedding ring, thereby unwittingly passing on the curse.

Sometime later, inevitably, Brynhild discovers the nature of the deception. She is filled with rage at having been tricked into breaking her oath. Her husband was not the man brave enough to pass through the wavering flame after all. She, therefore, arranges for Sigurd to be assassinated in his sleep before killing herself. The cursed ring then finds its way into the possession of yet another doomed soul. In the end, Gjuki and all his descendants end up dead.

The dark storm cloud that looms over Norse mythology is, of course, Ragnarök. This is the Norse vision of the end of the world. Indeed, the end of the universe as we know it. The prophecies say Ragnarök will be preceded by a time of war and a great winter that will last three long years. According to the Sibyl's Prophecy it will be a time of strife and conflict in which brother will be pitted against brother: the age of the wolf.[12]

Then all chaos is unleashed. The gods and the heroes of Valhalla will fight one last apocalyptic battle against the forces of chaos. The Fenris wolf will break free, and the Midgard serpent will emerge from the outer seas. Loki will also break free of his prison to join armies of frost giants and the dreaded ship Nagalfar, steered by the giant Hrym. Surt (the Black One) will come to Midgard from the fiery world of Muspell. He wields a flaming sword with which he sets all the world on fire and splits the sky apart.

The gods will succeed in slaying horrors like the Fenris wolf and the Midgard Serpent but at a terrible price. Most of creation, including many of the gods themselves will be destroyed in the conflagration. The old universe will be no more but, we are told, 'the earth will shoot up from the sea, and it will be green and beautiful'.[13] A new world will then be founded by two people named Life and Life Yearner. The prophecies of the Viking pagans were unable to see beyond this time to predict the future of the next world. This, they testify, is beyond the wisdom of any man.

The pagan world of the Viking Age may not have ended in such an apocalyptic way, but it ended, nevertheless. In a sense a new world did emerge to replace it – the Christian world of the high Middle Ages.

Tales from the Island of Destiny

Mythology in the Plantagenet world was also influenced by Irish tradition. Some Irish stories would, for example, serve as an inspiration for medieval tales like 'Sir Gawain and the Green Knight'. By way of another example, Irish myths surrounding the mysterious fairy race would come to have a profound influence on how medieval Britain regarded these otherworldly beings. However, when looking at medieval England and Wales, we should draw a distinction between the influence of Irish and native Brittonic/Welsh mythology. Although they represent two strands of a shared Celtic heritage, they should not be considered inter-changeable.

Irish Celtic traditions were less well-known in mainland Britain during the early Middle Ages though some Irish stories were transmitted across the water by traders and migrant settlers. Irish influence was particularly in evidence along the coast in south-west Scotland and north-west Wales during the early post-Roman period. However, few such settlers found their way further inland to England.

Contact with Irish culture intensified during the Plantagenet period from 1171 onwards. It was from this time that the Plantagenets sought to carve out a kingdom for themselves in Ireland, centred on Dublin.[1] In this sense Irish, mythology represented a relative late influence on mainland Britain. Classical, native Celtic, Anglo-Saxon, and Norse influences all had a significant cultural impact earlier.

As is the case with Welsh, Norse, and Anglo-Saxon myths, what survives of Irish mythology exists only in medieval documents. The age of these stories is difficult to determine for certain and most were produced in the form in which we know them between the tenth and twelfth centuries.[2] The earliest surviving copies are found in twelfth-century manuscripts which contain contemporary versions of tales that are doubtless versions of older tales originating from far earlier times – just as with the works of Taliesin and the *Mabinogion*.

These stories contain echoes of pagan times, referencing old Irish deities and supernatural beings. That said, the influence of the Christian writers who recorded them for posterity can be seen in the texts, just as is the case with early Welsh, Norse, and Anglo-Saxon literature. For example, in the story of 'The Wasting Sickness of Cú Chulaind' we find a reference to the biblical Adam.[3] We do need to exercise some caution when looking at Irish mythology. These are the stories of the Irish Celts after all, not the British Celts. We must, therefore, be reticent to use them as a guide to Celtic culture and belief in pre-Roman mainland Britain.

Irish mythology, like Welsh, lacks any form of cogent creation myth or narrative. Instead, it provides us with a narrative of a series of migrations as different peoples arrived to claim Ireland (the Island of Destiny). It also provides us with tales of the adventures of Irish heroes. Most notable amongst these heroes is Cú Chulaind, who might be regarded as something of an Irish Hercules.

One of the early mythical races said to have lived in ancient Ireland were the Fomorians (or Fomóri). Their name may imply that they were underworld giants, either that or some form of watery underworld demon. Originally, they may well have been visualised as evil spirits, dwelling underwater, deep beneath the earth and, indeed, we are told that their forms were so ravaged by the sea that they were difficult to describe.[4] They are generally referred to as monstrous creatures, such as in 'The Destruction of Da Derga's Hostel' where they are depicted as three-headed sea monsters, sporting three rows of razor-sharp teeth. In later tales, they are portrayed as sea-raiders (perhaps recalling the Viking raiders who plagued Ireland from the ninth century onwards).

Another supernatural race of Irish origin is the enigmatic Tuatha Dé Danann. It is believed that at least some of the Tuatha were, in the dim and distant past, based on old Celtic deities amongst the early inhabitants of ancient Ireland, eventually being supplanted by the Irish themselves. The name literally means 'the people of Danu'.[5] Danu appears to have been an old Celtic goddess about whom virtually nothing is known for certain. Indeed, as the folk of Danu, they may have originally been seen as her divine children. However, after Ireland's conversion to Christianity in the fifth century, tales concerning pagan deities or demi-gods would have been problematic. Consequently, the Tuatha Dé Danann were re-imagined simply as supernatural entities rather than gods.

Medieval tales concerning these entities speak of an immortal race that possessed strange supernatural powers. According to Irish folklore, these entities retreated into a supernatural otherworld after the Irish themselves arrived on the island. It was a mysterious realm that could only be accessed via the ancient barrows dotted around the Irish landscape. Since these mounds are known as *sídhe* (pronounced 'shee') in Irish, these entities, and their descendants, were later referred to as *aes sídhe* ('people of the mound'). In addition to dwelling within ancient mounds, the Tuatha Dé Danann also had the ability to conceal their whereabouts within a magical mist. They could avoid human contact most effectively if they wished, only interacting with humankind when it suited them.

The mythical banshee, who seems to have appeared later in the Middle Ages, was a form of *aes sídhe*. This entity would lament the dead with her eerie wailing, cries. Rather disturbingly, she had the ability to foresee impending death and so her cries were a sure sign of approaching doom. A particularly famous member of the *sídhe* was the Morrigan (whose name translates to something approximate to the 'Phantom Queen').[6] The Morrigan may have originally been a Celtic deity associated with war and fate. Certainly, she appears to have had the gift of prophecy, able to foretell death, defeat, or victory in war. She was also a shape-changer, able to adopt different forms, perhaps most notably a crow. In more human form, she appeared either young and beautiful or as an old hag but seems to have been able to take the form of virtually any animal.[7]

The Tuatha Dé Danann were said to have brought four treasures with them when they first came to Ireland. Each of these treasures held potent supernatural powers. One was the Stone of Fál, which is reputed to have roared with joy when the rightful king of Ireland set his feet upon it. The second was the spear of Lugh, that would always hit its mark when thrown and that could be made to return to the hand of its owner when called. The third was the Sword of Light which no one could resist once it was drawn in anger. The fourth was the cauldron of the Dagda, which was a cauldron of abundance, reminiscent (and probably inspired by) the cornucopia of classical antiquity.[8]

The people of the *sídhe* were a magical and dangerous folk. In the wooing of Étáin, King Echu Airem must compete with the *sídhe* lord Midir for his Étáin. But competing with someone like Midir is far from straightforward. Midir uses magic to transform himself and Étáin into swans to elude his mortal rival. Even when Midir is finally forced to promise to send Étáin to the king, he sends him fifty women, all of whom look exactly like Étáin. The hapless king then must choose just one of them![9] Early stories of the Tuatha Dé Danann, the Brittonic Annwfn and the Norse and Saxon elves would eventually feed into the evolving high to late-medieval concept of fairy folk.

In addition to stories about the mysterious Tuatha Dé Danann, Irish myths from the early Middle Ages told many stories of the deeds of Irish heroes. These stories are often grouped together in 'cycles', containing tales with shared themes and characters.

Perhaps the best known of these traditions is the Ulster cycle (so called because these stories concern Ulster and Connacht in the first century). Many of these deal with the heroic deeds of the Irish hero Cú Chulaind. These tales feature enchantments, magic, curses, legendary weapons, and the intervention (for both good and ill) of the enigmatic Tuatha Dé Danann. And, of course, there are no shortage of battles and heroic fights. The influence of Cú Chulaind and his heroic deeds can be seen in later medieval stories.

The tale of the 'Bricrui's Feast' is found in the early twelfth century *Book of the Dun Cow.* It tells of the heroes of Ulster who contend with each other for the hero's portion at the feast. The matter is finally settled by the arrival of a giant at their hall who challenges all to a most unusual duel. The giant dares any man brave enough to strike off his head in one unopposed blow, saving one condition: that he allow the giant to return the blow the following night. One of the heroes accepts the challenge and strikes off the giant's head in a most spectacular fashion. But, to the horror of all present, the giant rises, collects his head and his axe, and leaves. The giant returns on the following night to return the blow, only to find that his opponent has fled. Several more heroes accept the challenge with the same result, much to the giant's chagrin.

Finally, the hero Cú Chulaind volunteers. As before, he smites off the giant's head. As before, the giant collects his head and leaves. As before, the giant returns the following night. But this time he finds Cú Chulaind waiting for him. Cú Chulaind does not flinch and kneels to receive the blow. But the giant does not strike off his head. Instead, the giant praises him for his courage and declares him the true hero of Ulster and the only man present worthy of the hero's portion at the feast.[10]

The tale of the 'Bricrui's Feast', of course, foreshadows the tale of 'Sir Gawain and the Green Knight', which followed centuries later. The original written versions of tales like 'Bricrui's Feast' may well date all the way back to the seventh or eighth century. However, as with other early medieval tales, they could well have been inspired by even earlier oral folk traditions. Pinning down a precise time for the origins of such tales is virtually impossible.

As with the tales we find in Norse and Welsh mythology, the versions we have were collated during Christian medieval times. It is, therefore, hard to say how much of an earlier pagan influence survives unfiltered by later Christian editors. Perhaps in the earliest versions of some of these stories, the Tuatha Dé Danann may have been portrayed more clearly as gods. But not in the versions that survive. In that which survives, the identity of such entities is more blurred, certainly supernatural but not necessarily gods. *The Book of Invasions*, rather frustratingly, tells us that only some of these entities (their men of arts) were considered gods but that many were not. Indeed, sometimes it is hard to tell men and women apart from *sídhe*.

Druids and those employing druidic magic feature in these stories. But how closely do the druids we encounter in Irish mythology reflect the pagan druids of the pre-Christian period? It is impossible to say. The druids of Irish mythology can appear as sorcerers wielding potent magic. For example, the witch Fúamnach uses druidic magic to transform her love rival into a scarlet fly by striking her with a wand of scarlet rowan.[11] Alternatively, druids appear as simple wise men, gifted with the power of prophecy.[12] Perhaps such examples reflect genuine powers that pagan druids claimed to possess. Or perhaps they simply reflect a memory of the old druids, no more than fictional embellishments, appearing long after the druids themselves had disappeared.

As with all these old stories, all we can hope to see are echoes of a pagan past. We cannot escape the fact that these tales come to us in a form that Christian writers were happy to record. How true they were to the pagan originals is ultimately unknowable. What is without doubt, however, is the fact that the old pagan world died, and in its place, a new medieval Christian world emerged.

Conversion and Transformation

Paganism had all but entirely disappeared from Western Europe by the time the first Plantagenet king was crowned in 1154. The Old Norse paganism still held sway in parts of Scandinavia but even here, Christianity was very much in the ascendence. Nevertheless, the Plantagenet world was now (and had been for some time) solidly part of Western Christendom.

However, medieval Christianity was experienced very differently from Christianity today. One key difference was that the great majority of Christians were illiterate. Even literate Christians rarely had access to a bible. Therefore, bible study played no part in most peoples' faith. Complete copies of the Bible were mostly reserved for Christian scholars, often working in monastic orders and locked away from the general population. These scholars and thinkers devoted their time to studying and interpreting scripture and helping to shape church doctrine. They were essentially the custodians of orthodoxy.

Outside of this relatively small group, even most parish priests lacked access to complete bibles. Typically, priests would deliver their services using several agreed texts. These liturgical books included a brevity, a salter, an antiphoner, a legendary, an ordinal, the missal and gradual, and the manual. The brevity contained most of the information required for conducting services. The salter and antiphoner contained psalms and chants to be sung during services. The legendary contained lessons and stories from the Bible, the church fathers, and the lives of saints. The ordinal provided priests with a practical guide to what needed to be included or excluded from specific services on specific days. The missal and gradual contained details required for performing the mass, while the manual contained instructions for performing pastoral services such as baptisms, weddings and administering last rites.[1]

Whilst most priests lacked access to a comprehensive bible, their salters provided them with a complete copy of the psalms. All the psalms would be read or (ideally) sung in services across the course of a week, on every week of the year. The medieval liturgy mandated that selective readings from the Old and New Testament also be sung (or at least read out) over the course of the year. These were provided within the liturgical books supplied to the clergy, rather than being taken directly from a bible. What was sung or read to the congregation was, therefore, heavily proscribed and, of course, delivered in Latin. Stories concerning the deeds and teaching of saints and church fathers were just as likely to feature in church services as bible stories.

All this meant that medieval Christianity, as it was experienced day to day, was often more orthopraxical than orthodoxic. That is to say that medieval Christianity was far more about singing, chanting, participating in rituals, listening to music, experiencing the smell of incense, and the spectacle of light shining through a stained-glass window. Bible stories were learned from song, oral storytelling, religious plays, and art, not from reading or study. A local priest might or might not choose to elucidate on Latin singing or chanting from the Bible with a translation in the local vernacular. All of this meant that the lived experience of participating in religion was far more important in defining faith than a detailed knowledge of the Bible.

Services were delivered in Latin and, at least officially, this was all that was required. However, many local priests introduced prayers, announcements, and translated elements of the service into the local vernacular to cater for the needs of their congregation.[2] Even though the congregations' understanding of Latin was generally very limited, this doesn't mean it held no meaning for them. Latin was the language of an older, grander age; a language that carried potency, authority, and genuine ritual power. Literal understanding was not required to experience its sound and cadence as a potent element of ritual.

What common folk learned at the parish church depended on what a priest knew, how literate he was, and whether he had access to all the necessary texts. This varied greatly, depending on a priest's education, the religious material he actually possessed, and his willingness to translate Latin rituals for his flock. Whilst most priests were literate, not all were. Literacy was supposedly a requirement of their vocation, but some priests were only semi-literate or had received an inadequate education.[3] It was also the case that not all priests had access to all the liturgical texts they were supposed to. So, what a typical parishioner knew about Noah, Adam and Eve, or other biblical stories depended very much on the priest.

Such things as the Lord's Prayer, although recited in Latin as the Pater Noster, were widely taught. People would learn it orally and memorise it by repetition, even if they might not even understand its precise meaning. Assuming your local priest chose to translate bible readings for his congregation, such readings would probably be the only time many people encountered the Bible directly.

Since religious festivals commemorated important events in the Christian calendar, most people would have known at least something of the stories behind these special times and often such festivals were based around the deeds of various saints and martyrs. As a result, church goers would hear numerous stories of these saints and martyrs and the various miraculous wonders associated with them. They might also hear fantastic apocryphal tales of the miracles of a particular saint that would not be accepted as remotely reliable in modern Christianity. For an illiterate villein or husbandman, it probably wasn't always clear as to which of these stories came from the Bible, and which did not.

Many aspects of medieval religion would not be regarded as orthodox by most Christians today. Medieval beliefs surrounding holy relics, sacred pilgrimage sites, visions, prophecies, and so forth may seem highly fantastic, and quite alien to a modern audience. But, to a medieval audience, such things were an accepted part of the way they viewed the world. Medieval Christian belief and practice influenced the character of myths and legends from this period. Religious stories did not need to be (and often were not) rooted in scripture and some might be regarded as only tangentially Christian. But all of them were framed within a medieval Christian cosmology as it was understood at the time.

The history of conversion, whereby early missionaries brought Christ's message to pagan peoples, was clearly seen as a great triumph for the church. It was also a key source of stories of martyrdom and miracles. When considered in this context, it is not surprising to find that, in some cases, apocryphal stories of such events could easily develop into fantastic mythical tales, sometimes emulating older biblical stories of miracles, revelation, and conversion. Those saints who played a key role in bringing Christianity to the British Isles were routinely associated with tales of miraculous deeds. Saint Augustine, who brought Christianity to the Anglo-Saxons, is a typical example. Bede tells us Augustine performed numerous miracles to demonstrate the truth of the Christian message to the people of Kent.[4]

However, folk traditions and customs are strong things, not easy to change. Therefore, the conversion process was often one of transformation rather than revolution. Old customs, traditions, and stories were not simply eradicated and replaced by Christian ones. Rather, old customs and beliefs were often reinvented or adapted to reflect a Christian worldview. Stories from the Bible and tales of the miraculous deeds of saints were actively blended with and overlaid upon existing cultural beliefs. The existence of holy wells provides a good example of this. Saint Augustine's medieval biographers relate a story in connection with his mission to Dorset. The eleventh-century hagiographer, Goscelin, claims Augustine miraculously conjured a well into being by striking the ground with his staff.[5] The well assumed miraculous properties, capable of providing healing, imbued as it was with the power of the saint.

Sacred wells, with magical healing properties, were also a feature of the pagan world. They are present in Celtic, Roman, and Norse mythology. The Roman period spa at Bath is a classic example. The sacred properties of Bath's thermal springs were important enough for the Romans to name the place Aquae Sulis (literally the waters of the goddess Sulis). Sulis was a local Celtic pagan goddess who assumed the identity of Sulis Minerva at the Baths (a religious merging of local Celt and pagan Roman identity). She was venerated by both Romans and local Celts, since local archaeology demonstrates that both peoples presented votive offerings here inscribed with their own languages.[6]

So, the idea that a well could have sacred or curative properties would have been very familiar to the pagan people whom the early saints aimed to convert. Pagan belief in the power of sacred wells was so ingrained that early attempts by the church to stamp out the veneration of such places met with little success. In the end, it often proved easier to simply appropriate the idea of sacred wells and 'Christianise' them.

In an even more overt example of transformation, the Bede tells us that pagan temples, rather than being destroyed, were often re-purposed as early churches. The idols were thrown out and replaced with crosses and other Christian symbols, but buildings and sites were otherwise retained intact as sacred places.[7]

The poems of Taliesin, *Beowulf*, the *Eddas*, and early Irish literature provide a rich source for pagan mythology. However, as we have seen, these are pagan stories retold by Christians. And, in each case a Christian filter is often in evidence. Taliesin frequently mentions Christian themes in his poems, even those with a strong pagan flavour. In *Beowulf*, we are told that the monster Grendel is the descendant of the biblical Cain. The prologue of the *Prose Eddas* explains why it is that the Norse gods in the stories are not true gods (since there is but one true god). Old Irish myths mention biblical Adam.

Most certainly, pagan customs and superstitions could and did survive into Christian times. At least a few people were still practicing paganism in Kent in the early eighth century, a full century after the kingdom had theoretically converted.[8] Overt paganism would ultimately disappear over the centuries, of course. Nevertheless, many pagan superstitions and customs would endure in a form that would be re-imagined within a Christian worldview.

In time, medieval Christian culture began to develop myths and stories of its own. Over the centuries it evolved a rich tapestry of stories and beliefs surrounding miracles, visions, prophecies, holy sites, and relics. Medieval Christian mythology developed most extensively in three key areas.

Firstly, and most obviously, were the tales associated with the numerous saints and martyrs. Ever more spectacular tales of miraculous events, mysterious happenings, and encounters with fantastic supernatural entities flourished throughout the period. Secondly, is the mythology that sprang up surrounding the relics and sacred sites associated with these saints. In many cases, these relics seem to have inspired a greater number of miraculous happenings than the original saint. Even things touched by these relics could, in their turn, come to radiate holy powers! Thirdly, was the evolution of Christian mysticism and the belief in ecstatic visions and apocalyptic prophecy this inspired.

These beliefs would reach a spectacular zenith during the Middle Ages before fading from Western culture, from the Early Modern period onwards. For Christianity, and perhaps for Europe, the world would never seem quite so full of miracles and marvels again.

Saints and Martyrs

The cult of saints became a major feature of the Christian faith during the Middle Ages. By the time the Plantagenets came to power, the number of saints outnumbered the number of days in the year to a very considerable degree. Countries, cities, and towns commonly had their own patron saint who could be called upon for divine assistance in the hour of need. And, if you had a problem, there was almost certainly an appropriate saint who you could count on for help. Going on a crusade? Perhaps you might consider praying to Saint George for aid? Are you a fisherman, hoping for a bountiful catch? Pray to Saint Andrew. Is your cow sick? Pray to Saint Francis.

In some ways, the cult of saints had parallels with older pagan practices. In pagan polytheism, you'd pray to different gods for aid, depending on the power and portfolio of the god concerned. If you were a sailor, you'd pray to a sea god. If you were a farmer on the other hand, you'd pick a god who served as a patron for agriculture. Also in pagan times, the tombs of ancient heroes and revered religious sites would attract pilgrims, just like the saints' shrines. In ancient Greece, pilgrims regularly visited Delphi, hoping to receive prophetic guidance. Alexander the Great visited the tomb of the hero Achilles to pay his respects and, presumably, benefit from at least some of Achilles' heroic legacy rubbing off on himself.

That said, the cult of saints took these ideas and developed them in a uniquely Christian way, going far beyond anything we see in earlier times. One key element that features in many of the saints' stories related to martyrdom, something we don't see to the same extent in earlier beliefs. Of, course, this was largely inspired by the history of Christianity itself. Early in the life of the religion, Christians were often persecuted, subjected to legal penalties, tortured, and killed. This was true of some of Christ's disciples (as well as Christ himself) and for a great number of other early Christians leaders.

At various times, pagan Roman emperors imposed mass persecutions on religious minorities such as the early Christians. Emperors such as Nero and Diocletian provide us with perhaps the most infamous examples. During these persecutions, Christians were tortured and executed in a wide variety of ways, ranging from crucifixion to being torn to pieces by wild beasts in the arena. These early martyrs were much revered by the medieval church.

Early stories of Christian saints, therefore, often contained some quite distinctive elements. The first was the story of their mission, which usually involved the conversion of pagans and the foundation of new Christian communities. The second was the story of miracles associated with the saint. These miracles were invariably produced as a demonstration of the power of God to inspire the conversion of doubting souls.

The third was often martyrdom. The saint would be taken, tortured, and killed in the most horrific ways by their pagan persecutors. However, whilst a fate of torture and death might seem like failure, such a grisly end was often re-packaged as an inspiring tale of holy triumph. And so, tales of martyrdom came to follow a set formula. Saints would meet their ends stoically. They would endure any degree of pain and suffering and yet remain unwavering in their convictions. The power of God would enable them to endure their personal passion, seemingly unmoved by the pain, safe in the certainty of their own salvation. These were tales not simply of human courage in the face of adversity, but of miraculous resilience. The martyrs were elevated beyond the natural limits of human endurance and courage to the level of the divine superhuman.

And finally, and increasingly inevitably, followed the fantastic tales and miracles associated with saintly relics. A typical early example from the post Roman period, and of particular significance for early medieval English Christians, is the story of Saint Oswald. Much of what we know of the life of this saint comes to us from the Venerable Bede, who wrote just a couple of generations after Oswald's death. Saint Oswald was an Anglo-Saxon king who'd played a key role in spreading Christianity amongst the Northumbrians in the mid-seventh century.

Oswald came to prominence at a time of struggle between paganism and Christianity amongst the northern Anglo-Saxons. He famously defeated his adversaries at a battle Bede calls *Hefenfelth* ('Heavenly field'). Bede makes much of Oswald's erection of a cross prior to the battle and attributes his triumph to divine aid. However, Oswald's opponent in this battle was not a pagan but another Christian – King Cadwallon of Gwynedd. Despite this, Bede regarded Cadwallon's Celtic form of Christianity as no more than a false veneer. For Bede, this wild form of what he saw as faux-Christianity could never adequately mask the savage tyranny of a king more pagan than Christian.

The site where Oswald erected the Heavenfield cross quickly became associated with miraculous events. Bede informs us that a travelling monk who'd broken his arm had it healed simply by coming into possession of a piece of moss, scraped from the surface of Oswald's cross.

Oswald's primary achievements were undoubtedly the stability he brought to Northumbria and his patronage of the church. He famously founded the Christian community at Lindisfarne and several other churches and monasteries across his kingdom. Despite his secular power, Bede is at pains to emphasise Oswald's Christian virtues: his humility, kindness, and generosity.[1]

In one famous story we are told that Oswald, sitting down to a feast next to Bishop Aidan, ordered his food to be distributed to the poor begging in the road outside. This so impressed the bishop that he clutched Oswald's right arm and said, 'May this hand never wither with age.'[2] Inevitably, the right hand of Saint Oswald became a potent relic after his death.

In the end Oswald was slain in battle, fighting against the heathen Mercian King Penda. Not strictly speaking a martyrdom, but close enough to position Oswald as a man who died for his faith. The place where Oswald fell, Bede tells us, became so infused with holy power that many later pilgrims were able to find healing there. So great a reputation did the curative powers of this site acquire that people began taking away samples of 'holy' soil. Enough soil was eventually removed to scoop away a large pit, fully deep enough for a man to stand inside!

Bede's treatment of the various miracles and holy sites associated with Oswald's relics is extensive. So extensive, in fact, that he devotes more time to covering them than he does to telling us about the life of Oswald himself! Such miraculous and inspiring stories were a portent of things to come.

In around 1260, in Lombardy, a Dominican friar by the name of Jacobus de Voragine, sat down to compile a book entitled *Legenda Aurea* (*The Golden Legend*). He wrote it with the intention that its circulation would be limited to the clergy. It was designed to serve as a useful reference resource, providing priests with material to add engaging colour and edification to their sermons. And its content? *The Golden Legend* was primarily dedicated to detailing the lives of saints and martyrs, arranged in the calendar order of their feast days. This made it easy for a priest to drop a story about a saint into his sermons at the appropriate time of year.

The Golden Legend drew on a wide range of sources of varying provenance. Not all of these were especially reliable. However, Father Jacobus chose to deal with this little problem in the same manner as Herodotus. That is to say that he included apocryphal stories anyway with such qualifications as 'Whether any of this is true we leave to the reader's judgement'.[3] Potential factual flaws aside, at the time of its publications, the *Legend* represented perhaps the most comprehensive collection of hagiographies on the lives of saints. *The Golden Legend* was an instant smash hit and was destined to become one of the most popular books of the Middle Ages. It would serve as inspiration not only for sermons delivered from the pulpit but also for artists and secular writers, who'd seek inspiration from the *Legend* throughout the period.

History has since seen the *Legend* fall from favour. Its fantastical tales of saints and their miraculous exploits epitomised exactly the kind of Catholic beliefs that early modern Protestants found most offensive. Jacobus de Voragine's enthusiasm to literally include as much detail as possible, even if the provenance was questionable, would not survive the Catholic Reformation. In time, it would be supplanted in the Catholic tradition by more scholarly hagiographies, such as Butler's eighteenth-century *Lives of the Saints*. De Voragine's *Legend*, therefore, represents a lost world of miracles, martyrs, and relics, long vanished from European culture. But for a time, in medieval Europe, it was this vision of the world that reigned supreme.

Even when it was first published in 1260, *The Golden Legend* nostalgically harkened back to a lost age of martyrdom as most of the saints Jacobus de Voragine selected for his hagiographies had been dead for centuries. Even though there were more saints closer to his era that he could have chosen for his collection, de Voragine preferred to dwell on the early period of Church history. Inclusion of saints from the post-Roman period are very much the exception rather than the rule.

This focus enabled de Voragine to dwell on dramatic tales of martyrdom, so common to the lives of these early saints. His style chooses to present us with saints who were already more celestial than mortal. Unwavering, resolute, and aided directly by a divine power that enables them to endure the most extreme human suffering with effortless serenity. These are men and women capable of miracles that confound and frustrate their persecutors, overawing them with the power of heaven. In short, these are not poignant human stories that necessarily evoke sympathy. They are, quite literally, legendary tales of holy heroism. The reader is supposed to feel inspired with awe and wonder at the deeds of these saints, not feel sympathy or empathy. Indeed, how can one feel empathy for someone who has already transcended the human condition; for someone already more part of the kingdom of heaven than the mundane world?

The Golden Legend's version of the tale of Saint Agnes provides a good example. Agnes was a young teenage girl of around 13 years old, living at the end of the third or early fourth century. She was a devout Christian who pledged herself to a life of celibacy. Several young men nevertheless tried hard to win her affections. Amongst them was the son of the Roman prefect. The *Legend* tells us his advances were robustly rebuffed since Agnes had already betrothed herself to Christ. 'Go away, you spark that lights the fires of sin, you fuel of wickedness, you food of death!', she cries.[4]

Despite this knockback, the young man persists. At first, he and his father attempt to persuade her. When this fails, they resort to increasingly coercive tactics. When all else fails, Agnes' faith is eventually used to condemn her. The angry prefect has her dragged to a brothel, where she is stripped and humiliated. Despite this, her faith protects her. Her hair miraculously grows to cover her modesty and the brothel is filled with a blinding celestial light, radiating from her guardian angel. The men who lust after her flee from the holy light, but the prefect's son is undeterred. He then attempts to rape Agnes but is instead strangled by the devil. As Agnes explains to the prefect, by consenting to do the devil's work, he fell prey to the devil's power.[5] However, Agnes demonstrates the power of God by raising the boy from the dead. The prefect's son is miraculously converted by his experience and begins preaching Christ's message at once. The local pagan community then turn on Agnes, claiming she has used some kind of sorcery to befuddle the wits of the prefect's son. The authorities seize Agnes and attempt to burn her. However, divine power prevents the flames from harming her. In the end, she can only be killed by being stabbed in the throat.

On one level, this is a story about a young girl being sexually assaulted by the son of a powerful politician. She is persecuted and killed for offending the powers that be and remaining true to her faith. Likely, this was, in essence, the simple and tragic truth behind Agnes' story. However, at no stage in this medieval version of the story does young Agnes show the slightest fear or doubt. And, at every turn, divine power works through her to thwart and confound the machinations of the secular powers. Even when faced with death, Agnes remains serene, channelling a holy power that is manifestly more than a match for the authorities. Agnes, far from appearing a victim, is recast as a holy champion, always in ultimate control of the situation.

A particularly important saint from a Plantagenet point of view was, of course, Saint George. Edward III dedicated the Order of the Garter in his name and, by the reign of Henry V, he was firmly established as England's patron saint.[6] The original Saint George was most likely a Christian officer in the Roman army who was martyred for his faith in the early fourth century. In *The Golden Legend* we are presented with a story in two distinct halves. This first half tells us about Saint George the dragon slayer and the second concerns Saint George the martyr. Both reflect the fact that the original man had been a soldier but the *Legend*'s version recasts him with a description that makes him sound much more like a chivalrous, medieval knight.

The dragon slaying story follows a narrative that we would now recognise as a trope. A community is plagued by a dragon that can only be placated by feeding it livestock. However, when the supply of livestock runs out, the people resort to offering human sacrifices. In the end, a maiden is chosen and sent out to her doom. On the road she meets Saint George who, unable to ignore a damsel in distress, promptly rides off to despatch the dragon.

The dragon slaying completed, the *Legend* moves rapidly on to describe how Saint George and others are persecuted for their faith and martyred. The two stories are not directly connected by anything other than the fact that George appears in both. George, we are told, filled with grief at the persecution of so many Christians, lays aside his wealth, his possessions, and his military life to follow the path of martyrdom. His death, however, does not go unpunished. The Roman official responsible for his execution is struck down by an avenging divine fire sent down from the heavens.[7]

Saint George's dragon is by no means the only dragon to appear in *The Golden Legend.* In the tale of Saint James the Greater, the disciple splits a fire-breathing dragon in two by making the sign of the cross.[8] Saint Martha confronts a dragon in southern France, subduing it with the sign of the cross and binding it with her girdle.[9] In the tale of Saint Margaret, we are even told that she was eaten alive by a dragon before making the sign of the cross and bursting out unscathed from its belly![10] This latter story is a step too far even for de Voragine, who feels compelled to admit that he does not personally believe it. His personal scepticism, of course, does not prevent him from relating the story anyway.

The saints in the *Legend* not only have to confront dragons but also demons. In the tale of Saint Simon and Saint Jude, the saints are called upon to confront a group of pagan priests in the city of Samir. The local pagans try to entice the saints to venerate their temple idols, but the saints demonstrate their idols are demons by performing an exorcism. The demons are cast out of the idols which they angrily smash before fleeing from the saints. The enraged pagan priests then proceed to murder the saints. This naturally incurs the wrath of God who destroys the temple with lightning.[11]

These fantastic tales of miracles and marvels clearly resonated with a medieval audience. There is no denying their widespread popularity. One might wonder why it was that tales of marvels, wonders and supernatural heroism had such strong appeal? Why was it that a more human portrayal of these saints was not preferred? Certainly, it would have been possible (as indeed happened later) to present a more sober and scholarly account based on more reliable sources. This would have cut out many of the more fantastic details and presented more human and (to our modern eye) more believable and empathic stories. But perhaps this wasn't what people wanted or needed in the Middle Ages.

The reality of medieval life for many people was harsh. Life was often violent and short. Famine, disease, and war represented more common and more immediate dangers than we can possibly appreciate in our comfortable modern age. Living in such a world, is it so surprising that many people would prefer stories about marvels and miracles to tales of human suffering and tragedy? Perhaps what you really need is wonder and marvel, escapism, and heroism and, yes, perhaps hope.

The saints and their ability to call upon divine aid provided the chance, however slight, that tragedy and suffering might somehow be miraculously avoided. Or, even if tragedy proved unavoidable, it could at least be endured and transcended. Saints and martyrs could also supply a way to rationalise tragedy when it did strike.

After the Battle of Agincourt, in 1415, the French struggled to make sense of their spectacular defeat. How could it have been possible to lose so many good French knights on a single day? Where was the justice? Where, indeed, was God? Looking at the date of the battle the answer soon became all too apparent. The Battle of Agincourt had been fought on Saint Crispin's Day. Saint Crispin, amongst other things, had his tomb in Soissons, in France. Prior to Henry V's invasion of France, the French had been fighting a vicious civil war for control of the court. On the one side was the Duke of Burgundy's faction, on the other was the Armagnac faction. In 1414, the year before Agincourt, an Armagnac army besieged Burgundian-held Soissons. On taking it, they proceeded to sack it and massacred many civilians. The French army at Agincourt, as it turned out, mainly consisted of Armagnacs. The link, in the medieval mind, was clear. The French tragedy at Agincourt on Saint Crispin's Day could only be an act of divine punishment. The Armagnacs had clearly offended the saint by their actions at Soissons and Agincourt saw God's justice done upon them.[12]

The power of the saints was very real. Real in the sense that their stories clearly had the power to influence and inspire people throughout the Middle Ages. People strongly believed the saints had the power to protect and nurture those who petitioned them for aid. But they also believed the saints had the power to intercede for God's punishment upon anyone who dared harm those under their protection.

Relics and Holy sites

It is the sixth century. The old pagan world is dying but the new medieval Christian world is still very young. The wife of a man called Seratanus is suddenly and inexplicably struck dumb. What should he do? First, he calls upon the services of a traditional Roman diviner, a *harioli,* who attempts to treat his wife with herbs. It does not work. So, Seratanus decides to give some new-fangled magic a go. He calls upon the services of a Christian, who anoints his wife with oil and dust from the tomb of Saint Martin. Miraculously, the woman is cured![1] Whether she recovered by the power of relics, by the comforting words of her Christian nurse, or simply by natural means – it does not really matter. The fact is that a new form of magic has been born to replace the old.

Relics and holy sites associated with saints and biblical stories were destined to become a major component of medieval Christian belief. Previous times had seen their share of sacred sites, attracting their share of pilgrims and the concept of magical or sacred items was also nothing new. However, the relics and holy sites of the Middle Ages took the mythology surrounding such things to a whole new level.

Legendary items from pagan times, like swords and shields wielded by Greek heroes, were regarded as having magical or sacred properties. In this sense, they were no different from relics. However, the magical properties of these pagan items derived directly from the god or otherworldly force that had created them. What made the shield of Perseus special was its divine creator, not simply the fact that Perseus himself owned it.

The Christian concept of relics and sacred sites was different. These things held sacred power because they were associated with a holy saint, or a miraculous event, or a particular bible story. They were special by association. In short, their proximity to someone or something holy, in and of itself, was enough to make them holy. In this manner, holy power could be transferred from a saint to an object he or she had owned or from a miracle performed by a saint to the place at which the miracle occurred.

These places and objects had the power to offer many things. A path to redemption from sin, divine favour, miraculous healing, or even the power to punish enemies of the faith. These items and places assumed a sacred potency that is uniquely characteristic of medieval Christian belief. We might well ask how and why this came about? It is especially intriguing given the relatively limited biblical precedent for such beliefs.

The New Testament contains stories that bear witness to the fact that proximity to Christ or an Apostle can facilitate miraculous healing. It provides examples of people being healed by touching the clothing of Christ. Indeed, healing could come simply by touching a scarf that Apostle Paul had touched, or even by passing through the Apostle Peter's shadow whilst both still lived.[2] But these particular avenues to miraculous healing happened whilst Christ and his apostles were still living and usually in reasonable proximity. It is quite some leap to go from this to believing that a finger bone of a martyr who's been dead for four centuries can bestow miraculous healing. Indeed, sixteenth-century Puritans would no doubt argue that it was far too much of a leap – a leap into superstition. Nevertheless, whatever our personal thoughts on such matters, the fact is that it was a leap that was made. But how? Indeed, why?

Part of the answer must lie with the crucifixion story so central to the faith. Christ's example of suffering on the cross provided a path to redemption. So, in a sense, the idea that extreme sacrifice generates a powerful divine reward was baked into Christianity from the start. Since so many early Christian martyrs suffered similarly extreme ends, the sacrifice of the saint naturally assumed a potent spiritual significance. It is not hard to see how the idea that saintly sacrifice had the power to yield potent spiritual dividends evolved.

In the late Roman period, the state persecution of Christians, which had lasted for three centuries, abruptly came to an end. Suddenly, Christianity went from state enemy to state religion. All the suffering, the fear, the persecutions, the tortures, the executions, the need for secrecy, the need to hide, the need to flee – was over. What an incredible release it must have been!

What had previously remained hidden or, at the very least, practiced with discretion, could now be openly celebrated, making it possible to openly mourn the martyrs and even openly celebrate their lives and deeds. This ecstatic emotional release is encapsulated by the words of Bishop Vitricius of Rouen, in a sermon preached to celebrate the arrival of saintly relics at his Cathedral in 396: 'In this time there is no outpouring of blood, no persecutor pursues us, yet we are filled with the joy of triumphs. So, we must immerse ourselves in tears, and release our great joy in lavish weeping!'[3]

John Chrysostom, living around the same period, advocated visiting the tombs of martyrs to remember them and, by honouring their memory and their deeds, obtain divine blessing.[4] Thus, commemoration rapidly morphed into veneration. The remembrance and contemplation of the life and deeds of the saint was the original source of divine favour. But this soon evolved to encompass the objects and places associated with that saint and their deeds. Thus, an object became a holy relic, and a tomb became a pilgrimage site.

The relics and tombs of saints had to be held somewhere, typically in cathedrals, abbeys, and priories; spaces controlled by the church. People had to make the effort to visit these places if they wanted to benefit from the divine favours that might be obtained and thus the concept of pilgrimage was born. Pilgrimage, of course, was a big deal. You had to leave your home, your family, and your livelihood behind you and take to the road, sometimes for weeks. During that time, you wouldn't really be earning any money, you'd be reliant on your savings and the charity of others along the way. The road itself might be difficult, it might even be dangerous. Being a pilgrim, by definition, involved sacrifice.

There were many reasons why you might go on a pilgrimage. Perhaps a family member had been gravely ill, and you'd promised God that you would go on a pilgrimage if their life was spared. Perhaps you were going in the hopes of receiving healing for an affliction from which you were suffering. Or maybe, to give thanks for surviving a battle or atone for some wrongdoing. In the early days of pilgrimage, you might wear a simple russet cassock, patched with crosses to signify you were on a spiritual journey. You might also wear a wide-brimmed hat, sporting a pewter badge or two – mementos of past pilgrimages you'd made. However, by Chaucer's time, in the late fourteenth century, these customs were regarded as anachronistic. By this time, most pilgrims simply wore their everyday clothes.

The ultimate pilgrimage would be to visit the Holy Land and the various sacred places linked to the life and death of Christ. These places and the relics they contained represented many of the most potent in Christendom. Perhaps the most sacred site in all Christendom was the Holy Sepulchre in Jerusalem. Even after the crusaders had been driven from the Middle East, it was still possible for pilgrims to visit the Sepulchre. Although Muslims subsequently controlled access to it, they were happy to let pilgrims visit the site. Here, it was possible to visit the Holy Basilica and to see the actual site of Christ's tomb. The rock at the entrance of the tomb had been drawn aside during the resurrection. Here, you could touch the sacred rock, see the sacred tomb, and experience the very site where Christ himself had been resurrected. You could also visit the hill at Calvary, the place of the Crucifixion, where the attendant monks would point out a rock, stained with the blood of Christ. Other sacred relics you could see at this extraordinary place included the head of Adam, the stone where Joseph of Arimathea had washed the body of Christ after the crucifixion, the garden where the risen Christ had appeared to Mary Magdalene, the place where the Holy Cross had been buried and much more.[5]

For some, a visit to Jerusalem was an overwhelming spiritual experience. When the English mystic, Margery Kempe visited in the early fifteenth century, she described receiving a vision of Christ, standing before her. Whilst visiting the hill of Calvary, she fell to the ground and was unable to get up, writhing around and crying out, gripped by a vivid ecstatic vision of the Crucifixion.[6]

Henry Bolingbroke (later Henry IV) spent the best part of a year on a pilgrimage to the Holy Sepulchre in 1393/4. His experience was of a different character to Margery's. For one thing, he took with him a large entourage and was entertained at several European courts enroute. He was the first English royal to successfully make a pilgrimage to the Holy Sepulchre and, in doing so, he earnt himself considerable prestige. In his case, the purpose of the pilgrimage was primarily one of enhancing his reputation by demonstrating his piety.[7]

However, Henry was exceptionally rich. He could easily afford to make such a long trip. His formidable military entourage, not to say his own considerable martial skills, meant the road held few dangers for him. The political brownie points he earned in the process made it well worth his while. For most ordinary folk, such a lengthy and potentially hazardous (not to say expensive) journey was out of the question. Of course, for a devoted spiritual mystic such as Margery Kempe, no amount of risk or inconvenience could deter such a pilgrim. Nevertheless, most pilgrims were of humbler means than Henry and lacked the zealous faith of Margery. Fortunately for them, there were no shortage of pilgrimage sites, with their own relics and saints' tombs, scattered across England. These were much better suited to the needs of the ordinary pilgrim.

The most important pilgrimage site in England was Canterbury Cathedral and its lavish shrine to its martyred archbishop, Thomas Becket. So famous was this place that as many as 200,000 pilgrims came to pay their respects every year. The shrine itself was truly magnificent, lavishly decorated with gold plate, and studded with precious jewels, including a particularly large ruby. Visitors could buy small sacred vessels containing holy water mixed with a tiny drop of the martyred saint's blood. These sacred vessels were said to have beneficial healing powers. You could also buy pewter badge souvenirs depicting scenes and images of the martyr's death.[8] Unsurprisingly, the income for the cathedral was significant. All the gold plate and precious jewels had to be paid for somehow!

The second most popular holy site in England was Walsingham Priory. It famously contained a shrine to Mother Mary and a replica hut that was supposed to be an exact copy of the house the holy family had lived in at Nazareth. Even though it was a replica and not the original, this was still enough to mark it out as a holy place. Visiting pilgrims underwent a lengthy religious ritual experience. They would first arrive at a small chapel, around a mile and a half away. There, after praying, they would remove their shoes and make the rest of the journey barefoot. On arrival at the priory, they would make an offering before kissing the finger bone of Saint Peter. They would then visit the sacred Nazarene hut for further prayer and meditation, perhaps drinking from one of the two holy wells there. Here, or so it was said, drinking the holy waters had the power to grant a pilgrim whatever he or she truly desired. Finally, pilgrims would visit the sacred shrine of Mother Mary herself. There they would pay their respects to the most sacred relic in the priory – the Holy Milk of the Virgin Mary.[9]

The act of visiting such sites was, therefore, an entire spiritual experience that went far beyond simply seeing a relic or praying at a shrine. And, often, these sacred places were lavishly decorated with magnificent riches, well beyond the day-to-day experience of most pilgrims. These were truly places of awe and wonder. Places where it was possible to come close to touching and experiencing the divine. Places, perhaps, for healing, for redemption, or to give due thanks for divine aid already received.

Over time, a gloriously rich mythology evolved concerning the origins and histories of sacred relics. Stories of miraculous discoveries, links to holy saints and biblical figures, and the many miracles enabled by them. One of the most fantastic tales pertains to perhaps one of the holiest relics in all Christendom – the Holy Cross on which Christ himself had been crucified. The full telling of the myth surrounding its finding can be found, of course, in *The Golden Legend.*

This tale begins a long time ago, not long after Adam was cast out of the garden of Eden. Adam, now an old man, is in frail health. His son, Seth, sets out to the gates of paradise in search of a cure. He asks the Archangel Michael for oil from the Tree of Mercy but is refused. Man, for his sin, may no longer enjoy the fruits of paradise. Instead, the Angel provides Seth with a cutting from the tree and instructs him to plant it on the mountain of Lebanon. Seth returns with the cutting, but he is too late; by this time his father is dead. And so, Seth buries Adam and plants the sapling on his grave.

The years pass and the sapling grows into a great tree. One day, King Solomon is passing by and is greatly impressed by the tree's beauty. He has it cut down with the intention of using it to build himself a forest house. However, his builders cannot find a way to use the tree and so they put it aside. The tree is instead used as a bridge across a pond. A little while later, the queen of Sheba comes to visit. She receives a vision: one day the saviour of the world will hang from this wood. Overcome with awe, she immediately kneels and worships it. She then informs Solomon that one day a man will die upon this tree and that, as a result, the kingdom of the Jews will be destroyed. Solomon, fearful of this prophecy, buries the wood so that it might never be found.

Time passes and a miraculous spring bubbles to the surface where the sacred wood is buried. Its holy waters have the power to heal the sick. Nevertheless, it remains hidden until the time comes for the crucifixion when the wood floats to the surface of the pond and is taken by Christ's executioners to use in the construction of the cross. After the crucifixion, the cross is hidden once more and remains concealed for nearly three centuries. Then, miraculously, it is rediscovered after an extensive search by Helena, the mother of the Christian Roman Emperor Constantine.

It is at this point that our story takes a darker, antisemitic, turn. Helena's attempts to find the cross, we are told, are hindered by Jerusalem's Jewish community. Fearing that the finding of the cross will spell the end of their religion, the Jews resolve to keep its location hidden. Helena, however, identifies a Jew by the name of Judas who knows the location of the cross. Judas is at first unwilling to reveal what he knows, so Helena resorts to coercion and has the hapless fellow starved for seven days. Eventually, Judas agrees to show her the location and, as soon as he leads her to the place, we are told 'the earth suddenly quaked and a mist of sweet-smelling perfumes greeted their senses'.[10] This leads to the instant conversion of Judas, who claps his hands together with joy when he realises that Christ is truly the saviour. Seeing the error of his former ways, Judas is baptised and changes his name to the more Christian sounding, Quiriacus. Eventually the good Quiriacus even becomes a bishop!

And so, the True Cross is found! However, there is a problem. Helena did not just find one cross but three. One was the cross of Christ but the other two were the crosses of the criminals who'd died with him. How to tell which was the True Cross? Clearly some kind of miraculous revelation was required. Fortunately, one was duly provided. The three crosses were erected in a square and, after a time, a funeral procession passed by. The deceased was brought to the first cross – nothing. Then the next – also nothing. Then on being brought before the third, he miraculously came back to life! There was now no doubt. This was indeed the True Cross!

After this time pieces of the cross were distributed across Christendom, preserved in silver casing. Helena brought back a large piece for her son, the emperor. In addition to wood, there were also nails, and even these were treated with great reverence. And so, goes the tale of the finding of the True Cross.

Most holy sites and relics were not so grand as this of course. Nevertheless, they all served as a source of spiritual inspiration and comfort for medieval pilgrims. But we shouldn't get too carried away with the marvellous myths of *The Golden Legend.* At this point, it's worth considering a cautionary tale. The promise of divine aid offered by relics and sacred sites could sometimes have tragic consequences.

In the middle of the fourteenth century, as the Black Death swept across Europe, many people feared they were seeing the end of times. Between one third to a half of the entire population was dying. Such carnage had never been seen before and some feared that, perhaps, no one would survive. It seemed almost as if the Angel of Death was sweeping mercilessly across the world.

In the absence of any effective medicine and with no scientific understanding of the unfolding pandemic, there was little people could practically do. For most people, all they had was their faith. To many it seemed that only a miracle could save them and so, in search of a miracle, many set off on a pilgrimage to a sacred site. Here, perhaps, a saint might hear their prayers and intercede to save them from the pestilence. Or perhaps a holy relic might provide them and their family with divine protection. However, as people gathered at holy shrines in search of miraculous salvation, they created the ideal conditions in which infection could spread. Perhaps their pilgrimage gave them hope in dark and desperate times, but, for many, it also gave them a deadly infection.[11]

There can be few more tragic chapters in human history.

Visions, Prophecy, and Mysticism

From its earliest beginnings visions, prophecy, and mysticism have played a role in Christianity. Afterall, such phenomena feature prominently in several bible stories.

The Venerable Bede relates several stories featuring visions and prophecies from the early history of the church in England. A particularly striking example concerns a Northumbrian man by the name of Drythelm Cunningham. Bede tells us that he became gravely ill and, despite his family's prayers, one night, he died. The next morning whilst his family were still grieving, a miraculous thing happened. Drythelm, seemingly inexplicably, came back to life and was restored to full health. This near-death experience had a transforming effect on Drythelm, who immediately set aside worldly concerns to become a reclusive monk. He dedicated his life to prayer, lived simply, frequently fasted and dived into icy rivers as a form of self-mortification.

So, what had happened to Drythelm to bring about this epiphany?

When questioned about his experience he related how, during the time when he'd been dead, he'd received a powerful revelation concerning the afterlife. He claimed that, after he left his mortal body, a handsome man in a shining robe came to him as a guide. This fellow first led him through a terrifying valley. On one side was a raging inferno, on the other an icy wasteland, blasted by fierce snowstorms. He could see people tormented on both sides of the valley. Those in the fires leapt across to the snowstorms when they could bear the heat no longer. Those in the snowstorms leapt into the flames when the cold became too much for them. And so it was that they leapt from one to another in endless torment. And, yet, his guide told him that what he was seeing was not hell.

Next, his guide brought him to the edge of a vast black chasm. The guide disappeared and he found himself suddenly alone in this dark place. Great fires burned deep in the chasm, and colossal gouts of flames spewed up from the unspeakable depths below. Within the flames he could see tormented souls, burning like sparks in the fire. Then he saw a gang of devils, dragging a small party of whimpering souls down into the chasm, the devils' laughter merging with the pathetic screams of their captives, as they hauled them down into the flames. Then the devils returned and surrounded him, threatening him with tongs. But just then his guide returned, and the devils fled.

His guide took him next to a great wall of light and then, though he did not understand how, he found himself and his guide beyond the wall. Suddenly he was in a beautiful meadow, filled with happy people in white robes talking and laughing. He wondered if this might be heaven, but his guide told him it was not. Then they continued across the meadow and passed near to a place filled with a brilliant celestial light, sweet scents, and angelic singing. It seemed a most wonderous place, but his guide would take him no further.

At this point, his guide explained the meaning of what he had seen before returning him to life. The valley of fire and ice had been a purgatory where sinful but repentant souls were purged of evil before finally being permitted into the kingdom of heaven. The fiery chasm was the gate of hell and once a damned soul passed down into the flame there could be no return for them. The wonderous meadow was a place where those who had lived a good life came before being admitted to heaven. The wonderous place of celestial light was heaven itself, to which only the saintliest are directly admitted. Those within the meadow are destined to join them in time but were not yet so pure that they could be admitted at once. With the vision explained Drythelm's guide departed, and he was returned to mortal life, a much-changed man.[1]

In Drythelm's case his vision inspired him to live the ascetic life of a holy man. However, visions could potentially come to anyone in the Middle Ages, given the right conditions. Often, they served as a source of genuine religious inspiration but sometimes they could inspire violent fanatical zeal.

The crusades, especially the First Crusade, inspired a fierce appetite for holy war in a great many people across western Europe. It was preached by the pope and the church as a righteous campaign to free the Holy Land from heathen oppression. Of course, many of the crusades' leaders had secular as well as religious motives. For some, as second sons of powerful lords, it was their chance to carve out a personal fiefdom in the east, perhaps their only chance. For others, like Richard the Lionheart, it was all about personal glory. Nevertheless, the role played by religious fervour, for many, cannot be denied.

No better example of this can be found than at the siege of Antioch during the First Crusade. It was June 1098. Antioch had fallen to the crusading army after a long siege. However, the Muslim east, though greatly divided, had finally set aside its differences to unite behind a single powerful leader, Kerbogha. He now marched on Antioch with a view to re-taking it and crushing the crusaders once and for all. His army of some 40,000 outnumbered the crusaders by a factor of two to one. Now it was the crusaders who were besieged.

In early June, Kerbogha's great army encircled the city, and by 10 June, the crusaders were all but completely hemmed in. Things looked very bleak. However, just at this time a poor peasant crusader announced that he had received a vision from Saint Andrew. According to his vision a potent holy relic, the spear that had pierced the side of Christ upon the cross, was buried within Antioch's walls. A search was duly conducted and, sure enough, this wonderous relic was discovered.

Things were growing desperate by this time since the defenders were running out of supplies. However, the discovery of the sacred spear brought hope. Another vision from Saint Andrew revealed that battle could not long be delayed and the faithful should prepare themselves with a five-day fast. Five days of fasting, meditation, and prayer followed. One can only imagine the psychological impact of this upon the most zealous amongst the crusading army.

Having whipped themselves up into a fanatical frenzy, the crusading army charged out of Antioch on 28 June, with the holy spear carried before them. The attack caught the besieging army a little by surprise. Some of the crusaders even witnessed a fantastic vision during the ensuing battle. On a nearby hillside, they claimed to see a company of knights on white horses, waving white banners. These knights, they swore, were led by Saint George, Saint Mercury, and Saint Demetrius, encouraging the crusaders to victory. Sure enough, their zeal was rewarded for, as they saw it, God gave the faithful total victory that day. A miracle? Or perhaps a combination of religious fanaticism, a surprise attack and the shaky loyalty of some of Kerbogha's commanders serve as more practical reasons for the Muslim defeat.[2]

One might explain such visions, in this case, in terms of a combination of fanaticism coupled with days of fasting and zealous meditation. If some crusaders had been fasting, praying, and meditating late into the night for several nights, actual visual hallucinations can't be ruled out. Whatever the truth, there is no doubting the power such visions exerted over the psychology of those involved.

When we think of religious mysticism, it is Eastern religions rather than Christianity that often come to mind. It is certainly true that mysticism is not a label many people would associate with Christianity today, even many Christians. However, from the early eleventh century onwards, these supernatural experiences became increasingly interwoven with a broader movement of Christian mysticism and as the Middle Ages wore on, claims of visions and/or the gift of prophecy continue to feature in records.

But what do we really mean when we speak of 'mysticism'? In essence, mysticism emphasises a lived spiritual experience over theological or philosophical scholarship. It might perhaps take the form of a vision, an ecstatic religious experience, or similar state of heightened spiritual awakening. It can be felt and experienced but is not easily explained or codified by logic. It can be something as simple as a feeling of peace and tranquility induced by prayer and meditation. Or it can also be a truly life changing epiphany. In many ways, mysticism is reminiscent of Taliesin's concept of the *awen*. The difference is that the mysticism of the high Middle Ages was inspired by Christianity.

A certain tension between learned scholarship and lived faith was present within Christianity right from the start. Saint Paul himself was sometimes scornful of philosophy and knowledge born from intellectual scholarship. For him, faith and a strong spiritual communion with Christ represented the key to salvation. This is perhaps most clearly articulated in Colossians, 2:8. Here, Paul warns against paying heed to the philosophies of men, dismissing them as empty deceits. Such logic, he argues, is part of the world of men, divorced from the true wisdom of Christ.

So, it is little surprise that, ever since the earliest days of the church, mysticism had always been present. That said, it proved to be far more a feature of the Eastern Church than the Western. And, despite its appeal, it was also recognised that it had a dangerous side. Placing a stronger emphasis on spiritual experience rather than doctrine naturally encourages a far more personal form of religion. Taken too far, it can make religious belief more subjective as well as more personal. It is this subjectivity that can, unrestrained, stray into unorthodox belief and even heresy. At its most extreme, mysticism was a strong feature of the early Gnostic forms of Christian belief, denounced as heretical during the second and third century.

During the early Middle Ages, the Western church was still very much finding its feet. It was not yet the dominant cultural institution it became by the high Middle Ages. Thanks to the process initiated by Charlemagne's *correctio*, the Western church became an increasingly important centre of theology and doctrine. As its power and influence grew, so too did its wealth and, consequently, its ability to promote and foster scholarship, learning and theological thinking.

This could and did lead to some church scholars actively engaging in related disciplines such as philosophy, science, medicine, and even political thought. The intellectual life of the West was further stimulated by the crusades, which brought closer contact with new ideas from the Islamic world and Eastern Orthodoxy. An interest in mysticism was, no doubt, stimulated by these broader cultural horizons, especially through greater contact with Eastern Orthodoxy, which had a stronger and richer tradition of mysticism.

By the twelfth century, this reached critical mass, leading to an explosion of scholarship and intellectual speculation. The century saw the founding of several universities and significant monastic reform in which the Cistercian movement featured prominently. In the early twelfth century, both the Cistercian and church thinking in general were heavily influenced by Saint Bernard of Clairvaux.

Saint Bernard is noted for several things. He was a staunch defender of the rights of the church and a keen champion of orthodoxy. He took a prominent role in preaching the crusades. He co-founded the Knights Templar, providing them with their religious rules.[3] He also founded numerous monasteries. He was certainly an energetic and prodigious scholar, writing numerous books, sermons, and letters. His work had a profound influence on the development of canon law. He was also a prominent early proponent of mysticism in the Western church.

In Bernard's case, he certainly did not reject rational scholarship in favour of mysticism but, rather, saw the two as intimately interwoven. For Saint Bernard, study and scholarship provided the necessary foundations on which to build. But simply understanding correct doctrine was, in and of itself, wholly inadequate. The goal was to experience a spiritual relationship with the living God. Contemplation, prayer, meditation, and a life lived in Christ's image were then required to truly experience the divine. For Saint Bernard, only divine love, not reason alone, could reveal ultimate truth. This spiritual experience could be felt, and it could grant a profound inner wisdom as to the nature of the divine, but it could never be adequately explained in words.

Saint Bernard's concept of mysticism was (and remains) fairly mainstream in Christian religious thinking. In Bernard's time it was quite innovative. However, in terms of his orthodoxy, Bernard remained a conservative and his view of mysticism would remain strong throughout the Middle Ages (and beyond). Others would follow him, most of whom would tread an equally orthodox path. However, the embrace of mysticism would also lead to some more extraordinary, unorthodox, and sometimes even heretical outcomes.

For some, mysticism led them to draw closer to a pantheistic outlook. If the divine can be directly experienced, and if such experiences can visit anyone, it can, therefore, also be experienced by Muslims or Jews. Cardinal Nicholas Cusanus, preaching in the fifteenth century, believed that, whilst Christianity represented the purest faith, divine truth could be discovered anywhere in God's creation. This meant that it must be possible for a Muslim or a Jew to directly experience divine grace. Cusanus did not overtly claim to be a pantheist, but he came so close to being one that viewing him as orthodox strains credibility.[4]

Mysticism also led to some people crossing the line into the realms of the doctrinally unacceptable. Meister Eckhart, writing in the late thirteenth and early fourteenth century, believed that God was present throughout all his creation. These beliefs led to no fewer than twenty-eight of his ideas being condemned by Pope John XXII. The most controversial being: 'The eye with which I see God is the same as the eye with which God sees me.'[5] Such a pronouncement sounded dangerously like Gnosticism. At least Eckhart did not go so far as the Gnostics in drawing the conclusion that, since the divine is present within us, our personal salvation also lies within us.

A particularly striking aspect of medieval Christian mysticism manifested itself in the form of individuals who claimed to have vivid visions and ecstatic spiritual experiences. These experiences were not necessarily considered unorthodox or heretical (although they sometimes were). Nor were they considered symptomatic of some kind of hallucinatory psychotic episode (as some might be regarded today). Nevertheless, they were certainly considered extraordinary. And what made them more extraordinary was the fact that some of the most prominent examples are to be found amongst medieval women.

Perhaps the most famous of these women was Hildegard of Bingen; an abbess living and writing just a little later than Saint Bernard. In addition to being a renowned mystic, she was also a poet, a naturalist, composer of music, and writer on a wide variety of topics. As a mystic, Hildegard claimed to have received several vivid visions. These were so powerful that they affected her physically prior to experiencing them. She described her experiences in dramatic fashion, as a powerful, searing fire from heaven, piercing her heart. This holy fire, she claimed, granted her a profound insight into the meaning of the Gospels and other religious writings.[6] Hildegard received several similar visions, each one granting her spiritual insight into the nature of the divine and the more esoteric meanings of scripture. She believed that what she witnessed were reflections of the living light, a direct personal connection with the voice of heaven.

Inspired by these visions she wrote a book – *Scivias* (which literally means 'showings'). In this work, she describes her visions and elaborates on their meanings by dividing it into three parts. In the first part, she describes how she was called by God to write the book, before proceeding to describe visions which relate to the creation and the fall of man. The second part deals with visions relating to the sacrifice of Christ and the sacraments. The third, and longest part, relates to revelations concerning the coming kingdom of God. Her accounts are not limited to prose but also include various musical compositions. These are provided to enhance the experience of contemplating her revelations. Like Saint Bernard, the mystical experience must transcend mere words to impart true wisdom.

There were some within the church, even at the time, who were a little sceptical over the validity of Hildegard's claims. However, she received support from the aged, but revered, Saint Bernard. This was enough to persuade the pope that her visions were genuine.

Hildegard was by no means the only female mystic. There were many others who experienced similarly powerful spiritual revelations, especially in Germany. Mysticism came later to England than the Continent. However, of the four most prominent English mystics, whose identities are known, two were women. One of these women was Julian (or Juliana) of Norwich. In 1373, Julian fell gravely ill. So ill, in fact, that she was given the last rites. However, whilst on what she thought to be her death bed, she received several powerful visions of the passion of Christ. These included seeing the image of Christ bleeding and feeling a great sense of divine love. These ecstatic spiritual experiences inspired her to write the *Revelations of Divine Love* – the earliest attestable work by a woman written in the English language.

Testimonies of visions of the sort recounted by Hildegard or Julian were not prophetic in nature. Rather they described ecstatic religious experiences that brought religious teachings to life and gave them meaning. They attempted to inspire the faithful to engage more deeply, at an emotional level, with Christian stories and themes, such as Christ's passion.

However, there were other mystics from this period for whom mysticism was not simply about a heightened spiritual experience, it was also about prophecy. The most prominent of these medieval prophets was Joachim of Fiore. Joachim was a Cistercian monk who devoted a considerable amount of time to studying the Bible. By the 1180s he began writing, espousing theories and speculations about various biblical passages. He claimed to have been inspired to see hidden meanings and connections that others had missed. He claimed these esoteric revelations led him to a deep understanding of the history of the world. More importantly, they furnished him with an understanding of the future yet to come. These revelations, according to Joachim, were a gift from the Holy Spirit.

Joachim was particularly concerned with predictions of the apocalypse that appear within the cryptic Book of Revelation. He was by no means the first person to make specific predictions about the future based on this book. Rupert of Deutz, writing in the early twelfth century had, for example, interpreted the image of seven trumpets and seven angels as representing seven judgements. According to Deutz, some of these judgements had already transpired and others were yet to pass. But Joachim went further than simply seeking to decipher the meaning of allegorical texts.

Using an esoteric approach, Joachim predicted that an event he termed the 'consummation of ages' would occur in the year 1260. Joachim saw the history of creation passing through three distinct ages. The first was the age of God the Father. This age had lasted until the coming of Christ, since which time, the world had entered the age of the Son. During the third age, yet to arrive, the full power of the Holy Spirit would manifest. This would lead to the rise of a new order of spiritual men destined to lead the church during its final years.

They would be persecuted but would, of course, ultimately triumph. These men, he believed, would herald a new era of enhanced spiritual understanding and enlightenment. Only then would the true meanings of scripture be revealed to man in all their glory. Joachim prophesied that 1260 would see the dawn of this spiritual third age.[7]

However, Joachim's predictions inevitably had an apocalyptic element, as all memorable prophecies tend to have. This third age would herald the beginning of the end of times. It would be the role of the new breed of spiritual men to prepare the church and the world for the trials of the coming apocalypse. Joachim predicted that the antichrist would arise at this time and that he would be a false pope.

Joachim made these predictions based on what he termed 'spiritual intelligence'; a special insight granted to him as a gift of God. To enter this higher spiritual state required preparation and study. Joachim had studied scripture, prayed, and mediated until his spirit was finally ready to receive the gift. At this point, the Holy Spirit granted him spiritual intelligence and the ability to understand scripture with a deeper spiritual wisdom. Then, and only then, was it possible to interpret the hidden meanings of holy scripture and receive prophetic insight.

Joachim's revelations proved popular. However, there were also many within the church who were sceptical. Most believed Joachim to be genuine but wondered if some of his views might be misguided. In 1215, some of his views on the nature of the Trinity were condemned as being in error. Nevertheless, the church was at pains to make clear that Joachim himself had not been a heretic. Despite this set back, Joachim's views enjoyed a strong revival starting in the 1230s when groups of Cistercian and Franciscan monks embraced his ideas.

Amongst this emergent generation of Joachites, Gerard of Borgo San Donnino is of particular note. In 1254, he went a step further than Joachim by suggesting that the Old and New Testaments would be superseded by a new Eternal Gospel that would come into being in the year 1260. At this time the duty of preaching this new spiritual gospel would fall to holy men who fully embraced Christ's example of poverty and chastity. This, of course, was not only a challenge to orthodox theology but also a challenge to the structured hierarchy of the church itself (whose senior members were not remotely poor).

Such ideas were increasingly condemned by churchmen. Of course, as 1260 came and went, Joachim's predictions became increasingly untenable. The commission of Arles of 1263 condemned his work as 'pernicious'[8] although the man himself was still not labelled a heretic. The final nail in the coffin for the Joachites came from the quill of Thomas Aquinas. Aquinas rejected Joachim's approach and recommended a return to Saint Augustine's more conservative views on prophecy.

The experience of the Joachites made the church more wary of would-be prophets. Of course, it was not possible to condemn prophecy entirely since it was clearly an attested biblical phenomenon. However, Augustine's view was that, whilst prophecy can still be granted by God, the age of prophecy as recorded in the Bible came to an end in the post scriptural age.

The fact that the mysticism of the twelfth and thirteenth centuries had generated some false / misguided doctrines led to increased scepticism about the phenomenon. If teachings and prophecies arising from such experiences could be false or misguided, many reasoned, what had been the source of this falsehood? Could the devil be at work in some cases? Could it be that demons had misled some people? Concerns of this nature became increasingly common during the fourteenth century. The extent to which demons could influence false prophecy was, according to both Saint Augustine and Thomas Aquinas, severely limited by God. However, as the fourteenth century wore on the idea that demons were often permitted by God to tempt the unwary as a test of faith gathered popularity.

Despite these growing reservations, Joachim's concept of prophecy remained surprisingly durable. His specific prophecies may have been discredited but his views as to how prophecy might be experienced remained popular. The fourteenth century would see an increasing number of prophets and mystics emerging from the laity. These were often, but not necessarily always, people with at least some education. Some would follow Joachim in making dramatic predictions of the end of days. Others simply preached dire warnings of troubles in store for the church if it failed to reform.

In 1378, the Western church experienced schism. Two rival popes, one in Rome and one in Avignon, vied with each other for authority. This fracturing of church authority would not be resolved until 1417. During this period, prophecies of doom held a particular poignance. Also, the fact that papal authority was contested made it harder for the church to formulate a coherent response to any rogue prophets. The increasing proliferation of prophets and mystics, not only from the clergy but also the laity, is testimony to how widespread and deep-rooted mysticism became.

Nevertheless, by the fifteenth century, concern over the possibility of false prophecy and demonic forces was on the rise. It would come to a violent head with Joan of Arc in the late 1420s. Joan claimed to have received visions from God instructing her to take up arms against the English and drive them from French soil. The French court was sceptical but to ignore a genuine prophecy would have been tantamount to defying God and so it was guardedly decided to give Joan a chance. Her spectacular victory at Orleans seemed to vindicate her claims of divine inspiration and so a legend was born.

However, when Joan was finally captured by her English and Burgundian enemies, it became politically necessary to discredit her. The easiest way to do this was to demonstrate that her visions had been false, perhaps inspired by malicious forces. This, coupled with Joan's habit of dressing as a man for practical reasons on campaign, proved her undoing. Her accusers jumped on her claim that her crossdressing had been endorsed by her visions. This seemed to them like an obvious proof of demonic influence. Joan's lack of scholastic learning left her tragically ill equipped to defend herself against such accusations.[9] It would lead to her being burnt at the stake by her enemies.

In time, of course, Joan would be rehabilitated and eventually sainted. Too late to save poor Joan from the flames. However, her fate shows that views on prophecy, visions and mysticism had changed by the fifteenth century. The fear that malignant forces might mislead and deceive had become very real; real enough to see someone condemned and burnt as a heretic.

Despite this, the church itself never arrived at anything like a definitive position on prophecy and visions during the Middle Ages. On the one hand, the power of God to grant visions and prophetic powers could not be denied. On the other, the potential for false or even malicious doctrines to be spread by false mystics was of great concern. In the end, the issue would not even be formally addressed until the Fifth Lateran Council in the early sixteenth century.

Magic in the Middle Ages

The medieval church was clearly disapproving of any form of supernatural or religious belief that did not fall within its definition of orthodoxy. Most obviously, this led to the condemnation of paganism and rival religions such as Islam or Judaism. Heresy, once clearly identified and defined, was also treated as a serious threat. However, beyond these obvious sources of spiritual opposition, there was a panoply of other supernatural beliefs that did not conform to Christian teaching. These weren't always associated with any specific rival religion or heretical sect. Principal amongst these was a very mixed bag of practices, traditions, and superstitions that might be collectively labelled as 'magic'.

The medieval church condemned the practice of magic, sorcery, and witchcraft. Where magic was used with a harmful intent; to curse someone or to enlist the aid of demons, it was viewed particularly seriously. This form of 'maleficent' practice, especially where it involved a political dimension, could lead to overt persecution. The Latin language used in the medieval Vulgate Bible only advocated death for the practice of maleficent magic (i.e., where it was intended to cause harm to someone). However, it nevertheless condemned the practice of magic in general as sinful.

Although magic was proscribed, the medieval church avoided proactive persecution of witches and magicians. For much of the Middle Ages, the church usually recommended penance for practicing magic, rather than imprisonment or death. A harsher view was only likely to be taken where heresy of some kind was also involved.

Different European secular powers took different stances in relation to magic. Often, secular powers only acted if the magic was deemed to be maleficent. However, investigation and prosecution usually relied on local people coming forward to make an accusation of wrongdoing. In the case of Plantagenet England, there were no secular laws against witchcraft. Witchcraft was not made illegal in England until the Witchcraft Act of 1542. Indeed, England did not even have any formal laws against heresy until 1401.[1] If an

English witch or sorcerer chose to openly confess their sins, the church would require them to do penance. However, in the absence of proven maleficence, they were very unlikely to face any punitive consequences beyond this.

But what kind of practices were being condemned? How was magic practiced in the Middle Ages and what beliefs lay behind it? Before we even get to that, perhaps we first need to consider a more fundamental question – what exactly is 'magic'?

The answer is not as simple as it first appears. Is using oil and dust from the tomb of Saint Martin to cure an afflicted woman, religion or magic? Is using willow tree bark (which contains aspirin) as an herbal remedy to relieve a headache, magic or science? At what point does superstition end and religion begin? At what point does something cease being science and stray into the occult?

Heavenly bodies certainly have the power to physically influence the world. The sun determines the seasons, the moon influences the tides. That much is science. Perhaps, then, an understanding of the movement of heavenly bodies might provide foresight of auspicious times to act (or warn us of bad times to act)? Might that also be science? And how can these boundaries be clearly defined in a world like medieval Europe, where scientific knowledge is so limited?

Defining the boundaries between these different concepts is problematic. If we say that casting a spell is clear evidence of practicing magic, does that make it any easier? Some medieval spells incorporated quotes from the Bible or were delivered as if they were a Christian prayer. So, at what point does a prayer cease to be a prayer and become a 'spell'?

And what exactly was a 'witch' or a 'sorcerer'? The fact was it was far from easy to classify that many people into categories such as these. Most medieval people who practiced magic did so casually and occasionally rather than vocationally. The number of people who made a living from the practice of sorcery or witchcraft was only a vanishingly small proportion of all magic practitioners. Most people who practiced magic did not think of themselves as witches, mages, or sorcerers.

We face two significant problems in attempting to define and categorise magical belief in the Middle Ages. The first lies in the fragmentary nature of what survives in the written record. Partly, this reflects the fact that magic, as practiced by the majority of common folk was largely transmitted by oral tradition. But equally, it reflects the fact that many magic writings were considered heretical or maleficent. Hence, when they were discovered by the authorities they were often burnt. A considerable volume of such material was destroyed during the height of the early modern witch hunts (between 1550 and 1650).

The second challenge is that medieval magic was not one single homogenous belief system. It was, in truth, a mixture of beliefs, superstitions, and occult practices, derived from a hotch-potch of different cultures and traditions. To stand any chance of untangling all of this, we need to consider the different traditions that helped to shape the medieval understanding of magic.

One of the most influential sources for medieval magic was classical antiquity. The Roman world had encompassed most of Europe and, as a result, occult beliefs from pagan Rome spread across the entire continent. Roman beliefs were in turn influenced by earlier traditions, including Classical Greece, Ancient Egypt, and Mesopotamia.

The Romans themselves had an uneasy relationship with magic. Certain magical practices (such as curses) were viewed with anxiety and hostility. The Romans were also very uncomfortable with anything they saw as highly exotic, alien, and, basically, 'not Roman'. They were especially suspicious of Persian Zoroastrian priests and sorcerers, whom they referred to as *Magi* (from which we derive the word 'magician').[2] Part of the discomfort stemmed from the fact that Persia was Rome's great Eastern enemy. This served to exacerbate the sense of 'otherness' and danger associated with magi. Yet, of course, other magical practices such as divination were performed by Roman priests and, therefore, deemed entirely acceptable. Roman pagans even saw certain aspects of Christian ritual as dangerous forms of exotic magic.

The medieval world inherited a significant number of important texts on magic from the classical world. These included such things as Ptolemy's work on astrology, the magical theories of Plotinus the Neo-Platonist, and a collection of occult writing attributed to an enigmatic ancient sage known as Hermes Trismegistus. For the medieval mind, classical magic traditions harked back to truly ancient knowledge, associated with great lost civilisations. It was, therefore, viewed with a special reverence. For this reason, some medieval magical texts, such as the *Liber Juratus Honorii* (likely written during the thirteenth century), purported to have an older classical origin.

The practice of magic in pagan Rome is better documented than within pagan Celtic, German, and Norse cultures. However, these other pagan traditions represented a second important source of magical belief in the Middle Ages. Whether we consider Roman, Celtic, or Germanic practices, there were some common threads of belief running through these different cultures. A belief in divination and prophecy is present in all cases. Another common thread relates to stories involving shape-shifting – a central theme in Ovid's *Metamorphoses* and frequently referenced in the writing of Taliesin, Irish myths, and the Norse *Eddas*. Celtic, Scandinavian, and Germanic traditions all speak of otherworldly beings such as elves, dwarves, and fairy-like creatures, possessing strange supernatural powers.

The types of pagan magic most likely to inspire fear were spells, such as curses and other harmful magic. This form of magic was present in all pagan cultures. In the Roman world, if you wished to curse someone, you might take a lead plate, write a curse on it in Latin, and then drive nails through it. Having created your cursed tablet, you would then try to plant it somewhere within the intended victim's house. Old Norse sagas speak of curses working in a similar way within Scandinavian paganism. A witch could cast a curse by scraping a smooth surface on a piece of wood, inscribing it with the right runes, chant some incantations, and seal it with blood. If this cursed item then found its way into the possession of the intended victim, their fate was sealed.[3]

The third major influence on medieval magic was Christianity itself. Official church doctrine condemned magic, of course. Practicing magic could be seen as an evil act or, at best, foolish and misguided. For the most part magic was seen as resulting from demonic deception. This certainly does not mean to say that the practice of magic was automatically associated with devil worship. It usually just meant that a sorcerer had been tempted into error; fooled by the deceits of a demon. Despite this theological hostility, Christian practice featured prominently in a great many medieval spells and occult rituals. Many spells incorporated prayers, excerpts from liturgy, or quotes from the Bible, seeking to invoke the aid of God. Indeed, some of the people who practiced magic were, in fact, clerics!

To these traditions we must finally add the impact of Arabian occult belief. This became especially prominent because of contact with the Islamic world during the high Middle Ages. Arabic traditions were transmitted via Moorish Spain or through direct contact with the Middle East during the crusades. Arab scholarship in the fields of astrology, astral magic, and alchemy were particularly influential from the twelfth century onwards.

A final influence came from occult practices absorbed from Jewish esoteric beliefs. Some of these were adopted via the various diaspora communities scattered across Europe. Other Jewish esoterica found its way into Europe via the increased contact with Palestine that followed the First Crusade. All these different traditions fed into the medieval understanding of magic and the occult. It is little surprise that the reality of medieval magical practice was truly a mixed bag.

Another grey area comes in drawing a distinction between magic that people practiced on the one hand and stories about magic on the other. Stories and poems about magic obviously show us something of what people were thinking about magic at the time. However, these tales are not always easy to interpret. In some instances, these stories were clearly meant to be taken as fictional. But in some cases, it is hard to say how a medieval reader may have interpreted them. Would they have been read as fiction, myth or, perhaps, taken it as a genuine illustration of how magic was supposed to work? It is hard to say.

If we think of magic these days, we might think of witches. This conjures up the image of a sinister female practitioner of sorcery. It is an image that has its roots in the distant past. Classical stories present us with some of the earliest images for how women were associated with magic. Often women were portrayed as using magic to charm men into falling in love with them. In some of these tales, the women concerned were portrayed sympathetically, even tragically. In others, the women are portrayed as scheming and manipulative. Occasionally (but only occasionally), the classical female witch was portrayed as utterly evil. How much of this would people have regarded as pure fiction? How much was seen as a genuine representation of how people thought women commonly used magic?

The witch Erictho is described by the classical writer Lucan in the most horrific terms. She is an ugly hag, whose powers are drawn from the underworld. She practices necromancy and raises zombies. She snatches bodies from tombs for her dark rituals. She even engages in cannibalism, feasting on the flesh of children she has kidnapped and murdered.[4] The description of Erictho is an early stereotype that became almost universally applied to witches during the Early Modern period. However, in medieval times this particularly dark image of witchcraft was not yet ingrained in the cultural consciousness.

In early modern Europe, a common belief in relation to witches was that their magic gave them the power of flight. The iconic image of a witch on a broomstick comes to mind. The idea of flying female witches has its origin in earlier pagan beliefs. A belief held in Roman times, that was primarily Germanic in origin, was that certain women could transform themselves into *strigae* at night. Such creatures took the form of screech owls and represented an early image of the 'night witch'. Another classical belief was that some women, who served the goddess Diana the huntress, would sometimes ride out on night hunts. Often, they were depicted riding on wild animals but were sometimes said to fly.[5] Such women could be either benevolent or malevolent in nature. However, although such beliefs were embedded in both Roman and Anglo-Saxon folk tradition, they were largely regarded as misguided pagan superstition by the early medieval church. People who believed such things were either thought of as ignorant or as having been deceived by demonic illusions. Such errors could be corrected by confession, repentance, and penance. Punishment beyond this was generally not warranted, as long as no one had been harmed.

Despite this, it is important to say that the practice of magic, in the early Middle Ages was no more likely to be associated with women than men. The early medieval concept of magic, especially from the perspective of church thinkers, tended to view it as being primarily centred on divination (especially the forms of divinations performed within pagan cultures, most notably

Roman). In pagan Rome, of course, divinations were often more likely to be performed by men than women. By the same token, magicians and sorcerers were more likely to be seen as male rather than female vocations. There was no sense that women were any more likely to practice magic than men.

All forms of magic were generally viewed (thanks mainly to the influence of Saint Augustine) as demonic. That is to say that it was believed that demons deceived magicians into trusting magic was real. Church theology taught that it was not possible to predict the future using magic, since only God could know the future. If you believed you could use magic to foretell the future, you were either foolish or you'd been deceived by a demon. By the same logic, women could not really transform into *strigae*. However, they could be deceived into believing it was possible by demonic illusion. All this in no way meant that practitioners of magic were seen as devil worshippers, even if it was thought they had been influenced by demons.

By the time of the Plantagenets and the high Middle Ages, thinking had moved on. During the thirteenth century many people began acknowledging another kind of magic existed – natural magic. This magic drew power from natural forces (herbal healing being an example).[6] The boundaries between this form of magic and physical science could be (and often were) blurred. It was also not always clear where the boundary between this form of magic and demonic magic lay. Many church thinkers continued to insist that the distinction was a false one and that all magic was ultimately demonic.

In providing an overview of magical belief during the period it is perhaps helpful to draw a distinction between two different broad categories of magic. There was, inevitably, some overlap between these. However, the distinction often lay in the people who practiced magic as well as the type of magic practiced. In effect we might regard them as separate, if related, magical cultures operating within medieval society.

The first is what we might call 'common magic'. Magic of this sort was often simple, drawing heavily on traditional folk beliefs and superstitions. In a sense, we might call it folk magic. It might include herbal remedies, charms and other simple spells that did not require costly magical paraphernalia or access or rare and expensive books. Magic of this kind could be (and was) practiced by non-scholars and much of it was accessible to semi-literate or illiterate people. These folk traditions might also involve magic rituals, simple spells, and charms or possibly nothing more than superstitious belief. The simplest forms of common magic could be practiced casually, when the necessity arose, by just about anyone.

The second broad area consisted of occult practices that required a certain level of education to access. This form of magic was usually studied from books written in Latin, so was only accessible to Latin literate sorcerers.

These books might contain extensive astrological charts and instructions for creating horoscopes, esoteric alchemical formulae, or complex magic rituals. The rituals involved could be elaborate and often required expensive magical paraphernalia to perform. Formal study and a scholarly background were usually essential if you wished to be anything more than a dabbler. For this reason, we might call it 'learned magic' rather than common magic, since to practice it required scholarship. Learned magic was, therefore, more exclusive: inaccessible to all but the best educated members of society.

Learned magic benefited greatly from the influx of knowledge from the Arab world during the twelfth and thirteenth centuries. This included many classical texts that had been lost to the west, but which had survived in the east. They had been translated from Greek into Arabic and further developed by the Arabs themselves. Additional occult material from Jews, Persians, and Indians was also transmitted via the Arabs to Europe during this period.

In the twelfth and thirteenth centuries, as more of this material became available, Western scholars set about the task of translating it from Arabic into Latin. The result was an influx of new scholarly occult and magical knowledge from the East. It led to a golden age in the practice of learned magic from the twelfth century through to the end of the Middle Ages.

Common or Folk Magic

In considering how magic was practiced in the medieval world, it is first important to consider who practiced it. In fact, magic was widely practiced by people from all walks of life, including members of the clergy. However, only a tiny number of these people actively identified themselves as witches or sorcerers.

The common forms of traditional magic, as outlined by Professor Richard Kieckhefer[1] encompassed such things as:

- Herbalism and healing magic.
- Blessings and adjurations.
- The use of amulets and talismans.
- Divinations and popular astrology.
- Curses and charms.

Much of this might be termed 'folk magic' but it could literally be practiced by anyone, including wealthier commoners and members of the nobility. The key to common magic was accessibility. It was largely transmitted orally or, when communicated in written form, often written in the local vernacular. Crucially, it did not require any great academic scholarship and you did not need expensive books and ritual components to master it. It was mostly regarded as foolish ignorance by the church. However, when it was misused to harm others, it was likely to be viewed as maleficent magic or sorcery. And, in that case, it was often treated far more seriously.

Herbal healing was widely practiced in medieval times. Here there was a considerable grey area between magic and medicine since some herbs clearly had genuine medicinal properties. The most important source of herbal healing were the monasteries and abbeys. Monks frequently provided hospice care and such medical assistance as the times allowed. This usually included the provision of herbal remedies.

In addition to monks, there were also lay healers known as leeches. In this instance, the word 'leech' is derived from 'læca' – the old English word for a physician. The modern English word 'leech' comes from this. It evolved from the fact that these physicians often employed leeches for bloodletting treatments. We know less about these physician leeches than we do about the monks, except that they appear to have been itinerant healers. Some practiced medicinal herbalism just like the monks but at least some combined herbalism with magical or occult practice.

Learning their art probably involved some form of apprenticeship and much of the craft was probably transmitted orally. Such limited written sources we have for leechcraft include the Anglo-Saxon *Leech Book of Bald* (which dates from the tenth century). The book combines herbalism with religion and magic. Some prescriptions are simple herbal remedies. Some are herbal remedies that require a mass or prayer to be said over them to imbue them with healing potency. And some required a magic ritual or spell to be performed. Consider this instruction for the application of an ointment for example. The patient is instructed to apply the ointment at night, scratch their neck and drip the blood into running water. Whilst doing so they must spit three times and command the illness to depart with their blood and spit. Having done so, they must travel home in silence.[2]

Another work known as *Lacnunga*, from the eleventh century, provides further examples of remedies practiced by leeches. *Lacnunga* often attributes the cause of disease to the work of evil elves. This indicates a clear pagan Norse or Anglo-Saxon, rather than Roman or Celtic, influence. For this reason, many of *Lacnunga*'s spells and potions were designed to drive off or counter the influence of elves.[3] Again, Christian prayers and themes are integrated into magical formulae. In one instance, for example, a herbal preparation must be mixed with a stick inscribed with the names of the four Gospels written in Latin.

Healing treatments could involve all manner of herbs, plants, blood, honey, milk, or various parts of animals. In the case of prescriptions that involved magic, this might require a ritual of some sort in either the collection, preparation, or application of a potion. Perhaps a particular herb had to be gathered under a full moon to be effective. Maybe you needed to use a particular type of tool to harvest a plant. You might need to obtain the ashes of a raven by burning its body in a particular type of pot. You may need to recite a prayer or invoke the aid of a saint. In many cases herbalism, Christian prayer and magic rituals were blended.

Local superstitious practices could often incorporate elements of Christianity. The combination of magic with prayer or liturgy was quite common. So, is singing a phrase from Christian liturgy around your cattle to keep them from harm every evening a form of prayer or a spell? Various Christian charms appear to have been employed to evoke supernatural effects. Depending on your perspective, the result could either be classed as magical or miraculous. Examples include the Jordan Charm, intoned to staunch the flow of blood from a wound; 'Just as the Jordan stopped, so may your blood stop flowing.'[4] There was also the Charm of Saint William, used to ward off cankers among other things. Then there was the Charm of Saint Eustace, used to ease pain in women.

Such practices rarely, if ever, attracted persecution by either church or secular authorities. Charms of this kind, far from being considered socially unacceptable, were widely embraced. In the early fourteenth century, Edward II's official court physician actively and openly advocated their use. The grey area that lay between religion, misguided superstition, and magic, was indeed large. But, in the age of *The Golden Legend*, should we be surprised?

Consider one medieval community that practiced a 'Christian' ritual, recorded in a twelfth century manuscript. The ritual concerned was a blessing used to restore fertility to a barren field. It took a day to complete and was performed by a priest. It began at sunrise when four clumps of earth are dug up from the corners of the field. The earth is then mixed with an herbal infusion, holy water, oil, milk, and honey whilst reciting a passage from the book of Genesis in Latin. After further prayers, a mass is said over the earth before it is finally sprinkled back over the field at sunset. Christian blessing, or magic ritual?

Amulets and talismans were also used in medieval magic. Again, the more common forms of these items could be created and used by anyone. They were usually made from plants, wood, bone, fabric, or other parts of animals. In general, they could be constructed from virtually any material that was readily and cheaply obtainable. These objects usually served to provide magical protections from sickness, from enemies or perhaps demons. The only real distinction between amulets and talismans was that a talisman would have some kind of magical or religious phrase inscribed on it. Often, these phrases would be written in Latin and might include such things as the various names of God, of magi, or saints, and so on.

In more elaborate examples, the talisman might incorporate a complete magical phrase, such as the SATOR-AREPO magic square (shown below)[5]:

S A T O R
A R E P O
T E N E T
O P E R A
R O T A S

This magic square drew its power from Christian mythology. At first sight, the words appear meaningless. However, if you read it horizontally or vertically in any direction, you'll see the same words repeated. The first recorded example of it dates to the earliest period of Christian history in the first century. It was based on a combination of the Pater Nosta (Lord's Prayer) and the letters 'A' and 'O' (signifying the idea of Christ as Alpha and Omega). You'll note that you can spell the words 'Pater Nosta' by re-arranging the letters in the square.

The link between a protective magical talisman and Christianity may seem a little odd. However, what is a holy relic if not a form of protective amulet? Creating a talisman like the SATOR-AREPO magic square did not necessarily require the creator to be fully literate or even that educated. At a rudimentary level, you just needed to be able to copy letters onto a piece of cloth. You may have known something of the words you were writing but you did not need to be able to read them. Surprisingly, there were many people in medieval England who could write but not read. They were employed as scribes, copying written documents for their lord's records. They were trained to accurately copy the written word but not to read it. The fact that you might not be able to read the words on your talisman did not even matter. It was enough to know that these were ancient magic words that provided you with powerful protection.

A significant amount of occult belief in the Middle Ages focused on divination, the interpretation of omens and various forms of prophecy. As we have seen, Christianity itself was a source of religious prophecy but, alongside this were a wide variety of different forms of magical divination and omen reading. These practices were officially condemned by the church. However, this did not prevent them from becoming very popular and it certainly did not prevent them from being openly practiced.

One divination technique was oneiromancy, which dealt with the interpretation of dreams. The art of oneiromancy could be transmitted by oral tradition but there were also medieval dream books containing detailed instructions as to how to interpret the meaning of dreams. The English King Richard II was a strong believer in oneiromancy (as well as other forms of divination). After having the earl of Arundel executed, Richard was troubled by dreams of the ghost of the dead earl. So seriously did he take these dreams that he had Arundel's tomb exhumed to check he had not risen from the grave.[6]

Other forms of divination relied upon reading signs and omens in nature, seeing meaning in the flight of birds or animal calls, much like the old Roman auguries. Chiromancy used palm reading to foretell the future. Oenomancy attempted to determine the future through the study of names.

Popular astrology, of a simplistic sort, could be used by uneducated folk to read omens without a detailed knowledge of the zodiac or horoscopes. For instance, you might read significance into the basic lunar cycle, or a lunar eclipse, or the appearance of a comet.

The line between divination and simple superstition could be a blurred one. Simple daily events such as hearing a raven cry three times, finding a horseshoe or encountering a black cat might be interpreted as lucky or unlucky. Even natural phenomena like a thunderstorm at a particular time of year might be taken to signify something. Some people even attempted to receive occult guidance for their future actions by rolling dice or using herbal fumigations.

There were a few people who specialised in this kind of common magic, and these individuals could be regarded as witches or sorcerers. And, of course, in addition to the kinds of magic we've been discussing it was also possible to use such magic in a maleficent manner. In general, if you cast a spell with the intent of bewitching someone or cursing them, you were then dealing with the kind of magic that people feared most. Even love potions were seen as a form of bewitchment by many. If you used a love potion to seduce a married person for the purposes of adultery, then that would be considered maleficent.

Curses could be cast by creating cursed talismans or amulets and hiding them in the victim's house, very much reminiscent of old Roman and Norse practices. Or perhaps you might create a wax image of someone and stick the image with pins or a dagger to harm them. Sometimes magic could be used in a maleficent way by transferring a malady from one person to another.

The Italian witch Matteuccia claimed to be able to create a potion that would cure lameness. However, it achieved this when the intended subject cast the potion into the street. The aim was that their lameness would be transferred to a random passing stranger.[7] Matteuccia, unlike most other magical practitioners, was a well-known vocational witch, who seems to have attracted many paying clients. In her case, her practice of maleficence led to her prosecution and eventual execution in 1428. She was, in fact, one of the earliest examples of someone being burnt at the stake for witchcraft (rather than heresy) in the late Middle Ages. As was the case with many of these rare early witch trials, there may well have been a political dimension to her prosecution (she was associated with at least one powerful political figure whose reputation would have been damaged by her conviction).

But Matteuccia was fairly exceptional. Perhaps a better indication of how someone might practice common magic in the Middle Ages can be found in a document known as the Wolfsthurn book from the Tyrol region. The book was written in the local German vernacular. It was clearly produced by someone literate but not by someone with a high level of education (who'd be more likely to use Latin). The author appears to have been involved in the day-to-day management of a castle estate. As such they were almost certainly drawn from the German equivalent of the English yeoman class. These were commoners, employed in the service of a Lord as a household retainer of some kind. If they needed to deal with such things as the estate accounts, mundane written correspondence, and other documents, they would receive a basic education.

The Wolfsthurn book contains a mixture of notes and observations relating to the management of the estate. This included helpful tips on how to manage the cellars, how to deal with rat problems, practical agricultural information, and so on. But interspersed with this, we find prayers, herbal remedies for illnesses, healing charms, spells and even rituals for homespun exorcisms. Sometimes it uses cod-Latin chants or incantations that, when translated, might be little more than a mixed jumble of meaningless words and phrases. Mostly, it sticks with the local vernacular.[8]

The Wolfsthurn book shows us someone (who could have been a man or woman), who used magic on an occasional and casual basis, as and when the need arose. They almost certainly did not consider themselves to be a witch or a sorcerer. Clearly, their primary vocation involved working on their lord's estate, not casting spells, or brewing magic potions. Most of their knowledge came from folk traditions rather than academic study. What this book does show, however, was that magic of this kind was just an ordinary part of everyday life for at least some (and possibly for many).

Learned Magic

Unlike common magic, learned magic required at least some formal education, either as a cleric or within a university. The people who practiced it often shared a similar educational background to practicing priests and church theologians. Indeed, to produce the books used for this kind of magic required access to a scriptorium and access was generally only available to clerics and their students.

One important field of occult science in medieval times was hermetic alchemy. Prior to the twelfth century, only fragmentary alchemical information was available in the West. However, from this period onwards, an increasing amount of material was translated into Latin from Arabic sources. A variety of works attributed to an ancient scholar known as Hermes Trismegistus proved particularly influential. These works were collectively referred to as *Corpus Hermetica* and although they were most famous for alchemy, they also dealt with astrology and magic. They were translated into Latin in renaissance Italy during the mid-fifteenth century and quickly became very popular.[1]

Hermes Trismegistus was well-known in medieval Europe and was widely believed to have been a great scholar from the classical world. He was seen as being as wise and authoritative as Aristotle or Plato. Many even believed that he was an ancient contemporary of Moses. The name Hermes Trismegistus simply translates to 'Hermes thrice great'. It is a name shared by the Greek god Hermes (Mercury to the Romans) who, as well as being the messenger of Zeus/Jupiter, was also the god of wealth and fortune in trade.[2]

The work present in *Hermetica* was produced by a mix of authors over several centuries. Some of the earliest were produced by Greek scholars working in the second or third centuries, probably in Alexandria. However, many were later Arab additions and elaborations. Thus, the Hermes Trismegistus we find in *Hermetica* is something of a gestalt creation, rather like Taliesin. The primary impact of this work was in the field of hermetic alchemy, which reached the height of its popularity during the very late medieval and Early Modern periods.

At its core, alchemy taught that by distilling and refining certain materials it was possible to create various fundamental elements. The goal was to produce a pure element referred to as the philosopher's stone which could be used to transmute baser metals into gold. To practice this art required an extensive laboratory of sophisticated equipment to provide what you needed to boil, refine, distil, and purify materials used in the alchemical process. This obviously required a lot of money and free time and alchemy was certainly not an occupation for the poor (although some certainly became poor through practicing it). The process itself was an art that had to be learnt from a master and only then could you hope to acquire access to secret knowledge necessary to complete your work.

The descriptions of the work found in material like *Hermetica* were shrouded in their own, highly cryptic, esoteric language. You had to know how to interpret the hidden meanings of what you were reading to get your formulation and process just right. The spirit of this esoteric occult language is perhaps best summarised by the text of *The Emerald Table*. This was supposedly taken from the tomb of Hermes Trismegistus, but its provenance can only be dated as far back as an Arab source, writing during the eighth or nineth century:

> That which is below is like that which is above and that which is above is like that which is below to do the miracles of one only thing. And as all things have been and arose from one by the mediation of one: so, all things have their birth from this one thing by adaptation. The Sun is its father, the moon its mother, the wind hath carried it in its belly, the earth is its nurse. The father of all perfection in the whole world is here. Its force or power is entire if it be converted into earth.[3]

With instructions such as this, it is perhaps not surprising that refining the perfect formula proved so elusive. This did not deter people from trying, however! The lure of the power to create gold from baser metals and the intoxicating prospect of secret knowledge, ensured there were no shortage of alchemists.

Whilst the efforts of alchemists were in vain as far any gold was concerned, their work fuelled scientific advances in laboratory equipment. The study of chemistry and pharmacology in later centuries would be built on the foundations laid by hermetic alchemists. Since some modern medicines are worth more than their weight in gold, you might argue that alchemy ultimately worked.

More popular and widespread than the practice of hermetic alchemy was astrology. Many people knew at least something about the subject. However, to prepare a credible horoscope that someone might be willing to pay for required more advanced knowledge. This involved access to books and star charts and an ability to read and write Latin. Professional astrology was, therefore, the preserve of scholarly men.

In the early medieval period, astrologers based their art primarily on the limited surviving classical sources available in the west. However, from the twelfth century onwards, contact with Moorish Spain and the Middle East saw an increasing volume of knowledge imported from the Islamic world. This included Abu Ma'shar's *Greater Introduction* to astrology (translated into Latin in 1133) and Ptolemy's *Tetrabiblos* (translated from Arabic versions in 1138). All this new knowledge allowed the production of more detailed and learned horoscopes than ever before.

The boundaries between astrology and astronomy had always been a little blurred. On one level, astrology was a form of divination – exactly the kind of thing you'd expect the Christian West to condemn out of hand. But it was not as simple as that. Many European monarchs, nobles, senior clergy, and even popes employed the services of astrologers. Indeed, medieval European university education routinely taught the fundamentals of astrology. Students learnt about the different constellations of the zodiac, the movement of these constellations in the heavens and the movement of planets. You'd also become familiar with certain basic astrological principles. You might learn, for instance, how being born when a particular planet was present in your star sign might impact your personality.

Some people saw astrology as a natural science rather than magic. The stars and planets were visible in the sky after all. Their movement over time could be tracked and predicted. They clearly formed part of the heavens and, therefore, must work in harmony with the universe. In a sense, it could be argued that astrology was mainly concerned with reading meaning from God's harmonious creation.

However, the production of horoscopes involved making predictions about the future – surely that would count as a form of divination? From a theological viewpoint this was problematic. Certainly, making very specific predictions, such as foretelling someone's death was dangerous ground. The theological objection focused mainly on the fact that if a man's fate was pre-set, this implied he was unable to alter his fate. If a man was unable to alter his fate, then that denied him free will. Since God granted man free will, fate cannot be pre-determined and predicted in this way. Therefore, such specific predictions must involve demonic deception.

However, if, by reading the natural harmonies inherent in the movement of the heavens, one could discern more general insights – what then? Rather than foreseeing very specific future events, you might be able to foretell times when certain actions may be favourable. Actions, for example, such as when to get married, when to travel, when to start a war etc. And so, astrology was as likely to be regarded as a science as an occult practice by many, despite what church theologians taught.

From the twelfth century onwards, an entirely new field of learned magic was imported to Europe via Arab sources. It was a form of magic derived from astrology and known as astral magic. The concept behind it was that the power of heavenly bodies could be channelled to create a magical effect. By way of an example, to rid a palace of scorpions, the magician Thabit ibn Qurra recommends making a metal image of a scorpion when the constellation of Scorpio is in ascendence. You should then bury it near the infested site and empower it with the correct incantation. This would purge your palace of the pesky arachnids.[4] Astral magic could, of course, be used for a wide variety of other purposes. You could use it for divinations, to create protective wards, bewitch people, curse people, and so on.

Astral magic features most famously (or perhaps infamously) in an Arabian occult work, known by its Latin name *'Picatrix'*.[5] It first entered Western European culture through contact with Moorish Spain when it was translated into Latin during the mid-thirteenth century. *Picatrix* contains a range of spells and rituals, many of which would certainly have been regarded as demonic magic: spells for bewitching and compelling people, spells for compelling demons, and even a spell for de-populating an entire area. The power of demons was not simply implied or suspected but explicitly invoked.

Since *Picatrix* was an Arabian text, it addresses demons within a Middle Eastern context. It also draws heavily on astral magic which, again, was a product of the Middle East, not Europe. However, *Picatrix* and other works dealing with astral magic inspired new developments in a darker form of magic – ritual necromancy.

Necromancy and Demons

Grimoires and darker magical texts produced in the Middle Ages combined astral magic with exorcism rites performed in the Western church. The result was a strain of occult scholarship that focused heavily on tapping the power of demons, elemental spirits, and the invocation of astral powers. This form of sorcery represented the darkest and most feared form of magic, dealing overtly with necromancy and demonology.

Ritual necromancy represented an obscure but very real branch of medieval magic. As we might expect, it was most strongly condemned by the church. Grimoires containing details of these practices were often burnt when they came to light. However, practitioners were unlikely to be 'witches' as we might visualise them today (if we picture a witch as being a poor village wise woman practicing common folk magic). In the Middle Ages, the people who genuinely practiced ritual necromancy were almost always men drawn from the clerical class. Indeed, to study the rituals and spells outlined in these grimoires, you needed an education in Latin and Christian exorcism rituals. And this kind of education was simply inaccessible for medieval women. Preparation for many of the spells also required ritual cleansing, involving fasting, celibacy, and the kind of self-mortification practiced by monks.

Before going further, it is important to note that the medieval understanding of necromancy was different to ours. The word necromancy comes from classical Greek; *nekroi* (of the dead), *mantia* (divination). Originally, it specifically related to performing divinations by conjuring the spirits of the dead. This, indeed, was how the practice was understood in the classical world. However, Christian theology taught that it was forbidden to attempt to conjure the spirits of the dead. In general, it was believed that sorcerers were conjuring familiar spirits rather than real ghosts of the departed. In short, they were conjuring demons. These demons deceived the sorcerer into believing they were speaking with the spirit of a dead person. Consequently, necromancy became synonymous with conjuring demonic forces.

That said, the Bible makes it clear that it is possible to conjure the spirits of the dead (if God allows it). In 1 Sammuel 28, King Saul conjures the spirit of the prophet Sammuel to ask his advice. The spirit summoned is indeed the ghost of Sammuel. However, it is quite clear that the practice is strongly disapproved of. Sammuel's ghost rebukes Saul for turning away from God and practicing necromancy. In punishment for his transgression, Sammuel predicts Saul's death and the end of his royal line. However, the incident of Sammuel's ghost was generally seen as the exception rather than the rule. In general, spirits summoned for the purposes of divination were assumed, by church theologians, to be demons.

The church and secular authorities were especially keen to clamp down on divination magic of this kind. Copies of necromantic grimoires were often destroyed when they came to light, so few manuscripts survive. Such material as does survive is often fragmentary. However, one of the most complete surviving examples is a Latin grimoire known as the Munich handbook. It is a collection of several earlier works, compiled into a single handy reference volume. One section is in fact a complete book, entitled the *Book of Consecrations*. Other dark works were known to exist, of which mostly only fragments survive. Some are known only by the location in which they were discovered, such as the Paris manuscript, or the Prague manuscript. Others had names, such as the Sworn Book and the sinister sounding 'Death of the Soul'.

The Munich handbook deals primarily with complex magical rituals for the conjuring and commanding of demons and other spirits. It is based on a system of astral magic, combined with rituals from medieval exorcism. However, instead of using such rituals to banish or cast out demons, they are performed in an inverted way to summon and command them. This inverse use of exorcism indicates a form of magic designed primarily by and for people with a knowledge of such rites. That meant people with a clerical education. Throughout, these rites draw heavily on Christian theology. In the *Book of Consecrations*, the sorcerer is often instructed to offer prayers to God, to grant him the power over the demons he plans to conjure.

The rituals described in such material are often complex and time consuming. They typically involve using a variety of magical inscriptions and paraphernalia, including such things as ritual swords, rings, sceptres, tablets inscribed with images or, incantations. Many rites involve the use of fumigations and the burning of incense. This required a variety of herbs and oils such as frankincense and saffron, many of which were quite expensive. Sometimes, animal sacrifice was necessary, as was, in some instances, the need for a sorcerer to use their own sacrificial blood to either conjure or pay the demon.[1]

A distinctive feature of many of these spells lay in drawing magic circles on the floor. Several medieval moral anecdotes (known at the time as exemplars) feature cautionary tales of necromancy. Magic circles, in these stories, are shown as being used to protect the sorcerer and/or their client from demons. The sorcerer is depicted as standing within the magic circle to prevent the conjured demon from harming them. In one such tale, the sorcerer's client foolishly leaves the protective circle, only to have his neck dramatically wrung by the demon lurking without. In other accounts, it is the demon that is constrained within the circle.

However, the grimoires themselves show that magic circles may not necessarily have been used in this protective role. Their role simply appears to have been to facilitate the conjuring and commanding of the demon. When seeking knowledge from a demon it was necessary to use magic to force them to tell the truth. This was especially important since it was well-known that the devil was the prince of lies. The magic circle appears to have played a role in facilitating this.

To conjure and control demons, the words used in the rituals were often crucial. A necromancer might well invoke the various esoteric names of God, drawn either from Christian or Jewish traditions. A name that was often used was 'Tetragrammaton', a word used to signify the ancient Hebrew 'YHWH'. This was the true name of God, a word deemed so holy that it could not be spoken out aloud. The necromancer might also invoke the names of angels or demons. The power of an angel might be invoked to coerce the demon or perhaps the sorcerer might invoke the power of an arch-demon to whom the demon owed allegiance. The occult work entitled *Liber Anglis* (Book of Angels), contains numerous names of angels and demons that necromancers might use for these purposes.[2] Contrary to what we might imagine, demons were generally commanded to appear in forms that were not especially grotesque. Forms described in the grimoires include knights, kings, horses, sailors, dogs, black African men, or servants for example.

But why conjure such entities at all? What was supposed to be the end purpose of this magic? In general, necromantic spells and rituals fall into three main categories. The first is where demons are used to compel others to do the will of the sorcerer. This was achieved either by various forms of possession, by tormenting or haunting the victim, or simply by bewitching them. The second purpose is to create illusions which take on a partial (and temporary) tangible form. These include illusions to animate a corpse or, the inverse, to make the living appear dead. You might even wish to get the demon to take the form of an illusionary horse to convey you wherever you wish to travel. The third reason is to enlist the service of demons was for divination; to discover lost knowledge or useful secrets.[3]

At this point it is relevant to consider what exactly demons are. We take it for granted that we, pretty much, know the answer. However, our understanding of these supernatural entities has, in fact, been shaped over many centuries. Centuries during which the concept of what constitutes a demon, evolved, and adapted.

Daimons, as conceived by the ancient Greeks, were spirits that served as messengers between the gods and mortals. Some were malign and some benign. The early Christian concept of these entities positioned them as malign but was a little confused as to their nature. Early Christianity embraced several apocryphal scriptures later abandoned by orthodoxy. One of these, the Book of Enoch, was accepted as canon by many early Christians, including influential thinkers like Tertullian.

The Book of Enoch teaches that demons were Nephilim. The Nephilim were beings that resulted from human women conceiving children with angels that had somehow been tempted by mortal lust. The resulting race of Nephilim were, therefore, partly angelic and partly human. Since their existence was an abomination before God, God sent the great flood to eradicate them. This destroyed their physical bodies, but their spirits remained. These entities, according to Enoch, were demons.[4]

These ideas were eventually supplanted by the idea that demons were fallen angels, allies of Satan during his failed rebellion against God. However, if you read the Bible, actual references to fallen angels are scant. The most detailed account we get comes from the book of Revelation, 12:9, which explicitly states that Satan and 'his' angels were cast out of heaven.[5]

However, this account does not explicitly state that these fallen angels were demons. An early Christian who accepted the account in the Book of Enoch, might argue that a demon was Nephilim, whereas a fallen angel was something else. However, by the Plantagenet era, the idea that demons and fallen angels were one in the same was universally accepted. The concept nevertheless retained certain ideas that were reminiscent of pagan daimons and apocryphal Nephilim.

By the high Middle Ages, church thinkers had developed a fleshed-out view of demons, their nature, their powers, and their limitations. Demons were, like other angels, essentially spiritual rather than material creatures. However, they had been cast out of heaven. So, where were they? One theory was that they were in hell, suffering eternal fiery torment. However, some were clearly tasked with conveying the souls of the damned to hell and others roamed the earth, tempting and even possessing mortals. The latter is clearly attested to in the Bible.

Demons that dwelt upon the earth were thought to exist primarily in the air, amongst the upper clouds. They would come down from this realm from time to time to interact with mortals. In early Christianity, they were thought to be especially numerous in remote locations, such as deserts. However, they could potentially be encountered anywhere.

Whilst they were spiritual beings, they could assume physical form of a sort. These were not true bodies, like those of mortals, but semi-ethereal bodies formed from vapours in the air. Since these were not true bodies, demons could adopt a variety of different forms. They often appeared in foul, grotesque forms and, since their spirits were unclean, their manifestation could be accompanied by a foul stench. A multitude of different forms are described in medieval writing. There are terrifying beasts, great bear-like creatures with cruel talons, deformed pigs, apelike creatures, dragons, serpents, and demonic horses, to name but a few. Somewhat more disturbingly, some medieval descriptions of demons portray them as 'Ethiopians' or 'black men'. And, occasionally, they are described as men with 'hooked noses', playing on common antisemitic stereotypes.

Despite this, in necromantic rituals, the sorcerer could command a demon to appear in a fair form. Shape changing was, therefore, a common demonic power. A demon could (and often did) appear in beautiful forms if it suited their purpose. They could assume any disguise, appearing as humans or even as angels. Indeed, they were angels of a sort, of course.

Some would deliberately appear as beautiful people in an attempt seduce mortals and lead them into carnal sin. A demon in male form of this kind was known as an incubus and those in female form as a succubus. Whilst these demons worked to corrupt mortals with lust, and engage in carnal relations with them, they were not thought to be motivated by lust themselves. Instead, their motivation was simply to corrupt. Their satisfaction came from leading souls to damnation, not from any physical pleasure. Since they had no true physical bodies, they were thought to be incapable of carnal feelings.

It was often important to know the name of a demon, or of the arch-demon it served, to gain power over it. Many of the known names of demons and arch-demons came from biblical and apocryphal sources. Examples include Beelzebub (a name derived from a Philistine god) or Baal (a reference to a Canaanite god). The demon Azazel derived his name from a reference in the Book of Enoch to the demon Asa'el. Azazel became associated with tempting mankind with forbidden, hidden, knowledge. Mephistopheles first makes an appearance in German folklore in the sixteenth century. His name is a corrupted form of classical Greek which may suggest he was known of in earlier times. The term 'mephitic' which constitutes the first part of the name 'Mephistopheles', implies he had some association with noxious vapours.

There were, however, important limitations to demonic power. Although demons were angels, they were fallen angels. Since they had been defeated, they were fully constrained by God's will. God, therefore, placed restrictions on what demons could or could not do. They could not predict the future (only God himself had this power). However, due to their intelligence and immortal existence, they had great insight that made them far more skilled at anticipating future events than mortals. This might allow them to appear to have the gift of prophecy when, in fact, they did not.

Crucially, demons did not have the power to affect material change to God's creation. This meant that they could not physically harm people unless God explicitly permitted them to do so. This led to many medieval thinkers suggesting that any physical effects demons appeared to be responsible for were mostly illusions or deceptions. This did not, however, mean that they did not pose a very real threat.

The main way demons often chose to interact with mortals was to tempt them. Their goal was to corrupt your soul and consign you to eternal damnation, rather than to kill or physically harm you. For this reason, they would employ any trick in the book to persuade you to do the wrong things. This might include persuading a monk or nun to abandon their order, tempting someone to surrender to lust or terrifying someone into renouncing their faith.

Another tactic might involve possession. A demon or even multiple demons might possess someone, to make them sick, drive them to madness, or otherwise torment them. The aim, as ever, was to cajole someone or drive them to such despair that they abandoned their faith. There were also stories of demons harming or even killing people. However, this was only possible if God permitted it. And God would usually only grant such permission if the person concerned had strayed from a righteous path and thereby made themselves vulnerable. Those who had given their souls to Satan, either overtly or by some grave sin, might even be killed by a demon.

The extent to which demons were permitted to engage in such behaviour was, therefore, constrained by strict rules. In general, they were permitted to act only to test the faith of men. Often these tests could have the reverse effect of what the demon desired; to make the victim more, rather than less, holy. Medieval theologians believed that the holier someone became, the more attractive they became as a target for demonic temptation. Demons were, therefore, far more likely to be found attempting to lead a holy abbess astray than wasting their time with an avaricious merchant who was already damned. The twelfth century saw writers like Peter the Venerable and Herbert of Clairvaux vying to outdo each other with tales of resisting demonic temptation. The more demons assailed a monk, the logic went, the holier he must be.

Whatever trials demons might inflict on mortals, the church was clear that they were never able to test anyone beyond their capacity to bear it (since this was explicitly stated in 1 Corinthians 10:13). Trials, however, could be fairly extreme. Herbert of Clairvaux describes a demon sent to test him that took the form of a horrific dragon. The beast even launched itself at his face, threatening to devour him.[6]

In one particularly disturbing tale, Otloh of St. Emmeram, tells of how he was plagued by a demon who visited him at night in the form of a grotesque man. The demon proceeded to beat him savagely, returning night after night to administer further beatings. Otloh asked the monk sleeping in the bed next to him if he heard or saw anything of these demonic visitations, but the fellow swore he witnessed nothing. Despite this, Otloh claims, his back was completely covered in vicious injuries from the beatings.[7]

The possibility of possession was a very real fear in the Middle Ages. The reality of this phenomena was attested to in scripture and, consequently, several clerics practiced exorcisms. However, the sure-fire defence against all forms of demonic attack was a strong and unwavering faith. Reciting the Lord's Prayer, making the sign of the cross and other confident and sincere displays of faith were all highly effective in driving off or cowing demonic assailants.

Clearly, the demon summoning magic in the Munich handbook was a world away from the simple folk magic used by a humble farmer. The contrast between these different practices simply serves to illustrate the sheer diversity of occult belief during the Middle Ages. Magic and superstition, in a wide variety of forms, was pervasive in medieval society, despite the hostility and unease that existed within the church and wider society. Nevertheless, by avoiding maleficent forms of magic and political complications, many people were able to practice magic relatively freely for most of the Middle Ages.

This gradually changed as the Middle Ages wore on. Earlier in the period, magic was typically regarded as misguided superstition. Perhaps nothing more than a hangover from cruder pagan times. Church thinking was that sorcerers were either being deceived by demons or foolishly seeking to control them. Certainly, this was a sin that required penance, but it was not automatically considered synonymous with heresy or devil worship. Heresy, of course, was a different matter. Actively turning away from God was seen to present a far more serious threat to the church than magic in general. So, how and why did attitudes shift? How and why did magic and witchcraft come to be so closely associated with overt devil worship and heresy?

Heresy and Witchcraft

Since early times, the church had been concerned with protecting orthodoxy and eradicating heresy. The early church itself faced challenges from heretical versions of the faith such as Gnosticism (in the second and third century) and Arianism (during the late Roman period). It also had to combat paganism, whether that be Roman, Celtic, Germanic, or Norse in origin. Pagan practices often included magic, so you might think that magic itself would have been more aggressively targeted. However, for much of the early Middle Ages, the primary target remained pagan belief overall, rather than the superstitious practices that came with it. The feeling was that if belief in pagan gods and misguided heresies could be stamped out, then any associated superstition would likely fade with them.

Different secular powers took a patchwork of different approaches to dealing with magic. Most often they took their lead from the church. In the case of England, for most of the Middle Ages, little or nothing was done to suppress magic. Much of this can be explained by the fact that common magical practices were often dismissed as foolish local superstition. It was also regarded as something individuals did rather than being associated with any organised group or insidious conspiracy. There was no real concept of networks of witches' covens or cabals of sorcerers banding together to conspire against Christendom (unless they were overtly associated with a particular heretical group).

Another important factor was the lack of an organised church inquisition. Any investigation of alleged maleficence had to be undertaken ad-hoc in response to a particular allegation. The onus was very much on private individuals to come forward with a complaint. No one proactively looked to investigate or hunt down witches and sorcerers.

In the early Middle Ages, even the prosecution of heretics could be quite ad-hoc. Neither heretics nor witches were burnt at the stake at this time. The first confirmed burning of heretics occurred in 1022, in Orleans. A dozen priests were convicted and burnt for challenging key aspects of church doctrine.[1]

The church Inquisition first came into existence only in 1184. It was created, in the initial instance, to deal with the growing threat of the Cathar heresy emerging in Languedoc region of southern France. The Cathars were a heretical sect strongly influenced by Gnosticism and a concept known as dualism. For them, all material things were inherently corrupt and evil, the product of a flawed creator deity. This imperfect god, they argued, was not the true god. Only the spiritual aspect of humanity originated from the true god. Therefore, true salvation lay in a path of personal spiritual enlightenment rather than the sacrifice of Christ's crucifixion. Christ, for the Cathars, was a guide and teacher who shows us the path to Heaven but, ultimately, it was for human beings themselves to deliver their own salvation. The spiritual mysticism of the Cathars made them far closer to Buddhists than orthodox Christians in their quest for spiritual purity. For them, like Buddhists, salvation lay in freeing the spiritual self from all material connections.

Initially the Inquisition attempted to deal with the Cathars through teaching and persuasion. This stemmed from a conviction that heresy was a product of error and ignorance. As a result, it was believed that all that needed to be done to stamp it out was to explain to the heretic the error of his ways and, surely then, he would see the light and repent. This approach enjoyed some success but couldn't fully eradicate Catharism and a core of stubbornly fervent believers remained. Eventually, it became clear that firmer measures were needed. In the end, it required a crusade (the Albigensian crusade of 1209–1229) to dismantle the Cathar community. The church generally dealt with the heretics by forcing them to perform penance, go on pilgrimages, or join a crusade. However, those few that refused to abandon Catharism were eventually burnt at the stake.

One of the many aspects of Catharism that marked it out as dangerous in the eyes of the church related to the role of women. In the medieval church itself, the priesthood was purely patriarchal. Women had no official active role to play in teaching or preaching. The same was certainly not true of Catharism. In the Cathar faith, women could and did actively preach. Some women even became *perfectae* (the Cathar equivalent of priests). They were in the minority, but the mere presence of any such women stood in shocking contrast to the orthodox teachings of the church at the time.[2]

Catharism came to be regarded by the church as the most dangerous heresy encountered since Roman times. The role played by Cathar women raised the frightening prospect of female inspired heresy. The danger posed by non-conformist female belief had suddenly become very real in the minds of many. It was an important early step in the demonisation of female witches that would eventually coalesce in the early modern witch hunts.

Having established the Inquisition, heresies of all kinds became more actively investigated and prosecuted. During the thirteenth century, heretics could find themselves accused of consorting with devils, witchcraft, or sorcery as well as heresy. However, the primary focus remained fixed on the dangers of heresy. Indeed, to ensure Inquisition resources were used wisely, the pope ordered that accusations of witchcraft and sorcery should not be investigated unless heresy was involved.

However, the twelfth century had also seen some significant developments in learned magic. Learned magic, including the much-feared ritual necromancy, also became increasingly visible by the early thirteenth century. Greater visibility doubtless served to increase the perceived level of threat posed by magic overall. So, by the end of the thirteenth century, the Inquisitorial structure was fully in place and medieval society had become increasingly uneasy about the practice of magic.

These two changes culminated in an important event that occurred in the early fourteenth century – the arrest and trial of the Knights Templars (1307–1314). The Knights Templars were a crusading military order, established during the early twelfth century, to defend the Holy Land against Islam. Since their establishment, the order became rich and powerful, acquiring lands and properties across Europe as well as the Holy Land. The Templars' fall from grace was precipitated, in no small part, by the loss of the Middle Eastern crusader kingdom at the end of the thirteenth century. With the Templars driven from the Holy Land and, with no prospect of return in the foreseeable future, they lost their core raison d'être.

Despite being apparently redundant, the Templars remained rich and privileged. And, to many, it seemed they were far more worldly that their title, The Poor Knights of Christ and the Temple of Solomon, warranted. Suspicion also fell on the order because their initiation ceremonies were often (if not always) held in secret. These concerns were enough to raise some serious questions about their future. The final catalyst appears to have been allegations of heresy levelled at the order by a disgruntled former member.

The initial allegations were largely dismissed for what they were by most people. However, the French king, Philip the Fair, saw an opportunity to discredit the order and seize its valuable assets in the process. It was this political agenda that ultimately served as the driving force behind their arrest and trials. The nature of the allegations themselves were of particular importance.

The Templars were primarily accused of heretical practices rather than witchcraft or sorcery. This was no doubt driven by the official church criteria that witchcraft alone was not usually considered sufficient grounds for an investigation. However, the nature of the heresy of which the Templars were accused was of a character that strongly implied occult practice and ritual magic. They were accused of an organised and widespread conspiracy. This included some very specific and troubling allegations:

- That they widely practiced ritualised homosexuality.
- They denied Christ and spat on the cross.
- They maintained idols in the image of human heads. Some of these idols were said to have three faces and some were human skulls.
- That they worshipped these idols, believing this would bring them riches.
- That they wore ritual cords around their waists and touched the head idols with these cords during their rituals.[3]

During the torture-extracted confessions that followed, one brother even identified one of these 'head-idols' as a demon called Baphomet. This demon was first mentioned at the time of the First Crusade. Troubadours of the time used the name to denote Mohammed and a crusader claimed the local population prayed to this demon. Baphomet seems to have been mistakenly conflated with Mohammed on at least some occasions in the European mind.

The Templars were accused of effectively worshipping these demonic idols, channelling their powers to gain riches and make their lands fertile. Tapping the power of demons to gain material wealth, of course, was very suggestive of ritual necromancy, even if the accusation was not explicitly made. The accusation of wearing ceremonial cords might also bring images of ritual magic to mind. However, the use of ritual cords was also reminiscent of Cathar practice. Cathars who underwent a heretical initiation rite known as the *consolamentum* were thought to wear such cords. It was, therefore, potentially a charge designed to imply a connection with the Cathar heresy. Despite the specific nature of these charges, aside from confessions extracted under torture, the accusers were unable to produce any evidence. Not a single cord, head idol, heretical or magical book was ever produced at the trial.

The Templar trial nevertheless served as a template. It demonstrated that an organised heretical group could take the form of an insidious conspiracy of covert demon worship. It also implied strong links between heresy and learned magic as many people would have understood it. In the case of the Templars, they had not simply been guilty of being deceived by demons into false belief. They had been guilty of overt demon worship. This direct link with demon worship elevated the perceived threat posed by sorcery and witchcraft into more dangerous territory.

This opened the door to more overt prosecution of individuals for sorcerous practice during the fourteenth century. However, the number of individuals actively prosecuted remained very small across Europe and most prosecutions had a political dimension. In England itself, secular laws against witchcraft and heresy remained absent from the statute book throughout the fourteenth century. The first formal laws were introduced only at the start of the fifteenth century, by Henry IV, in the form of *De Heretico Comburendo* (literally 'concerning the burning of heretics'). It was a law that focused on the prosecution of heretics, which was brought in primarily to deal with the Lollards (an early proto-Protestant sect).[4] Witchcraft and sorcery were still not considered a serious enough threat to warrant specific legislation.

Across the whole of Europe, the earliest mass witch hunt occurred in Valais, in Switzerland in 1428. More than a hundred witches were discovered and burnt for practicing maleficent magic.[5] Although, here too the allegation of witchcraft alone was not enough to have prompted prosecution. The primary allegations included heresy, murder, and devil worship as well as sorcery. Following Valais, some religious thinkers began making far more overt links between magic and devil worship. Johannes Nider wrote a treatise on this subject in 1435–37 called *Formucarius*. In it, he argues that all forms of magic are a form of devil worship and that the two cannot be separated.

The reality of magical practice in the Middle Ages was that those people who genuinely practiced necromancy and demonology were virtually all men. Women, if they practiced magic at all, tended to practice common magic such as herbalism, folk spells, and charms. There were almost certainly far more women practicing common magic than there were men practicing ritual necromancy. Nevertheless, such women were more numerous and hence more visible. As medieval culture became increasingly hostile to all forms of magic, these women became increasingly vulnerable.

Nider's treatise aimed to alert people to the fact that the practice of magic and sorcery were far more widespread and dangerous than many imagined. In making his point, he specifically draws attention to women practicing common folk magic. This, Nider argues, is every bit as much a threat, in its own way, as the feared necromancers. Not only are women capable of actively practicing maleficent magic, but they are also more likely to succumb to this sin, in Nider's view. The emphasis on directly linking satanism with witchcraft and singling out of women as its primary practitioners, were both relatively new developments.

In England, an incident that occurred in the mid-fifteenth century illustrates how attitudes were changing. An astrologer consulted by Duchess Eleanor of Gloucester foolishly predicted that King Henry VI would fall ill and die in 1441. If such an event had occurred, Eleanor's husband, the duke of Gloucester, would become king. Eleanor certainly had an interest in magic and astrology for she also consulted a well-known witch by the name of Margery Jourdemayne (known as the 'Eye-Witch'). Unfortunately for all involved, Eleanor's husband had powerful political enemies, keen to find any way possible to discredit him in the king's eyes. Her astrologer, Roger Bolingbroke and her physician, Dr Thomas Southall, were accused of attempting to hasten the foretold demise of the king by means of necromancy. More specifically, it was alleged that they'd procured a wax image of the king from Jourdemayne, which, on melting, would bring about the king's death. Eleanor claimed the image had been procured for fertility magic to help her conceive, but it was to no avail.[6]

The duchess and her associates found themselves charged with 'treasonable necromancy'. It was a charge that would mean death for her acquaintances (though not the duchess herself). The practice of magic and astrology were still not considered crimes in themselves. However, when the nature of the magic involved maleficence directed against a king, Eleanor's occult dabbling was elevated to the far more serious charge of treason.

What was still absent from fifteenth-century society was a fully formed conception of witchcraft as it came to be understood during the Early Modern period. The mass witch-hunts of the sixteenth and seventeenth centuries were driven by a conviction that all witches were satanists. The idea that witches made pacts with Satan, met in covens, practiced black masses, black magic, and human sacrifice emerged during the fifteenth century. This particularly nightmarish vision of witchcraft became increasingly widespread as the century wore on. Nider represented an early articulation of it. However, it was not given its ultimate coherent vocalisation until a radical German inquisitor, Heinrich Kramer, published *Malleus Maleficarum* in 1486.[7]

Known as the *Hammer of the Witches*, *Malleus* not only cemented the view that witchcraft and satanism were synonymous, it also strongly identified the practice with women rather than men. In Kramer's view, witchcraft was the product of carnal lust, a sin to which he was convinced women were far more inclined.

By the dawn of the early modern age, the concept of *the evil witch* had taken shape in the European consciousness. It would lead to the mass witch-hunts that swept Europe during the sixteenth and seventeenth centuries. The old medieval laissez faire, if disapproving, attitude to magic would be swept away by the new fanatical creed of *Malleus*.

Ghosts and the Walking Dead

Stories and superstitions concerning the existence of ghosts, hauntings, and unquiet spirits are as old as civilisation itself. Just about every single ancient civilisation, whether Egyptian, Mesopotamian, Hellenistic, or Roman held some kind of belief in such entities. Ghosts and undead hauntings of various kinds were also a feature of other pagan cultures, whether Celtic, Germanic, or Norse. The Plantagenet realm, therefore, inherited a deep-rooted belief in ghosts and restless spirits from every single pagan cult present in the British Isles prior to Christianisation.

As we have seen, the medieval church strongly condemned necromantic practices aimed at summoning the spirits of the departed. It also held that spirits conjured by necromancy were, in fact, demons attempting to deceive the foolish. Despite this, church teachings were less clear on whether it was possible for ghosts to rise from the grave to haunt the living. Saint Augustine had been sceptical. He tended to take the view that people who claimed to see visions of the dead were either imagining it or being deceived by demons. Not everyone in the church agreed with this, but Augustine's views were influential and the church tended to remain sceptical on the subject of ghosts, as a result. Belief in ghosts was often regarded as a superstitious hangover from an ignorant pagan past.

However, though sceptical, the church remained open to the possibility of ghosts. Pope Gregory the Great taught that under certain circumstances those souls consigned to suffer purgatorial trials might return as ghosts. Furthermore, the Bible itself seemed clear that Saul had, indeed, spoken with the ghost of the prophet Sammuel. Of course, Saul was harshly condemned for conjuring Sammuel's ghost, reinforcing the prohibition on necromancy. However, it was hard to deny that a literal reading of the Bible left little doubt that a ghost had indeed been conjured. Under the right circumstances, and if God permitted it, contact with ghosts was a possibility that was difficult for any theologian to rule out.

Church scepticism of ghosts was also problematic when it is considered that visions and visitations of the saints was an accepted reality. Such cases were, of course, held to be exceptional. The saints were not just any old spirits of the dead after all. However miraculous such events may have been, they were undeniably examples of contact between the living and the spirits of those who had died.

In the medieval mind, there were three main reasons why the spirits of the departed might wish to return to haunt the living. The first related to purgatorial punishment. In early medieval belief, it was thought that a ghost might be condemned to return to the land of the living as part of their punishment. However, as the concept of purgatory as a specific dimension of existence in the afterlife took shape, this kind of manifestation was increasingly out of step with theology. Nevertheless, a ghost of someone in purgatory might still be permitted to visit the living to petition their aid in their search for redemption. The second reason for a haunting was potentially far more disturbing. If the departed soul was particularly sinful and the correct funerary rites had not been properly observed, the body might rise from the dead as a revenant. The third and final way would be when a ghost was permitted by God, an angel, or a saint to deliver a warning or a message to the living.

Some churchmen held that this latter case applied in the instance of the prophet Sammuel. King Saul sought the aid of the witch of Endor to summon the spirit of the dead prophet so he could seek his council. In Saul's case it seemed that God had intervened directly and permitted the departed spirit of Sammuel to be conjured. This was done specifically so that Sammuel's ghost could castigate Saul for attempting such a conjuring and to inform him of God's judgement upon him.

More often than not ghosts were regarded as spirits enduring purgatorial punishment. The medieval Christian generally believed damned souls went straight to hell when they died. However, only the souls of dead saints and martyrs were pure enough to go directly to heaven. For most ordinary folk, their souls were not pure enough to pass directly to heaven, even if they had been good Christians. Instead, they would first need to undergo a process of cleansing and purification in purgatory. Unfortunately, this cleansing process involved punishment, pain, and suffering. For some people, if their sins were grave, this ordeal could last a very long time, perhaps many centuries.

However, praying for the souls of the departed or, better still, performing masses for their souls, had the power to reduce the duration of their purgatorial punishment. The medieval church based this belief on 2 Maccabees 12:46 which encouraged the living to pray for the dead to free them from their sins. This meant that the living possessed the power to ease the purgatorial suffering of the dead which naturally provided a strong motive for souls trapped in purgatory to reach out to the living for aid.

Whilst many clergymen were suspicious of tales of ghosts, tending to regard them as foolish superstition, this was never a universally held view. Other clergymen not only embraced but actively encouraged belief in ghosts! Many of the medieval ghost stories that survive were, originally, the subject of sermons. Such stories served as useful moral lessons, promoting church teachings and instilling a suitable fear of purgatorial punishment amongst the faithful.

A good example can be found in a fifteenth-century manuscript concerning events that supposedly happened in 1373. This ghost story claims that a man from Haydock had been visited by the ghost of his former mistress. This ghost had been granted divine permission to approach her former lover to seek his aid. She implored him to help her, explaining that 'I can be freed from the punishment I am suffering, if masses are celebrated for me by good priests.' The ghost then provided her lover with several hairs from her head. To her lover's surprise, these hairs were black, even though her hair had been golden in life. Nevertheless, the man did as the ghost asked and found that, after the performance of each mass, one strand of hair changed its colour from black to gold. When all the hairs finally changed to gold, the woman's soul was freed from purgatory. The priest who originally wrote this story, ends his cautionary tale with the proverb, 'Praise be the power of the mass'.[1]

Another salutary clerical ghost tale, probably written around 1400, concerns the ghost of the canon of Newbury. This apparition apparently attacked a man whilst he was speaking with a ploughman in a field. The ghost launched a frenzied assault in which he shredded his victim's clothing. The ploughman was so terrified that he fled the scene. This ghost was corporeal enough to shred the clothing of its victim and, for its victim to eventually overpower it in a physical fight. We are then informed that, once the ghost was defeated, the man 'conjured it up'. It then confessed that it was the ghost of a canon of Newbury and that it had been excommunicated for stealing silver. It then begged the man to take the silver and return it to the prior in the hope that the prior might absolve the ghost of its sins. This, we are told, the man did, thereby allowing the ghost to rest in peace.[2] This reference to a man literally conjuring the spirit of a dead canon shows just how ingrained the concept of necromantic conjuration was in the medieval psyche. And this was despite all the church's efforts to stamp out such beliefs. In this case it appears as an almost causal reference in a tale written by a clergyman.

A key reason for hauntings stemmed from a ghost's desire to atone for past sins and/or seek absolution. However, there were other circumstances that could result in unquiet spirits returning from the grave to haunt the living. In some particularly horrific instances, they could return as the walking, corporeal undead. Usually, these horrific risings from the grave were the consequence of the ritual observances surrounding death and burial being ignored or polluted in some way.

The medieval rituals that surrounded death and burial were crucial in ways that it is difficult to appreciate today. Correct ritual observance ensured that the dead could rest in peace and helped to ease their path through purgatory to heaven. Ideally, you would have lived your life as a good Christian, regularly making confession and attending mass. Then, if you were near death, you'd need to make your confession to your priest and receive absolution and the last rites.

However, religious funerary rituals evolved to become increasingly elaborate and complex throughout the Middle Ages. They were all designed to ensure the soul of the departed enjoyed an easy passage to the afterlife. To experience an ideal death, tapers or candles would be lighted near to a dying person to ward off demons. Demons were thought especially likely to appear at this time. It was the last chance for a demon to claim a soul for hell after all. Once last rites were received and the person passed on, it was important to open the bedroom door and windows, so that the soul was not impaired in its journey. The corpse would then be ritually washed, wrapped in a shroud, and placed in a coffin. The body would then be conveyed to the church, ideally accompanied by bell ringers and candle bearers. Pall bearers should have been citizens of good repute. Once at the church, a funeral bier would be placed near the altar and the ritual of the Office of the Dead performed. The priest should also perform Vespers on the evening before Requiem Mass was said. The next day, there should be Mattins with lessons from the Book of Job. Then funerary rituals would culminate in a Requiem Mass for the departed soul, and a final Blessing of Absolution would be received. Only then, finally, could one safely be laid to rest in hallowed ground.[3]

It was an elaborate and fragile ritual balancing act. Should any element be disrupted, performed incorrectly, or missed, it could spell trouble for the departed. Any pollution of the sacred rituals could result in the spirit of the departed being unable to find peace in the afterlife. Under such unfortunate circumstances, the dead could literally rise from the grave to plague the living. And, of course, this possibility became even more likely when dealing with the corpses of those who had lived dissolute lives. This, then, represented the second significant way in which a haunting might occur.

The idea of corpses returning from the grave to haunt the living dated back to pagan times. In Old French such entities were called 'revenants', meaning 'returning', as in returning from the grave. They were a feature of old pagan beliefs that persisted into the Middle Ages.

William of Newburgh was an Augustine canon famous for writing the *Historia rerum Anglicarum*. It was a history of England, covering the period from 1066 up to 1198 (the time William finished it). William provided four different reports of revenant activity in the *Historia* to illustrate the nature of this phenomenon. He informs us that he limited the number of accounts to four because: 'to write down all the instances of this kind which I have ascertained to have befallen in our times, the undertaking would be beyond measure laborious and troublesome'.[4]

One of these cases occurred in Bedfordshire and concerned a farmer who accidentally stabbed himself with a knife, after tripping and falling. His wound proved fatal, and he quickly bled out before the appropriate rituals could be observed. The local priest did his best to mitigate this unfortunate circumstance. Nevertheless, his wife, aware her husband had not led an especially Christian life, consulted a local wise woman. Following her advice, the wife placed a jet bead on her husband's coffin in the hope that this would protect his corpse from demonic forces. She also hung 'mare stones' in the rafters of her house to act as an additional warding. But these were of no use. The farmer's corpse rose from the grave the very next night and forced its way into the marital bed. Terrified, the only thing his wife could do was pray to the Virgin Mary as the revenant's corpse crushed her.

Over the next few nights, the revenant continued to haunt its wife as well as many other local villagers. It even attacked local farm animals. The villagers sought the help of the local archdeacon who, in turn, consulted the bishop of Lincoln. The bishop, in turn, consulted with his colleagues. One of these, William de Montibus, master of Lincoln's cathedral school, claimed to have some knowledge of this phenomena. William told the bishop that such revenants were not uncommon and that the 'traditional' way the English dealt with the problem was to exhume the corpse and cremate it.

However, this old pagan remedy was problematic. Cremating the corpse might prevent the unquiet spirit from rising again but it ran the risk of damning the soul of the deceased. Instead, the bishop was determined to find a solution more in keeping with Christian teachings. In the end, he decided that a scroll of absolution might well do the trick. The revenant's coffin should be opened, and the scroll placed on the chest of the corpse. The bishop theorised that if the corpse was possessed by a demon, the sacred word would bind the demon into the grave. If, however, the body was possessed by the restless ghost of the farmer, the scroll would lay the ghost to rest. Either way, the revenant would not return.

Following the bishop's instructions, the body was exhumed. The corpse was found to be swollen with blood and the funeral shroud torn to shreds. It stank of decay but was still unnaturally warm and pliable. These were the sure signs of a blood-sucking fiend: a vampire. The scroll of absolution, sealed in a lead case, was placed on the chest of the revenant and the coffin re-sealed. It worked. The farmer's wife and the villagers were never again troubled by the revenant.[5]

Old pagan methods for dealing with such entities still appear to have been practiced in William's time. Indeed, William mentions instances where fearful locals took the law into their own hands. They dug up suspected revenants, chopped them to pieces, and burnt the remains. For them, it seems, these were the only tried and trusty 'old ways' that could truly protect their community from such horrors.[6]

The horrific concept of the revenant appears to have had its origins in old pagan Anglo-Saxon belief. Echoes of this belief can also be found in Scandinavian sagas that mention such entities as evil, plague-bearing undead with vampiric qualities.[7] The thirteenth-century *Eyrbyggja Saga*, suggests these beliefs were common across both pagan Anglo-Saxon and Norse societies. In this saga, we are informed of two revenants (often referred to in Norse mythology as *draugr*). In both instances, hauntings were the result either of evil nature in life or of a failure to observe necessary funerary arrangements.

In the case of Thorolf Twist-Foot, the man behaved violently and greedily in life, constantly scheming against his neighbours. In death, however, he was even worse. He returned as a *draugr* to haunt the villagers, spreading destruction and death when he rose from his grave at night. Eventually, his body was exhumed, moved to a remote location, and walled up to ensure he troubled the locals no more. We are informed that when his body was finally moved, it was extremely heavy, had acquired an ugly visage, and was fiendishly lacking in any signs of decomposition.[8]

The sightings of ghosts and apparitions could sometimes be taken as a warning or a portent. Occasionally, ghosts were permitted to appear to deliver a warning to the living. In such instances, a ghost itself was not the soul in peril so much as the living whom they'd returned to warn. In these circumstances, they could only manifest if God, an angel, or a saint permitted it.

One particularly fearful example of apparitions appearing as a warning to the living is recorded in the *Anglo-Saxon Chronicle* for the year 1127. In a deer park near Peterborough, we are told that:

> several persons saw and heard many huntsmen hunting. The hunters were dark, and huge, and ugly; and their hounds were all dark, and broad-eyed, and ugly. And they rode on dark horses, and dark bucks.[9]

Were these ghosts? Were they demons? Or some other kind of supernatural fiend? The chronicler does not say. The incident is an early reported sighting of the Wild Hunt in England. Such sightings, associated with spectral entities, were a feature of Anglo-Norman culture during the high Middle Ages. They were usually, but not necessarily always, taken to be a troop of restless souls (either bound for hell or purgatorial torment).[10]

Whatever the nature of the hunt, the manifestation recorded in 1127 was clearly taken as an ill omen. The chronicler attributes this dire portent to the appointment of Henry of Poitou to the abbacy of Peterborough. It is made clear that Henry received his appointment because of nepotism and corruption. Furthermore, this corrupt abbot had proceeded to strip the monastery of its wealth for his own personal enrichment. It came as no surprise that his appointment should be heralded by such an evil vision.

Not all manifestations of ghostly portents and warnings were necessarily seen as restless spirits. A fifteenth-century manuscript from Ely provides an example of such a haunting from 1389. Thomas of Ely was haunted for thirteen nights by a ghost who, on the thirteenth night, threw both Thomas and his son out of their beds. This apparition then summoned Thomas to follow the spirit to meet with Saint Ethelreda. Sure enough, the ghost led Thomas into the presence of the saint. She informed him that, as Thomas had honoured her in his prayers, she had decided to grant him a warning.

At the time, the region was suffering from a severe heatwave causing serious crop damage. Saint Ethelreda warned that if the people of Ely failed to do as she advised, the heatwave would only get worse. The heat would become so great that the lead on the church roofs would melt. To put things right, the people were pressed to resolve any unpaid church tithes and unproved wills. Furthermore, the prior and convent of Ely needed to hold religious processions every Wednesday and Friday for five weeks to petition God's mercy.

There was a problem, however. Thomas was a man of only modest reputation and it seemed unlikely that his claims would be taken seriously without the aid of a miracle. Therefore, Saint Ethelreda struck him down with an affliction and told him to take to his bed and wait. Then, on the saint's feast day, he should be brought to the tomb of Saint Ethelreda and, before witnesses, the words 'get up and walk' should be spoken. This was done as the saint commanded and, sure enough, Thomas was miraculously restored to full health before several witnesses. There was no doubt that a miracle had occurred. Consequently, the warning was taken seriously, and the advice of the saint duly followed.[11] In this case the ghost concerned had been sent as a messenger by a saint, so that a warning might be delivered to the living.

Another example of a ghost returning to warn the living of peril can be found in Sir Thomas Malory's epic, *Le Morte D'Arthur*. Towards the end of this tale, King Arthur gathers his forces for a final confrontation with his arch-nemesis Mordred. However, on the eve of battle he receives a visitation from the ghost of Sir Gawain who had only recently died. His appearance is so real that Arthur, at first, mistakenly believes that Gawain somehow still lives. However, Gawain swiftly disavows him of this and informs Arthur that he is indeed dead, but that God had permitted him to warn Arthur of his death. He goes on to advise

Arthur to delay his battle with Sir Mordred for one month so that Sir Lancelot has time to assemble an army to come to his aid. Should Arthur ignore his council, Gawain warns, both Arthur and Mordred will fall.[12] Tragically, Arthur ignores the ghost's warning and proceeds to give battle. Sure enough, Gawain's warning proves prescient, and both Arthur and Mordred are slain.

Of course, Malory's Arthurian ghost tale was dramatized fiction. It, nevertheless, reflects a belief that, by God's leave, ghosts could return to deliver warnings to the living. It was a tale that carried more weight because it was an Arthurian story. This placed it firmly within a highly respected and revered mythological tradition, central to the identity of the medieval elite.

It is to tales of King Arthur and chivalric mythology that we must now turn our attention. For the elite of the Plantagenet court, these stories were regarded as exemplars for their chivalric culture. In many ways, Arthurian lore came to be regarded as nothing more nor less than the chivalric foundation mythology of Britain.

Chivalric Mythology

The structure of the medieval world was such that its cultural values were largely determined by the upper echelon of society. The secular lords, along with its senior clerics, shaped the cultural and social priorities of their age. This, in turn, often determined what stories, myths, and legends were valued the most. And, since these people represented the most literate section of society, they also determined what was recorded for posterity. It is, therefore, a fact that the stories most likely to have survived are those that were most valued by the lords of the land. That does not mean to say that these tales were not also popular with the illiterate majority. Only that these stories were written primarily to please an audience of lords and ladies.

Key to the culture of Europe's medieval elite was the concept of chivalry and what that meant in shaping the image of a perfect knight. Part of what made the medieval knight different from warriors of previous times was the fact that he fought in a very different style. First and foremost, he was a heavy cavalryman, heavily armoured, and very well equipped. He had to be wealthy simply to afford to maintain himself in the field. His armour, his horse, and his weapons were all very expensive; certainly not the kind of equipment that those outside the ruling elite could afford. It was this technology that gave him his edge on the field of battle for most of the Middle Ages. Few enemies, aside from other knights, could withstand the onslaught of a heavy cavalry charge of massed knights. Military equipment was, therefore, a key part of knightly identity. A fine warhorse and a keen sword were treasured personal possessions, essential elements of his identity and status.

Naturally, the medieval knight was still a warrior. He inevitably shared some of the same values as warriors of earlier times. The pagan warrior-culture portrayed in *Beowulf* clearly valued valour, martial skill, and loyalty to a lord.[1] Pagan kings reinforced the loyalty of their warriors through patronage. It was an important two-way contract. The warrior provided strength of arms and loyalty and, in return, he could expect rich rewards from a grateful and generous lord.

These were also aspects of chivalric culture. However, as we all know, a true medieval knight sought (at least in theory) to live his life by a code that incorporated other values as well. The perfect knight was more than just a warrior, he also aspired to be a paladin – a champion of Christendom. As such, he was expected to protect the church, uphold Christian values, and lead a pious life. He was also expected to be a civilised and cultured man, familiar with court etiquette, courteous, and chivalrous in his dealings with high-born ladies. His reputation for honour, piety, and chivalry marked him out not only as a civilised and cultured man, but as a noble paladin worthy of respect, even reverence.

Chivalric culture evolved over time to create an ideal vision of knighthood. Not all knights were such perfect paladins by any means. Indeed, the reality very often fell far short of the ideal. But the ideal stood, nonetheless. And it was an ideal that was reflected in the literature of the age, literature that evolved its own unique mythology – the mythology of the perfect knight. It served both to inspire and validate the chivalric culture of medieval knighthood.

This new mythology would build on the older traditions of heroic tales such as *Beowulf.* However, it also needed to be accessible to the lords, ladies, and knights that attended the royal courts of Europe. Earlier in the Middle Ages, works in Latin, usually produced by clerics and usually dealing with classical or religious themes tended to dominate. However, not everyone could read Latin and not everyone could understand it, even when someone else read it out aloud.

During the eleventh century a new form of literature was born. It originated in France and was written in French rather than Latin. It had the merit that if it were read out or sung at a French or Plantagenet court, the lords, ladies, and courtiers present could all understand it. This made it accessible to a significantly wider audience.

These stories took the form of epic verse known as *chanson de geste* (which literally means 'song of heroic deeds'). The intended audience was lords, ladies, and knights. This group of people were highly literate and, therefore, able to read these tales. However, the verse structure of many of these stories meant that they were designed for performance. They would be either sung or recited out aloud as a poem. Typically, they would be performed at court or perhaps at a feast in a manor house by minstrels. When performed for an audience at a more local level, the stories could be transmitted not only to an audience of lords and ladies but also to their guests and servants. This allowed for stories to be heard and enjoyed by the illiterate members of these households.

The *chansons de geste* were stories centred mainly around the famous French King Charlemagne (768–814) and his knights. By the high Middle Ages, Charlemagne had attained a legendary status within the French speaking world. Tales concerning his court and the deeds of his knights provided fertile material for heroic tales of derring-do. One of the earliest and most popular of these tales is the *Song of Roland.* This was originally composed at some time during the mid-to-late eleventh century by a poet known only as Turold, or Turoldus.[2]

As with other such tales, historical accuracy was not the primary concern of the poet. This was historical fiction taken into the realms of mythology. Key events in the story were deliberately changed to suit the dramatic narrative. No attempt was made to hide these changes or pretend they were real history. Since this story was written for an educated audience, many of them would have been aware of this. In the song, the key event portrayed is the Battle of Roncesvalles. This battle was fought between Charlemagne's knights and the Basques and not, as the *Song of Roland* tell us, against the Spanish Moors. The Roland in the story is portrayed as Charlemagne's nephew. Whilst there was a real Roland present at this battle, he probably wasn't related to Charlemagne.

In this story, Roland is tasked with leading the rear-guard when Charlemagne's army returned to France from campaigning in Spain. He and his army are ambushed and massacred at the Battle of Roncesvalles by the Moors, largely due to the betrayal of Roland's stepfather, Ganelon. Despite putting up a fierce and valiant fight, Roland and his men are overwhelmed and Roland finally attempts to summon aid by blowing on a great hunting horn, the *oliphant*. Tragically, aid arrives too late. In a scene that possibly inspired Tolkien's treatment of the death of Boromir in *The Lord of the Rings*, Roland dies heroically, sounding his horn.

These early stories contain little in them by way of romance but do contain a strong Christian theme that is absent from pagan tales such as *Beowulf.* Roland and his companion Oliver are Christian paladins, fighting for a righteous cause, a theme that the story emphasises throughout. The Archangel Gabriel is depicted as watching over Charlemagne as he sleeps and as being with Roland as he fights the Moors.[3] Roland is martyred, and his soul carried to paradise by angels. It is a tale reminiscent of the martyrdom stories that appear within *The Golden Legend* – the valiant Christian knight, slain honourably in battle, fighting for a righteous cause against a heathen foe.

In such stories we see the symbols of knighthood described with a reverence not present in earlier tales. Roland's sword Durendal has a special, almost enchanted quality, imbued with the power of holy relics. Roland's companion Ogier's warhorse, Bierefort is also presented as something truly special, more noble than other horses.[4]

The story of Roland, Oliver, and the knights who fell at Roncesvalles made such an impact that, later in the Middle Ages, they were commemorated with cultish reverence. Chartres Cathedral became a centre of veneration for a cult of all things Charlemagne. Stained glass windows show Charlemagne's pilgrimage to Jerusalem and Charlemagne finding the tomb of Saint James on campaign in Spain. The famous legend of Roland is also depicted, celebrating the hero almost as if he were a saint. Roland's fabled sword Durendal was eventually 'discovered' and displayed as a holy relic at Rocamadour in south-western France.[5]

Such stories were seen as inspirational as well as aspirational. In accounts of the Battle of Hastings we are told that a minstrel by the name of Taillefer inspired the Normans by singing the *Song of Roland.* Whilst tossing his sword in the air and catching it, Taillefer sang of Roland's famous sword:

'Oh Durendal, how dazzling bright you are – You blaze with light and shimmer in the sun!'[6]

The story might well be apocryphal, but it clearly shows how inspirational the legend of Roland was thought to be for knights in battle.

The idea of a knight as a holy paladin would come to hold even greater significance with the launch of the First Crusade in the late 1090s. In preaching the crusade, Pope Urban II emphasised this new model of knighthood when he implored those who had formerly been robbers to become soldiers of Christ.[7] The idea of the Christian paladin took shape and was one that would inspire the formation of the military orders: the Knights Templars, Knights Hospitallers, and the Teutonic Knights.

The church provided the aspiring knight with holy purpose, serving to regulate his behaviour and inspire him to fight on behalf of Christendom. However, it was not simply a one-way street. The knight, for his part, could call upon the church and Christianity for validation of his actions. Banners and swords could be blessed by clerics to provide the knight with holy power in battle. Military saints like Saint Michael and Saint George could be invoked for martial aid. Knights even reported seeing saints appearing to aid them in battle. In this way, Saint George is reported appearing on a white charger to aid the Normans against the Saracens at the Battle of Cerami in 1063.[8] Divine aid, even if entirely imagined, can provide a potent moral boost in war.

Although the *chansons* did much to inspire the ideal of the paladin knight, they contained very little that might be regarded as romance. These early stories were all about the brave deeds of knights in battle. Female characters are all but absent, leaving little scope from romantic tales of fair maidens or damsels in distress. This emerged later, during the twelfth century, inspired in part by the influence of troubadours and their songs of courtly romance.

The new tales of chivalric romance began not with tales of Charlemagne but with a nostalgic reworking of older classical stories. As with the *chansons*, they were written in French. *Le Roman de Troie* (The Romance of Troy) was perhaps the most popular of these. Written by Benoît de Sainte-Maure in c. 1165 and based on Latin texts rather than Homer, *Le Roman de Troie* tells the epic tale of the Trojan War.[9] Like the original, this version features many epic battles (more than Homer's version in fact). However, it also adds in a love-triangle involving Troilus, a Trojan prince, Briseida, the daughter of Calchas, and the Greek hero Diomedes. This addition (almost certainly a fictional creation of Benoît's own making) served as inspiration for Chaucer's *Troilus and Criseyde* and, in time, Shakespeare's *Troilus and Cressida*. The addition of a romantic dimension makes it a chivalric romance rather than just a simple re-telling of an epic story from antiquity.

A second key French re-telling of a classical myth, written at around the same time was *Roman d'Enéas* (The Romance of Aeneas). This is pretty much a straight re-telling of Virgil's *Aeneid* in French verse. It digresses from Virgil's original in a few limited ways, however. It makes a lot more of the romantic relationships of Aeneas: first his torrid and doomed infatuation with Dido and then his relationship with his Latin wife-to-be, Lavinia.

In Virgil's version, Aeneas marries Lavinia as part of a political arrangement; there is very little made of any romance between the two. The writer of *Roman d'Enéas*, however, makes far more of the romantic connection between them. Lavinia becomes more central to the story, given considerable agency of her own. This moves the story from its original context as a piece of epic Roman propaganda to the realms of a medieval chivalric romance. The emotional struggles of the characters are now much more front and centre. Lavinia's feelings for Aeneas are now important, as opposed to the Roman version in which her feelings, desires and opinions are deemed so unimportant that they are not even mentioned.

The romantic love between Aeneas and Lavinia in *Roman d'Enéas* develops into a far more medieval tale. To win Lavinia, Aeneas must first win his kingdom. Despite the strong romantic elements in the story, most of the tale is dedicated to tales of war and deeds of heroism in battle. Aeneas fights to win his lady's hand in marriage just as a knight must win a lady's favour by feats of valour and battle honours.

This is an important aspect of how romance is portrayed in these stories. Romance, and the desire to win the love of a noble lady, is a spur to action that encourages the knight to accomplish great deeds of valour and heroism. The medieval knight, Geoffrey de Charny, who wrote extensively on chivalry, argued that love was important precisely because it inspired a man to great deeds to honour their ladies.[10]

However, the growth of chivalric romance was not only about inspiring men to great deeds. It was also about writing for an audience that included powerful women. The high Middle Ages saw the emergence in court circles of women who served as wealthy and powerful patrons. Women like the Empress

Matilda, who challenged Stephen for the throne of England just before the dawn of the Plantagenet age. Women like the formidable Eleanor of Aquitaine, wife of the first Plantagenet King Henry II. These women wanted to hear tales about other noble women, not simply tales of men.

Tales from the ancient world also provided writers of these romances with the opportunity to explore exotic faraway lands. The *Roman d'Alexandre*, based around tales relating to Alexander the Great, offered the opportunity to describe mysterious Middle Eastern lands. Such distant places were only just becoming more visible to Western Europe at this time because of the crusades. This contact with the Eastern world, inspired a new fascination with the exotic east.

Roman d'Enéas includes a few elements absent from Virgil's original, specifically added to conjure images of exotic marvels. These include a fantastic description of a crocodile (described as a serpent) and of Carthage's capitol building's eerie, almost supernatural, acoustic qualities. These seem more calculated to inspire a sense of wonder rather than for any other purpose. To the medieval audience, of course, Africa was a strange and distant land that few had ever visited. To Virgil's Roman audience, Africa was, by his time, just another part of the empire. For Romans, Carthage was alien only in so far as it had been Rome's ancient rival, not in so far as it was genuinely unfamiliar.

The Anglo-Norman culture of the Plantagenet court had come a long way since the Norman conquest. Under Henry II, the Plantagenets reached a new zenith of Anglo-Norman power, commanding an empire that included not only England and Normandy but also Aquitaine, Brittany, and most of Western France. The mythology of Charlemagne and the classical heroes were undeniably inspirational but, ultimately, they were not Anglo-Norman. Of course, the Plantagenets were French, but Charlemagne was nevertheless a hero of the kingdom of France, a kingdom increasingly viewed as a rival to Plantagenet power.

It was against this background that new chivalric romances began to appear in the latter part of the twelfth century. And these stories centred not on the paladins of Charlemagne's court or the deeds of ancient Greek and Roman heroes, but on Arthur, king of the Britons. Tales of Arthur and his knights of the round table that would ultimately become the central mythology of the Plantagenet age.

Arthurian lore came to constitute the third key strand of medieval court mythology across all Western Europe, not just in the Plantagenet realms. As one writer of these times, Jean Bodel, so succinctly put it, it was only necessary for a man of quality to concern oneself with three great Matters: the Matters of France, Britain, and Rome. By this he meant the legends of Charlemagne, Arthur, and classical heroes from the ancient world.[11]

However, Bodel was not quite correct in his assessment of the court culture of his times. There was a fourth 'matter' that also served as inspiration for the knights of Christendom. This fourth matter was perhaps so obvious that it is surprising that Bodel neglected to state it. And that source was, of course, the Bible. The martial deeds of biblical heroes such King David and of the warrior saints were every bit as important as the deeds of Arthur and Charlemagne in chivalric culture. And, of course, their deeds, by their very nature, provided most fitting exemplars for any aspiring paladin of Christendom.

Jean de Longuyon, writing in the early fourteenth century, identified nine chivalric champions from history who were particularly worthy of praise. There were three champions from Old Testament times: the biblical heroes Joshua, David, and Judas Maccabaeus. There were three great champions from classical antiquity: Hector, Alexander, and Julius Caesar. And, finally, there were three Christian paladins: Charlemagne, Arthur, and Godfrey de Bouillon, the leader of the First Crusade.[12] Together, these nine constituted the 'Nine Worthies', the great chivalric champions of medieval mythology. Of these, both Hector and Arthur were largely mythical. Of the others, many of their stories assumed a semi-mythical character (such as in the *Song of Roland*).

The idealised vision of the Christian paladin lay at the heart of the mythological world of the lords and ladies of medieval Europe. And, of course, for Plantagenet England, the most important of these paragons was undoubtedly King Arthur.

Arthurian Lore

King Arthur is probably the most significant and enduring character from British mythology. His legend has not only remained popular but has grown stronger over the centuries. But who was this mythical British king? Was he even real at all?

The twelfth-century history *History* of Geoffrey of Monmouth and Chrétien de Troyes' romances played key roles in elevating Arthurian lore to the Three Matters. But prior to these epic versions of Arthur's story, we have only fragments. We have enough to know that Arthur was considered a British hero earlier than the twelfth century. But, on the other hand, we have nowhere near enough to put together a clear picture of exactly how he was regarded prior to this time.

Many books have been written on the 'real' King Arthur. Many of them take the form of a detective story, forensically picking over old stories and fragments to reconstruct the historic Arthur. However, read any two of them at random and you will, like as not, read a different account of who this 'real' Arthur was. All that we really know about the historic Arthur amounts to a few fragments in old Welsh poems and tantalisingly brief entries in old chronicles and histories. These are enough to tell us he was respected as a heroic figure from the dim, twilight-years of early dark age Britain.

The earliest certain reference to Arthur is an old *History of Britain*, authored by a Welsh monk commonly known as Nennius. It was completed at some time around 830 AD. In this document, Arthur is identified as *dux bellorum*, or war leader. Such a title would have been appropriate for a late Roman military commander but does not mean to say that this Arthur was a king.

According to Nennius' version of events, Arthur was a British military leader who played a key role in defending Romano-Briton against Saxon invaders. Arthur, we are informed, fought, and won no fewer than a dozen battles. In the decisive twelfth battle, at a place called Badon Hill, Nennius claims Arthur personally slew 960 enemies.[1] Ever since, historians have been arguing over when exactly this happened, where it happened, and whether an historic Arthur

Above: Stories relating to the Trojan War and Aeneas were amongst the most popular classical myths in the medieval period. ('Trojan Horse', Giovanni Domenico Tiepolo, c. 1760)

Below: Reproduction of a Celtic Briton pagan village. Whatever remained of the mythology of Celtic Briton was preserved in early medieval Welsh stories and poems. ('Recreated Celtic Village', photo by Colin Smith; Museum of Welsh Life)

An Anglo-Saxon *scop* entertains his lord's household with tales of Beowulf and Wayland Smith. (J.R. Skelton, illustration, c. 1910)

Above: Viking longships terrorised northern Europe at the end of the first millennium. The Norse migrants who followed the raiders introduced their own stories and myths to the British Isles. (Nasjonal Digital Laeringsarena, 2021)

Below: The Tuatha Dé Danann were supernatural beings with mysterious powers who feature prominently in many early Irish legends. They may once of have been Celtic deities and would later serve as inspiration for evolving concepts of the medieval fairy. ('Riders of the Sidhe', John Duncan, 1911)

Left: The Venerable Bede provides us with a detailed account of the conversion of early Anglo-Saxon England to Christianity. (early illustrated manuscript; Virtual Manuscript Library of Switzerland https://www.e-codices.unifr.ch/de/bke/0047/1v)

Below: Jacobus de Voragine, holding a copy of his famous *Golden Legend* in the presence of Christ Crucified. ('Crucifixion', Ottaviano Nelli, fresco, 1375–1344; Trinci Palace, Italy. Photo by Georges Jansoone, 2008)

Saint Margaret hammering a devil. Saint Margaret was celebrated in *The Golden Legend* and medieval pageantry as a dragon slayer. In the east she was called Saint Marina and better known for her demon hammering. (Illustration from the saint's hagiography, printed in Greece, 1858.)

The reliquary of the holy Saint Nicholas, c. 1225–1250. Just one of the many thousands of holy relics that were venerated throughout the Middle Ages. (Treasury of Halberstadt, Inv. DS021. Kulturstiftung Sachsen-Anhalt. Photo by Bertram Kober/punctum)

Left: Hildegard of Bingen, the famous twelfth-century Christian mystic, dictating her visions to her faithful scribe, Volmar. (Illumination from Hildegard's *Scivias*, 1151; Miniature from the Rupertsberg Codex of *Liber Scivias*)

Below: A variation on the SATOR-AREPO protective talisman. (Photo by Fr. Latreille, 2009)

The work of the alchemist was an expensive and time-consuming process. It may not have ever led to the transmutation of any lead into gold, but it did lead to significant advances in laboratory equipment. (Image is taken from *The Ordinal of Alchemy*, c. 1477; British Library, Add. 10302, f.37v)

Saint Anthony assailed by demons. It was believed that demons were more likely to attempt to corrupt the saintliest people. So, if many demons attacked you, it was a sign of holiness! ('The Temptation of St. Anthony', Martin Schöngauer, engraving, c. 1480–1490; Metropolitan Museum of Art, New York)

The image of the demon Baphomet. Baphomet was venerated by the Knights Templar, according to their accusers. It is likely that the name 'Baphomet' was a corruption of 'Mohammed', stemming from the confused prejudices of the crusades. (From Eliphas Levi, *Dogme et Rituel de la Haute Magie*, Volume 2, 1856)

The dead rise from the grave! The horrific revenant – an undead corpse that returns from the dead to haunt the living. Revenants were the most fearful form of undead in medieval England. (c. 1500; Bavarian City Library, Munich, 2 Inc. c. to. 3893, fol. h.ii.)

The joust represented the epitome of chivalric culture by the late Middle Ages. (‘Joust between Pierre de Courtenay and the Sire de Clary’, miniature, c. 1470–1475; British Library, Harley 4379, f.19v)

The Song of Roland was one of the earliest *chansons de geste*. It formed part of the Matter of France, a series of chivalric myths, centred on Charlemagne and his court. (Philip the Good, *Grandes Chroniques de France*, c. 15th century)

During the high Middle Ages, Arthurian lore emerged as the defining mythology of the Plantagenet realm. ('The Last Sleep of Arthur', Edward Burn Jones, 1898)

Lancelot slays a dragon. Lancelot du Lac is perhaps the most iconic Arthurian knight. Yet, for all his valour and skill, he was not a 'perfect' knight. His adulterous relationship with Queen Guinevere stained him with a sin that prevented him from completing the Grail Quest. ('Lancelot Du Lac tue un dragon', illustration by Arthur Rackham, taken from *The Romance of King Arthur and his Knights of the Round Table'*, by Alfred W. Pollard, 1910; Photo by 206rosparks, 2016)

Right: Geoffrey Chaucer was the most prominent of a number of English writers who pioneered Middle English literature in the fourteenth century. (Portrait of Chaucer, Thomas Hoccleve, 1412)

Below: Coventry Pageant wagon. Medieval civic pageant plays are just one example of how stories could be transmitted to a largely illiterate audience. (‘Representation of a Pageant Vehicle at the time of Performance’, David Gee, engraving, 1793–1872)

Robin Hood and Guy of Gisborne compete together in an archery competition. Competitions of archery, wrestling, and other medieval sports were a common feature of early Robin Hood ballads and plays. ('Robin Shoots with Sir Guy', Louis Rhead, 1912)

Queen Guinevere goes a-Maying, perfectly illustrating how May Day was celebrated in medieval England. The queen and her court visit the woods and meadows to collect flowers and foliage with which to decorate themselves to celebrate the coming of summer. ('Queen Guinevere's Maying', John Collier, 1900)

The wild man or woodwose was a common theme in medieval art and made frequent appearances at summer fairs and in mummers' plays. In many ways, he was a quintessential bogeyman, representing everything medieval society regarded as savage and 'godless' in man's nature. ('Sigenot, Dietrich's fight with the wild man', from *Codex Palatinus germanicus*, c. 1470; Digitalisat der UB-Heidelberg, Heidelberger historische Bestände)

A faun. Walter Map's fairy tale of King Herla depicts the fairy king as a pygmy with the appearance of the classical god Pan. ('Johann Nepomuk Nestroy als Pan in Offenbachs "Daphnis und Chloe"', Emil von Hartitzsch, watercolor, c. 1870)

Above: Griffin image on the walls of the palace of Knossos. This Bronze Age representation of the beast perfectly illustrates its ancient pedigree. (Knossos Fresco. Photo by Cavorite, 2016)

Left: Mélusine discovered in her true form, an otherworldly hybrid of woman, fairy, serpent, and dragon. As was the case with other fay creatures, Mélusine appeared to occupy a perilous grey area between heaven and hell. ('Mélusine', illustration from *History of Magic* by Emile Bayard, 1870)

Saint George, surely the most iconic of all medieval dragon slayers. ('Saint George Slaying the Dragon', woodcut by an unknown artist, c. 1504)

Above: Celtic Carnyx horn from the Gallic sanctuary of Tintignac, Corrèz in southern France is the most complete example ever found. It is made from bronze and was around six feet in length when fully assembled. Carnyx typically featured the heads of creatures such as wild boars, serpents and dragons. This example dates to c. 150–c. 50 BC. (*Les Gaulois, une expo renversante*; Cité des Sciences et de l'Industrie, Paris. Photo by Claude Valette, 2012)

Below: Stonehenge. Geoffrey of Monmouth explains its origins with a story about how it was brought to England from Ireland to commemorate British warriors who fell fighting the Saxons. According to Geoffrey, it had originally been constructed by giants! (Photo by Diego Delso, 2014)

ever even existed. Since Nennius wrote three centuries after Badon, and since much earlier accounts (Gildas and Bede) fail to mention Arthur, these questions remain unanswered. All we can really say of Arthur is that he appears to have been an early sixth-century warlord, whether real or mythical. A man who built an enduring reputation for heroism in battle. And, perhaps, he really did play a key role in stemming the tide of Saxon invasion in the early sixth century.

By the twelfth century, Arthur was certainly regarded as a hero from Britain's dim and distant past. However, it took Geoffrey of Monmouth to transform him into a legend. Geoffrey's seminal work, *The History of the Kings of Britain* was written around 1136. It draws heavily on Nennius, Gildas, and a rich tradition of Welsh poems and folklore to create an epic narrative of British dark age history. Geoffrey himself claims his source was an ancient British book.[2] Whatever this book was, no copy survives and no one other than Geoffrey himself has ever claimed to have seen it. Some speculate this book might have been a compilation of sources: folk stories and fragments from the writing of Gildas, Bede, and Nennius. Some of the more sceptical would argue that Geoffrey simply invented all or most of it. The truth, like much of the history of post-Roman dark age Britain, remains shrouded in uncertainty.

Geoffrey of Monmouth was clearly an educated man. Although he hailed from the Welsh borders and had a detailed knowledge of Welsh folklore, he was almost certainly Anglo-Norman. He was a member of a French speaking Anglo-Norman elite, fully invested in the emerging chivalric court culture of his time. As such, he would have been familiar with the growing body of mythology surrounding Charlemagne and his paladins. He would have observed how France had acquired its own foundation mythology centred around Charlemagne. He would also have been aware of the importance of Aeneas in Rome's foundation myths. Britain, by contrast, had no such foundation mythology. Indeed, Britain had very little by way of written history at all. The period between the end of Rome and the establishment of the Anglo-Saxon kingdom of England represented a virtually blank canvas.

Part of Geoffrey's aim in writing his history, was to fill in these gaps; to provide a history for Britain covering a period which, in the twelfth century, was only poorly recalled. In doing so, he hoped to establish a foundation narrative comparable with Rome's Aeneas or France's Charlemagne. It was a grandly ambitious undertaking – to create a foundation myth for an entire people – and, it would have Arthur at its heart. Monmouth set about elevating Arthur from the status of poorly recalled hero from the distant past to that of a national legend. To weave a coherent foundation mythology from a ragged and disparate collection of fragments required no small degree of dramatic license and literary invention.

His history was, therefore, less history after the fashion of classical historians like Thucydides or Tacitus and more along the lines of Homeric or Virgilian mythology. He was not writing a *chanson de geste*, although as an educated man we would doubtless have been familiar with them. Instead of attempting verse, he sticks to his own earthy prose. He was also writing just before the time when chivalric romances began to become popular. As such, his history lacks much of the romantic content that can be found in such abundance in later Arthurian tales.

Geoffrey's history begins in early pre-Roman Britain, with an explanation of the origins of the Britons. This he attributes to Brutus, an early Roman senator and direct descendant of Aeneas, the Trojan founder of Rome itself. It is an incredible claim, clearly one that sits firmly within mythology rather than real history. This sets the tone for what follows. In the second part of his book, he tells us how two British kings, Belinus and Brennius, lead an army of Britons to sack Rome. This remarkable claim, like much of his work, is woven around fragments of historic reality. Belinus may have been a name taken from an old Celtic god. Rome really was sacked by an army of Gauls in c. 390 BC, led by one Brennus. Geoffrey gamely attempts to create a connection between his British Brennius and the historic Brennus by claiming that he married the daughter of a southern Gaulish king. It is all, nevertheless, highly implausible stuff.

Geoffrey's writing style is generally one of rumbustious action-adventure that moves along at an incredible pace. The narrative moves swiftly from one heroic fight to another, occasionally interspersed with the odd prophecy and the barest minimum by way of exposition. The reader hardly has time to catch breathe when one battle ends before a fight with a giant explodes into the narrative. One adventure ends only for someone to immediately receive a vision of a flying growling bear completely out of the blue. However, it is in his treatment of a post-Roman Britain beset by savage pagan invaders, that Geoffrey's epic really comes into its own.

Geoffrey incorporates some of Gildas' history in his handling of the post-Roman British leader *Aurelius Ambrosius* (the anglicised form of Ambrosius Aurelianus). He tells us how Aurelius battles with the first Saxon invaders to save the Britons from the brink of destruction. Gildas, the sixth-century historian, tells us that a commander of this name was indeed instrumental in stemming the initial Saxon invasion.[3] Geoffrey, of course, elaborates on the life of Aurelius, providing a far more detailed view of the man and interweaving elements of mythology. Aurelius is portrayed as a great leader of the Britons, but his life is tragically cut short when he is treacherously poisoned.

Following the death of Aurelius, the narrative moves on to the reign of his younger brother – Uther Pendragon. Uther, like his brother, must contend with Saxon aggression. He is triumphant in his defence of the land but, his victories over Saxon foes are not the end of his troubles. Uther becomes smitten with lust for Ygerna, the wife of his former ally, Duke Gorlois of Cornwall. This leads him to civil war. To keep his wife safe, Gorlois has Ygerna sent to Tintagel Castle where she can be more easily defended. Realising Tintagel cannot easily be taken by siege, Uther resorts to magic, enlisting the aid of Merlin to transform him into the likeness of Gorlois. This allows him to enter Tintagel and have his way with Ygerna unopposed. Through this act his son, the future King Arthur, is conceived. Uther triumphs over Gorlois and, with his rival out of the way, marries Ygerna. For her part, Ygerna appears to meekly accept this situation. Their pairing is hardly romantic to say the least, but represents one of the very few relationships that gets any more than a cursory treatment in Geoffrey's tales.

With Uther's death, Arthur becomes king, and it is under Arthur that Britain enjoys her greatest glory. The fact that dark age Britain was divided and a unified kingdom never materialised, let alone an empire, does not deter the intrepid Geoffrey. Arthur, he informs us, was a British Charlemagne. He subdued and drove out the Saxons. He conquered France! He even served as kingmaker in Scandinavia. His reputation in battle was unrivalled and he became the most feared and respected conqueror in Europe.

Geoffrey describes Arthur's arms and armour with the same kind of reverence used to describe Roland's sword in his chanson. Arthur's helmet, we are told, is fashioned from gold, and sports a magnificent dragon crest. His shield, Pridwen, bears the image of the Virgin Mary. Perhaps most impressive of all is his sword, Caliburn, which we are told was forged on the enchanted Isle of Avalon.[4] This is the first reference to Arthur's famous sword. Later 'Caliburn' would be renamed Excalibur.

Arthur's numerous triumphs on the field of battle earn him a great empire and a golden age for the Britons. In telling his tale, Geoffrey introduces us to several other now familiar characters from Arthurian legend. There is Arthur's seneschal, Kay, and Arthur's cupbearer Sir Bedivere. Arthur marries Guinevere who, we are told, is of noble Roman birth. We also hear of Arthur's two nephews: Gawain and Mordred.

Arthur's growing reputation eventually causes him to fall foul of the Roman emperor Lucius. Lucius demands Arthur submit to Rome and send tributes. Arthur, of course, refuses, thus setting the stage for a major confrontation. Arthur assembles a great army and marches across Europe to confront the Romans, leaving Mordred behind to rule Britain as his proxy. The matter is decided at the epic Battle of Saussy, at which Lucius himself is slain. Arthur now stands on the brink of the conquest of Rome itself.

Of course, this grand mythological epic bears no relation to the known history of this period. By the time in which Geoffrey places Arthur, the Western

Roman Empire had been gone for half a century. There was no Emperor Lucius, nor even any Roman leader of any significance of this name during this period. Northern Italy, at this point in history, was in turmoil as what remained of the kingdom of Ostrogoths fought it out with the Eastern Emperor Justinian for control of Italy.

Of course, Geoffrey cannot go so far as to suggest his Arthur succeeded in re-establishing the Western Roman Empire! And so, he brings his Arthur to ruin at his very hour of triumph. Just as the dust is settling on the victorious battlefield of Saussy, and Arthur is preparing to conquer Rome, he is betrayed! News reaches his ear that his nephew Mordred has seized his crown. Not only that, but Mordred has also seized his queen, Guinevere, and is living adulterously with her. Arthur returns to Britain and confronts Mordred at the fateful Battle of Camlann. Mordred is slain but Arthur is gravely wounded. His wounds force him to abdicate, and he sails off to the Isle of Avalon in search of healing.

Here, Geoffrey's story of Arthur ends. He does not tell us whether Arthur ever found the healing he sought. However, with Arthur's abdication, Britain's golden age was at an end. The final part of Geoffrey's history tells us of the decline of the Britons as they were eventually overwhelmed by the Anglo-Saxons. Geoffrey tells us that an angel dramatically pronounces that the Britons should never rule Britain again until a time prophesised by Merlin should finally come.[5]

As to what became of Arthur, Geoffrey does not tell in his history. In a later work, the *Life of Merlin,* Geoffrey tells us only a little more. On the magical Isle of Avalon Arthur's wounds are tended by nine sisters. All nine are sorceresses and shapeshifters. One of these nine, their wise and potent queen, is identified as Morgen.[6]

Geoffrey of Monmouth's *History* provided the foundations for the Arthurian mythology that emerged in the Middle Ages. Geoffrey's Arthur is a martial-action hero after the manner of the *chansons de geste*. As with the *chansons*, we also see a significant supernatural element built into Geoffrey's tales. We have prophetic dreams. We have Merlin's magic and the mysterious Avalon. We even have battles with giants. The Christian credentials of Arthur's court are strongly in evidence. Arthur's shield carries the image of the Virgin Mary. And much of the narrative focuses on the desperate conflicts between the Christian British knights and savage pagan foes (in the form of the Saxons).

What is lacking from Geoffrey's account, of course, is any significant element of courtly romance we commonly associate with Arthurian tales. Geoffrey's knights are undoubtedly valorous and highly skilled in war but their deeds and interactions mostly all take place on the field of battle. We see little to nothing of any interpersonal interaction at court and next to none between men and women. Arthur's court is shown as having magnificence and pomp, but the focus is very much on the many powerful men who attend to pay Arthur homage. The women enjoy court entertainments separately from the men and, aside from characters such as Queen Guinevere, few women are even named. The women in Monmouth's Arthurian court say virtually nothing and do very little except look nice.

But all this changes later in the twelfth century with the creation of some of the greatest chivalric romances of the medieval period, romances that feature several tales of Arthur and his knights. They stretch across themes of civilised court culture, romance, the chivalrous paladin, and the supernatural far further than Geoffrey's action-packed romps. And they were not written by anyone from the British Isles but by a Frenchman, Chrétien de Troyes.

Chrétien de Troyes wrote a couple of generations after Geoffrey and it is quite clear that Geoffrey was among his influences. Chrétien's knowledge of British folklore was no doubt augmented by old Breton songs and verses, the remnant of Celtic British culture in north-western France.[7] However, Chrétien was also influenced by the growing romantic movement of his times. This came in the form of the courtly love songs of the southern French troubadours and the emerging genre of chivalric romance. These troubadours included several women and the extent to which they were at the forefront of a cultural revolution cannot be understated.[8]

Chrétien wrote a series of discrete stories rather than a complete narrative history like Geoffrey. Each of these stories focus less on Arthur himself than on the deeds of his famous Knights of the Round Table. Each story emphasises the adventures of a particular knight. A key theme running through all of them is romance and tales of love between valiant knights and fair ladies.

In his earliest story of *Erec and Enide* (itself an adaptation of an earlier Welsh tale), the plot centres around the relationship between the two title characters and the trials and tribulations they experience together. Erec is one of Arthur's knights but although Arthur's court features in the story, it primarily serves as little more than a backdrop to Erec and Enide's adventures. Familiar characters such as Arthur and Guinevere appear but play a largely secondary role. Despite the couple's many tribulations they eventually find good fortune and become king and queen of Nantes. Enide, as a character, probably says more in a single page of this story than Geoffrey of Monmouth's Arthurian female characters say in total.

Chrétien adopted an approach where each of his tales focused on a particular knight and his adventures. Inevitably this would always feature a romance between the knight concerned and a lady. He adopts just this approach with the tale of *Yvain, the Knight of the Lion*. In this story the knight Yvain breaks a promise to his lady, causing her to reject him. He, therefore, sets out to win her back by performing a series of heroic deeds accompanied by a lion that he befriends after rescuing it from a dragon. It is a fantastic tale in which Yvain encounters such creatures as the dragon, a giant herdsman, and demons. Chrétien's fantastic tale appears to have been inspired by Welsh/Brittonic stories of the old Cumbric hero Owen, the son of Urien of Rheged. A variant of Chrétien's tales appear in the Welsh *Mabinogion* in the form of the tale of 'Owen and the Lady of the Fountain' and 'Geriant and Enid'. Both may well have drawn inspiration from the same original Brittonic folktales.

With works like *Yvain*, it is Chrétien, far more than anyone else, who transports us into the dream realm of romantic Arthurian fantasy. It is also Chrétien who first references Arthur's court, Camelot. Camelot, we are told, was located in Caerleon in Wales.[9] Caerleon has a long history and was once the location of a major Roman fort and, before that, an Iron Age hillfort. It could quite possibly have been used as a stronghold by a sixth-century British leader such as a historic Arthur. Chrétien is also the first to provide us with tales relating to some of Camelot's more famous knights, including Perceval and the iconic Sir Lancelot. Lancelot's story introduces us to the passionate adulterous affair between Lancelot and Guinevere. In Chrétien's story, their love affair remains secret and apparently has no negative consequences. Later writers, however, would pick up on this theme and provide Lancelot and Guinevere's love story with a more tragic ending. Chrétien's tale of Perceval also introduces us for the first time to the Holy Grail, probably the most iconic quest in Arthurian lore. Chrétien's Grail story raises more questions than answers about this relic, not least because the author died before he could finish it.

Following Chrétien, many others would add to the growing corpus of Arthurian lore. Few could match Chrétien's skill, however. Nevertheless, as the Middle Ages wore on, numerous tales of Arthur and his knights were written and circulated throughout the courts of Europe. During the early thirteenth century there was a shift in story-telling style as Arthurian tales began to appear in French prose rather than verse. A series of stories, which became known as the Vulgate Cycle (which simply means the 'common' cycle) appear at this time. These stories are sometimes also called the Lancelot-Grail cycle. They further developed stories surrounding the Holy Grail, Lancelot and his affair with Guinevere, and the character of Merlin.

These stories portray Lancelot and Guinevere's adulterous affair as having more serious consequences, contributing significantly to the disintegration of bonds of loyalty and honour that hold together Arthur's court. It causes a disunity that Arthur's nemesis, Mordred, exploits for his own ends. Thus, the affair eventually incites the conflict that brings a cruel and bloody end to the golden age of Camelot and the Knights of the Round Table.[10]

Tales of Arthur remained popular across medieval Europe throughout the Middle Ages. Writers continued to add to the mythology with each passing generation. These stories were perhaps most popular in France and England, but versions also appear in Germany, Holland, Italy, Spain, and Portugal. The Matter of Britain had indeed become an important part of medieval European mythology.

By the late fourteenth century, England was in cultural transition. The nobility of England had, ever since the Norman conquest, embraced a distinctly French culture. This meant that much of their literature was written in Latin or French. But this started changing during the fourteenth century. Richard II was the last king of England whose first language was French. The Lancastrian regime that succeeded him at the end of the fourteenth century increasingly adopted English as its official language. We can see this trend emerge during the fourteenth century as an increasing number of works in Middle English appear. By the end of the century, writers such as Chaucer and Gower had created the first great literary works in the English language.

This transition is evident in Arthurian lore from the period. Around the same time as Chaucer was working, an unknown English writer gave us the tale of *Sir Gawain and the Green Knight.* Gawain appears as a character in many other Arthurian stories, dating all the way back to Geoffrey of Monmouth. However, it would be for his legendary confrontation with the mysterious Green Knight for which he would be best remembered.

Later, by the mid-fifteenth century, the golden age of chivalry was more of a memory than a reality. The Middle Ages were coming to an end. If anything, the old bonds, and values of chivalry appeared to be breaking down as England was torn apart by the bloody Wars of the Roses. It was at this time that one man sought to draw together all the different Arthurian tales into a single coherent epic. His name was Sir Thomas Malory, and his *magnum opus* was the magnificent *Le Morte D'Arthur.*

As an epic, Malory's tale easily dwarfs the Arthurian stories of Geoffrey and Chrétien combined. It represents nothing less than the final refined medieval version of the Arthurian myth. In a reflection of how England had changed by this time, Malory wrote in Middle English prose, rather than Monmouth's Latin or Chrétien's French verse. It was also a work that came at the end of an era. The medieval fascination with tales of knights, valour, and chivalry still held sway but a new early modern age was about to dawn. Malory's tale of Arthur would be the last great medieval work of Arthurian lore.

Although the title of Malory's work might suggest it focuses on the death of Arthur (and by implication on his final years), it is a complete biography. It traces the story of Arthur's origins, his rise to power, and the court of Camelot. It is full of stories of the exploits of the famous knights of the Round Table and, of course, the famous quest for the Holy Grail. Only the latter section of the work deal with events leading up to the final battle with Mordred and Arthur's death.

Malory elaborates on the mysterious circumstances of Arthur's death, providing the story with a most poignant ending. As in earlier tales, the last we see of Arthur is of a gravely wounded king, sailing off to Avalon in search of healing. In Malory's version, three enigmatic queens, including Morgan Le Fay (by this time firmly established in Arthurian canon as Arthur's half-sister) bear him away on his final voyage.

Malory informs us that he can tell us nothing more for certain of Arthur's fate. However, he says that some men believe that Arthur is not dead. Perhaps, he muses, a divine power will allow Arthur to return in triumph one day. As if to confirm this, Malory tells us that on Arthur's tomb it is written: 'Hic iacet Arthurus Rex quondam Rex que futurus' (Here lies Arthur. The past and future king).[11]

Knights of the Round Table

Perhaps the best known and most iconic of the Knights of the Round Table is surely Sir Lancelot. He was first introduced to the world in Chrétien de Troyes' work. He is first mentioned in Chrétien's *Erec and Enide,* but it is no more than a fleeting reference. It is the story of *Lancelot, the Knight of the Cart* that firmly establishes him at the heart of Arthurian lore. Lancelot's story was written during a particularly significant period of Chrétien's career, when he was writing for the court of Countess Marie de Champagne. Unlike Geoffrey of Monmouth's Arthurian history, this story was conceived to entertain a powerful woman, rather than a male audience.

Marie was the daughter of the king of France and Eleanor of Aquitaine. She acted as regent for Champagne in her husband's absence on crusade between 1179 and 1181 and later for her son, between 1190 and 1197. She was also a well-known patroness of troubadours and writers, including Chrétien. Marie was, therefore, utterly unlike the Queen Guinevere we find in Geoffrey of Monmouth's history. Monmouth's fictional Guinevere plays no role in his tales save as a royal adornment; her sole purpose appears to be to look good at Arthur's side. She has no agency of her own, being relegated to the status of a prize for Arthur and Mordred to fight over. The real-life Marie, by contrast, had no shortage of personal agency. She ruled Champagne alone for a decade after all, and she no doubt wanted to hear stories about women who were more like herself. Chrétien wrote the *Lancelot* romance for Marie between 1177 and 1181, during the period of her first regency.

His *Lancelot* story is perhaps one of his most memorable, not least for the fact that this is the first time Sir Lancelot is firmly established as a central character in Arthurian lore. Some feel this character has his roots in earlier Welsh mythology. However, it is hard to demonstrate a definitive link between Chrétien's Lancelot and any earlier character. It is quite possible that Lancelot was Chrétien's own literary creation.

Lancelot's tale begins when Queen Guinevere is kidnapped by means of deception by a knight known as Meleagant. Meleagant carries her off to his father's kingdom, the kingdom of Gorre where she is imprisoned in a tower. The scene is set for a valiant rescue. Arthur's nephew Gawain is sent to retrieve the queen but shortly after he sets out, he encounters a mysterious knight with no-name. This knight is on the same quest, driven by a passionate love for the queen. This love is so intense that there is seemingly no task he will not attempt to rescue his beloved.

On the road, this knight encounters a dwarf driving a cart who appears to know something of where the queen has been taken. However, he refuses to reveal what he knows unless our knight with no-name accepts a ride on his cart. This is a most shameful thing since we are told that only criminals and invalids would ride upon a cart. However, our hero's love for Guinevere is so strong that he accepts a ride without hesitation, an act that brings him great shame. It also brings him no small amount of ridicule from those he encounters on his travels.

After a series of adventures in which our knight with no-name jousts, fights, and defeats several formidable foes, he eventually crosses the perilous Sword-bridge, to enter the Castle of Gorre. There he defeats Meleagant, frees Meleagant's prisoners, and, of course, rescues the queen.

Unlike Monmouth's tales, female characters play a far more prominent role in Chrétien's romances, especially in this story. They speak, express opinions, argue, and make requests and demands on our hero. Indeed, one brave woman even rescues Lancelot from imprisonment in a tower! Throughout much of the tale the identity of the knight of the cart remains a mystery. No one he encounters knows his name. And, with each victory in combat, this enigmatic traveller's reputation grows more formidable. Only Guinevere knows his identity, which she finally reveals to another lady as they watch Lancelot fight Meleagant.

It soon becomes clear that Lancelot's passion for Guinevere is matched by her passion for him. The highly charged sexual chemistry between them goes beyond the subtleties of most courtly romances of the time. Their love is far more than mere romantic flirtations or subtle exchanges safely confined within the boundaries of chivalrous etiquette. The couple eventually share a night of adulterous passion in bed together. It is left to our imagination as to what the couple do together in each other's arms that night. Chrétien hangs back from spelling it out explicitly, using the excuse that it should not be written about. Instead, he simply tells us 'the most delightful and choicest pleasure is that which is hinted at, but never told…Lancelot had great joy and pleasure all that night'.[1]

Of course, in the eyes of the medieval church, adultery was a grave sin. Nevertheless, Chrétien's tale of adulterous passion ultimately carried no negative consequences for the lovers. Or, at least, when the tale ends neither Lancelot nor Guinevere suffer any consequences for their adulterous love.

In short, they get away with it scot-free.[2] What is even more remarkable is the fact that such a story was written for a powerful woman. Its implied message appears to be that such a woman can indulge her adulterous passion with no ill consequences. It may, of course, have reflected a fantasy, but if so, it was Marie de Champagne's fantasy. Naturally, it made a compelling and enduring mark on Arthurian mythology. Later writers, picking up on this love affair, would use it to create a rift between Arthur and Lancelot that would divide Camelot. Lancelot and Guinevere's love would, in the end, have the most tragic consequences, triggering the events that lead to Camelot's downfall.

Aside from Lancelot, the most famous of Camelot's knights is surely Sir Gawain. Gawain had been a significant figure in Arthurian tales from the time of Geoffrey of Monmouth, but it is his adventure in the tale of the Green Knight for which he would be especially remembered. We do not know who wrote this tale. All we know is that he was a contemporary of Chaucer and that he wrote the story in English verse. As such it is perhaps the earliest Arthurian tale originally written in English.[3]

The basic plot combines familiar themes of chivalry, valour, and honour with a strong undercurrent of the supernatural in the form of wild, pagan magic. The story begins with Arthur and his knights feasting at Pentecost. Their festivities are interrupted as an intimidating giant of a knight rides into the court. He is not equipped with armour but carries a large, cruel-looking, axe. Most distinctively he is not only dressed in green, but his skin and hair are also tinged green, as if by some supernatural power.

The Green Knight lays down a seemingly insane challenge. If one of Arthur's knights will be so bold as to strike him a blow with the axe, he will return the blow in kind at the following New Year. Of all the knights it is Gawain who takes up the challenge. Taking up the axe, Gawain strikes, severing the Green Knight's head clean off. However, the knight does not die. Instead, he picks his severed head up from the floor and rides off. As he leaves his severed head tells Gawain to meet him at the appointed time to receive the return stroke at a place called the Green Chapel.

When the appointed time comes, Gawain sets off to keep his promise, as his honour compels him. En route, he stays at a knight's castle during which time the knight provides him with the spoils from each day's hunt. Three times the knight's wife attempts to seduce him. Each time Gawain piously resists her advances. Eventually, however, he agrees to accept the lady's green sash as a token, although he still refuses to succumb to temptation.

Not long after, he leaves to find the Green Chapel. Waiting there, sure enough, is the Green Knight. The Green Chapel is a strange place, not a chapel of the kind we might imagine but an ancient barrow in a wild, green, craggy vale. It is a place far more pagan than Christian; Gawain instantly feels that it has an evil aura. The Green Knight soon appears, carrying a great Danish axe, ready to return the blows he received from Gawain at Pentecost.

Gawain is honour bound to kneel and receive the stroke, just as he agreed he would. The Green Knight strikes but only nicks Gawain's neck rather than delivering a death blow. The Knight then reveals that he has spared Gawain and that he is in fact the same knight who has recently played host to him. Gawain's refusal to take advantage of his wife has shown him to be an honourable man. The Green Knight also reveals he was transformed by the sorcery of Morgan Le Fay, in the hopes that his terrifying transformation might frighten Guinevere to death. However, since Gawain has proven himself a worthy knight and since Morgan is Gawain's aunt, he should be spared.

Nevertheless, the Green Knight deals Gawain a nick in payment for the sash he took from his wife and concealed from him. When Gawain finally returns to court, he and the other knights agree that henceforth they will wear a green sash in honour of his adventure.

Gawain's tale contains strong moral messages concerning the importance of keeping oath, bravery in the face of death, and the virtue of upholding the chivalric code. However, it also contains supernatural themes from a distant pagan past.

Old Irish folk tales that long pre-date the fourteenth century serve as part of the inspiration for this story. Bricrui's feast features an almost identical story with the part of Gawain taken by the Irish hero Cú Chulaind and his nemesis is not a Green Knight but a savage giant.[4] In the tale of the Green Knight, this old story is re-imagined within a medieval chivalric context. Morgan's fay enchantments and the wild pagan nature of the Green Chapel appear in clear opposition to the civilised Christian world. Gawain, when he first discovers the chapel, clearly senses this, describing it as 'a desolate place, an ugly chapel, over-grown with weeds, well fitted for the green man to make his devotions in the devil's fashion'.[5] Morgan's magic and the supernatural powers of the Green Knight are clearly rooted in a wild and dangerous pagan past. It is for the Knights of the Round Table and Camelot to bring order, honour, and Christian justice to such a world. In this sense Gawain's ultimate triumph over the schemes of Morgan signify the triumph of the chivalrous Christian knight over the dangers of wild, ancient paganism.

The Knights of the Round Table came to collectively embody the value system of medieval chivalry in its purest form. Values that centred around martial excellence, valour, honour, court etiquette, and piety. Of course, there is little that was pious about Lancelot and Guinevere's love affair, but later writers were at pains to demonstrate that this sin had serious consequences. The counterbalance to Lancelot would eventually take the form of Lancelot's son Galahad. Galahad, whose story is fully rounded out in Malory's tales, is the perfect knight that Lancelot could not be. He has all the skill and valour of his famous father but, unlike his father, he is not tainted by the sin of adultery. Unlike his father, he is the chaste man, and, for this reason, it is he and not Lancelot who is able to succeed in the Grail quest.

The tales of the Knights of the Round Table are, we should remember, written largely for an audience of knights, lords, and ladies. They were conceived to present this audience with a vision of a chivalric, romantic, ideal to which they might both aspire and draw inspiration from. It is an ideal which most could never live up to. It is also an ideal that largely sanitises much of the violent reality of the medieval world.

However, Arthurian tales were also pure escapism, even fantasy. The inclusion of such things as dragons, giants, demons, relics, enchantments, prophecies, and the wild power of pagan magic gives these stories a strong supernatural flavour. Indeed, sometimes, especially with Chrétien, it is not always clear whether the story is taking place in the real world or in some otherworldly fairy realm. The boundaries between our world and the otherworld are blurred. The knights in these stories can sometime cross the boundary between the real world and this otherworld almost without realising. The division between the natural and the supernatural is porous, just as it was in the old Celtic tales from which Arthurian lore often drew inspiration.

And, although these stories are written within the context of a Christian cosmology, old pagan themes are frequently present. They include elements of magic and sorcery that are not necessarily condemned or even portrayed negatively in the narratives. This is despite such practices being disapproved of by the church. We should, therefore, be cautious about seeing these tales as nothing more than exemplars of chivalric virtue. They were so much more than that.

Merlin and Morgen Le Fay

Arthurian mythology came to feature two characters who are without question the most famous medieval sorcerers to endure into the modern age. The first was a man, the wizard Merlin. And the second was a woman, the enchantress, Morgen, also known as Morgan or Morgana Le Fay.

Merlin is a somewhat enigmatic figure whose mythological history begins in a context that probably had no direct association with Arthur. The earliest references to Merlin come from old Welsh poems that pre-date his appearance in Geoffrey of Monmouth's history.[1] In these early stories he is Myrddin Wyllt (meaning 'wild Myrddin' or 'mad Myrddin'). In this incarnation, he is a Brittonic warrior from Cumbria who fought in the Battle of Arfderydd. His lord was slain in the battle, and he was so shocked by the carnage that he lost his mind and went to live in the wilds. He may have been a bard, and he certainly appears to have possessed the gift of prophecy, rather like Taliesin.

These early Welsh stories served as Geoffrey of Monmouth's inspiration for his Merlin. He may well have had access to other old stories and oral traditions concerning Merlin that no longer survive. It is Geoffrey who gives Myrddin his latinised name 'Merlinus'. By Geoffrey's time, Merlin was clearly seen as a prophet. Indeed, Geoffrey devotes an entire section of his histories to relating the many prophecies of Merlin. These prophecies are presented as if they are the genuine revelations of a 'real' Merlin. Geoffrey offers us little, if any, explanation, or interpretation as to the meaning of these prophecies. They appear as enigmatic, highly allegorical revelations, written almost as a stream of consciousness.

From a theological viewpoint, such prophecies would surely have been regarded as divinations and, therefore, forbidden in the Bible. However, the fact was they were written down and circulated in Geoffrey's time with little or no criticism from the church. It is testimony to the somewhat laissez faire attitude to magic at the time. Writing about magic in this way was by no means seen as serious enough to warrant any form of persecution or censorship. We are, in fact, clearly informed that Merlin's powers have infernal rather than divine origins. Somewhat disturbingly, Geoffrey tells us that although Merlin's mother was human, his father was a demon.[2]

In Geoffrey's histories, as with later Arthurian stories, Merlin is primarily associated with the reign of Arthur's father, Uther Pendragon, and the early period of Arthur's reign. Merlin is perhaps most famous for the council and assistance he gives to Uther and his brother Aurelius before him. He plays a key role in facilitating Uther's seduction of Arthur's mother and is, as a result, instrumental in Arthur's conception.

Merlin, as a character, disappears from the narrative during Arthur's early reign in Geoffrey's history. After having helped Uther to magically disguise himself to seduce Ygerna, Merlin plays no further part in Arthur's story. Geoffrey does, however, tell us more of Merlin in a work called the *Life of Merlin*. Here, Geoffrey informs us that Merlin survived to a truly ancient age, outliving even Arthur. However, in an echo of the old stories of Myrddin Wyllt, we are told that Merlin spends time as a madman in the woods. Although he recovers his senses, he remains in the woods, in retirement, away from the civilised world.

Malory provides us with perhaps the definitive version of Merlin. His Merlin plays a more active role in Arthur's early reign. Many of Merlin's prophecies foreshadow future events in his narrative. He foretells the coming of Sir Galahad and warns Arthur that he should never lose Excalibur or the sword's scabbard. He plays a key role in shaping Arthur's world, facilitating events such as Arthur's birth and the finding of Excalibur. However, he is by no means all powerful. There are unfortunate events that, for all his insight, he fails to prevent. He fails to stop Arthur conceiving Mordred with Morgause (who, unknown to Arthur, is his half-sister). This is even though he can foresee the danger Mordred will pose.

In protecting Arthur from Mordred, Malory shows us a darker side to Merlin's character, perhaps more closely reflecting the demonic side of his nature. In an echo of Herod's massacre of the innocents, Merlin advises Arthur to kill all the children born one Mayday (the time when Mordred was born). This Arthur does, although, by a quirk of fate, Mordred survives.[3]

In the final analysis there is a certain ambiguity about Merlin. He generally aids Arthur's family, yet he has an undeniably sinister demonic heritage. His predictions and magical interventions can be helpful and sometimes save lives, yet children are put to death by his council. He predicts dangers but often cannot prevent them. Although he is often helpful, his help sometimes involves colluding in infidelity and deception.

This perhaps reflects a certain underlying tension in the very idea of someone like Merlin. He is, ultimately, a character based on old Brittonic stories. His prophetic abilities cannot escape the taint of paganism and his sinister powers are partly the product of his demonic origins. Attempts to accommodate such a character within a medieval Christian worldview is, therefore, understandably problematic.

Malory also relates what has now become the most familiar ending for Merlin's story, based on a variation of an earlier thirteenth-century tale. Now in his old age, Merlin becomes besotted with Nimue, one of the Ladies of the Lake. For a time, she accompanies him and eventually they end up in Cornwall. However, Nimue is most reluctant to bear Merlin's child, fearful of Merlin's demonic heritage. To avoid this, she uses her magic to trick Merlin into entering a chamber beneath a rock. Once he is inside, she uses enchantments to seal Merlin within. For all Merlin's prophetic powers, he is ultimately unable to avoid his own fate.

In some versions of this tale of Merlin's enchantment, Merlin's femme-fatal is not Nimue but another sorceress: Morgan, or Morganna, Le Fay. Aside from Merlin, Morgan is easily the most memorable sorcerous character in Arthurian lore. In many ways, she is a far more interesting character than Merlin. Tracing the history of how Morgan is portrayed between Monmouth and Malory can tell us a lot about how medieval society's attitude to women and magic evolved over the period.

Within Geoffrey of Monmouth's early tales, Morgen (as she was originally known) features only briefly. She appears in his *Life of Merlin* as the principal one of nine sisters who rule the Isle of Apples (Avalon). She is described as beautiful and wise, a gifted scholar, mathematician, and skilled in the arts of herbal healing. She also has the power of shapeshifting and the ability to fly. It is to Morgen that the wounded Arthur is brought after the Battle of Camlann. Arthur's companions leave him in Morgen's care, since she is the only one with the skill to heal him.[4]

Morgen then, begins her story as a mysterious queen, ruler of Avalon, a scholar, a healer, and shapeshifter. In this persona, Morgen is entirely benevolent, the healer queen of an otherworldly paradise. Her character is strongly influenced by Celtic ideas we find in the old Welsh and Irish folk stories. And her shapeshifting powers are reminiscent of the old world of Celtic bards and druids.

The word 'Morgen' itself has connections with mermaids, sea nymphs, and sirens. She is briefly mentioned in Chrétien's *Erec and Enide*, this time with the name 'Morgan Le Fay'. The addition of the appellation 'Le Fay' implies a fairy connection. The Welsh name 'Morgen' literally means 'of the sea', so her name can be read as meaning something akin to 'fairy of the sea'. However, Chrétien's Morgan, we are told, is Arthur's sister, which gives her a human identity. As with Geoffrey of Monmouth, she is only ever mentioned as a benevolent and gifted healer. There is not even a hint, yet, of the scheming femme fatale.

Her character in Arthurian lore experienced a significant evolution during the Middle Ages. In her earliest incarnations, she is always presented as benevolent and noted for her healing powers. Indeed, Gerald of Wales, writing in 1216, even describes her as a Celtic goddess, with the name Morganis.[5] Morgan's character began to change during the early-to-mid thirteenth century and the Vulgate Cycle presents us with a darker Morgan. Here, her identity as Arthur's sister or, rather, his half-sister is fleshed out. They share a mother: Ygerna. However, they have different fathers. Arthur's father is, of course, Uther. Morgan's father is Gorlois, the duke of Cornwall; Ygerna's first husband, although it is also hinted that she may be illegitimate. It is out of his lust to possess Ygerna that Uther kills Gorlois and takes Ygerna as his wife. This unfortunate shared family history creates an obvious source of potential friction between Arthur and Morgan.

The Vulgate Morgan learns her arts by studying in a nunnery and through an apprenticeship with Merlin. In this regard, she has been demoted from an otherworldly queen, very much Merlin's equal, to a very human student of the old wizard. From this point onwards she is typically portrayed as Arthur's half-sister rather than as a mysterious fairy sorceress. Animosity with Guinevere follows when Arthur's queen ends Morgan's love affair with a man named Guiomar. Morgan's later infatuation with Lancelot also brings her into conflict with Guinevere. This new Morgan embarks on a series of malevolent acts such as attempted abductions of Lancelot and schemes to expose Lancelot and Guinevere's affair. As her character evolves, she is increasingly depicted as ageing and ugly rather than young and beautiful.[6] Presenting her in this manner reflects the transition of the role played by her character, from benevolent and nurturing to malevolent and evil. Yet, despite all this, her role as Arthur's healer at the end of his reign is usually retained. The siblings, it seems, are ultimately reconciled.

As the thirteenth and fourteenth century wore on, Morgan gradually acquired an increasingly dark reputation. Over this time, Morgan's classic image as a malevolent sorceress takes shape. The Celtic, otherworldly, and largely benevolent Morgen gradually gives way to a more dangerous human Morgan Le Fay, willing to use her enchantments for maleficent ends. A sense of ancient Celtic mystery is replaced by growing late medieval paranoia concerning necromancy and sorcerous practice.

This evolution occurs in tandem with two significant changes in the way in which medieval society regarded magic. The first of these changes was the growth in the practice of learned magic over the period of the twelfth and thirteenth centuries. A commensurate level of unease concerning ritual necromancy would have been building over this period. This would have been especially notable amongst the educated upper classes who formed the core audience for Arthurian tales. Earlier in the period, the idea of witchcraft was largely seen as misguided nonsense. Sinful, certainly, but hardly anything to be taken too seriously. But these attitudes were changing as the twelfth and thirteenth century wore on.

The second change was the gradual shift in attitudes regarding female practitioners of magic. Originally magic was not necessarily any more likely to be associated with women than with men. However, as the Middle Ages progressed this view shifted. By the time we arrive at the fifteenth century, attitudes had radically changed. Nider's image of the female witch, driven to practice the dark arts by her lust, reflected the growing paranoia of times. It was a paranoia that influenced the last medieval incarnation of Morgan, encountered in Malory's tales.

Malory's Morgan appears driven purely by chaotic passions and a malevolent hatred of her brother Arthur's court (and especially of Guinevere). She is constantly plotting against Camelot in general and Guinevere and Arthur in particular. She is also unequivocally portrayed as an active practitioner of black magic. Her willingness to use enchantments to entrap Lancelot out of lust for him, is a typical example. It perfectly reflects the late-medieval fear of how the practice of maleficent sorcery by a woman was thought to work. However, this Morgan goes even further. She entraps Elaine of Corbenic in a boiling bath because she is envious of her beauty. She steels Excalibur's scabbard and gives it to her lover. She even attempts to slay her own husband at one point.

Malory's Morgan is a sociopathic woman, driven to acts of violence and maleficent sorcery by her lusts, her envious nature, and her thirst for power. Ominously, Malory even tells us that Morgan was well versed in the sinister arts of necromancy, directly linking her with maleficent sorcery of the worst kind.[7] Malory's Morgan is, in short, the embodiment of everything fifteenth-century churchmen like Nider and Kramer feared.

Yet, despite all this, Malory cannot escape Morgan's original role in Arthur's story. His tale returns to Morgan the healer who takes charge of the gravely wounded king on his last trip to Avalon. Given the darkly dysfunctional nature of Arthur and Morgan's relationship in most of Malory's saga, their sudden reconciliation at the end seems very out of character. However, Malory's inclusion of this reconciliation, demonstrates his desire to remain true to one of the core beats of the earliest Arthurian tales.

Morgan's character, even more so than Merlin, is something of a contradiction. During the twelfth century she is the benevolent fairy queen of Avalon, a healer, intellectual, and scholar. By the fifteenth, she is a malevolent necromancer, a slave to her own passions, wielding maleficent magic for her own selfish ends. Her transformation, in many ways, stands as a visible record of changing medieval attitudes to magic in general and to the female witch in particular.

The Holy Grail

Perhaps the most famous episode in all Arthurian lore is the quest for the Holy Grail. The story of the Holy Grail itself has a history that sits within medieval Christianity, as well as within Arthurian mythology. The Christian element of this legend holds that this relic was the cup used by Jesus at the last supper. This same cup was later used to catch the blood of Christ during his crucifixion.

The Grail was associated with Joseph of Arimathea, a man who appears in the New Testament. John 19: 39-40 informs us that Joseph retrieved the body of Christ after the crucifixion and attended to Christ's burial. Joseph also appears in apocryphal literature from the early Christian period, most notably the gospel of Nicodemus. It is obvious that various legends and stories were circulating concerning Joseph from early Christian times. Medieval stories of Joseph had a life of their own separate (albeit often related to) Arthurian lore. *The Golden Legend* tells us that Joseph was walled up in Jerusalem for forty years as punishment for his role in burying Christ. During his long incarceration he was miraculously sustained by a divine power.[1]

It is Joseph who was later reputed to have brought the Holy Grail to Glastonbury in England.[2] Joseph's association with the Grail and with Glastonbury seems to have appeared at a similar time to early Arthurian Grail stories and was most likely inspired by them.

The idea of vessels with magic properties also features in Celtic folklore. Ceridwan's cauldron, which served as the source of Taliesin's poetic inspiration, being an example of one such vessel. The cornucopia of classical mythology supplies us with another example of a vessel imbued with supernatural properties. However, cornucopias and cauldrons are not grails. The very first mention of a Grail in Arthurian lore, appears in Chrétien de Troyes' work *The Knight of the Grail (Perceval).* In Chrétien's tale, there is no mention of Joseph of Arimathea, nor does it even fully explain what exactly the Grail is.

Chrétien's Grail story is his most enigmatic work. It is enigmatic in terms of the mystery surrounding this Grail, the identity of the person it serves and its true nature. And it is also a mystery in so far as Chrétien himself never finished the story. He was working on it at the end of his career in the late 1180s and died (or his patron died) before he could complete it.[3] The ultimate secret of the true purpose and nature of this Grail, as Chrétien conceived them, remain a mystery to this day.

In Chrétien's tale, Perceval begins life as a Welsh country boy, largely ignorant of the ways of the wider world and certainly ignorant of knighthood and chivalry. One day he is hunting in the woods and encounters some knights. He is intrigued but his behaviour displays a painful ignorance of knights and their ways. He even ignores their leader's questions as he quizzes him about the nature of knighthood and his magnificent equipment. Such behaviour was hardly an appropriate way for a common country lad to interact with someone of knightly status. However, having met these knights, he decides he wants to become one and sets off to Arthur's court with this end in mind.

Much of the early part of the tale is taken up with Perceval's coming of age story. He acquires a fine suit of red armour, a good horse, and the equipment he needs to become a knight. He does services for King Arthur's court and thereby earns his status. He finds a mentor from whom he learns how to use his equipment and how to act and dress. He grows from an ignorant country bumkin into a formidable knight of considerable skill. He acquires a reputation, a castle, and a wife in the process. No doubt, Perceval's ignorance and unfortunate chivalric faux pas provided Chrétien's medieval audience with a considerable source of amusement along the way.

After a time, Perceval, now properly a knight, decides to return home to see his mother. It is on this seemingly ordinary journey that he encounters the truly extraordinary. Whilst attempting to cross a river he meets a man fishing in a small boat. The man informs him that there is no way to cross the river for many miles either up or downstream. Nevertheless, he generously offers Perceval lodgings at his nearby castle for the night.

When Perceval arrives at the castle, he is greeted by the nobleman he saw fishing in the river. His host cannot rise to greet him since he has been invalided by some unknown injury. His host grants him a gift of a most magnificent sword and treats him to a sumptuous banquet. During this banquet a mysterious procession of servants passes through the hall, enroute to serving some unknown person in the neighbouring chamber.

The servant at the head of this procession carries a white lance, its tip drips blood by means of some unknown supernatural power. Then come squires with magnificent candelabras. Then follows a maiden with the Grail. But this is no common Grail. It is an impressive golden vessel, richly decorated with jewels. It also shines with a supernatural radiance that is so bright that it makes all the other lights appear dim. Finally, another maiden follows bearing a silver plate.

Perceval wonders who's being served by this magnificent procession but as he is unsure of the correct etiquette, he does not ask. Indeed, he does not ask any questions at all, despite being clearly intrigued. Instead, he decides to stay quiet for the time being and ask one of the servants in the morning. When he wakes in the morning, he finds the castle utterly deserted. His host is gone and there is no sign of any servants. He tries to return to the chamber into which the Grail was taken but cannot gain access. In the end he can do nothing but set out again on his journey, unable to find answers.

Having left the Grail Castle, Perceval continues his journey to visit his mother, only to discover that she has died. His journey was in vain. He also learns that his failure to discover whom the Grail served and the nature of the lance, will have terrible consequences. He is told that his host, the mysterious Fisher King, is a virtual invalid because he was maimed by a terrible wound. If only Perceval had had the sense to ask about the Grail and the lance, the king could have been healed. And, once the king was healed, so too would the land be restored and much good done. Perceval, it appears, had failed the Grail test. Perceval also learns that the sword he was gifted, although magnificent, is also flawed. It cannot be safely used until it is properly repaired, but it can only be made whole again by the one who made it.

As time goes by the gravity of Perceval's failure begins to sink in. The mysterious Loathly Lady informs him that he is doomed. His failure to ask who the Grail serves is symptomatic of an inner spiritual failing. He has committed a grave sin of which he is unaware. That sin makes him unworthy, even though he does fully understand the nature of his sin.

He takes to wandering in the wilderness and experiences many misfortunes. He simply does not possess the inner wisdom he needs to find spiritual healing. This lack of inner awareness and lack of spiritual purity appears to lie at the heart of the Grail quest. The quest for the Grail is more an inner journey of spiritual enlightenment than a quest in the material world. Perceval beings his tale as an ignorant boy. Despite his clumsiness and many mistakes, he learns how to fight as well as any other knight and picks up the rules of chivalrous etiquette reasonably quickly. But spiritual wisdom, it seems, eludes him. Perceval literally does not know himself.

The maxim of the oracle of Delphi was 'know thyself'. It lies at the heart of Perceval's spiritual failings. Although he knows his mother, he encounters relatives on his journey whom he fails to recognise. He does not know his own cousin, even though she was raised in his mother's household. Nor does he know his uncles or, indeed, his grandfather. He does not even appear to know his own name when he is asked it. He simply guesses that his name is Perceval because it felt right.[4] Most importantly of all, he does not know who the Grail serves.

Perceval wanders the wilderness for several years. During this time, he lost his memory so completely that he forgot even God.[5] Eventually Perceval encounters some pilgrims. They inform him it is Good Friday and berate him for not worshipping the cross and contemplating his sins. Perceval learns from them of a local holy man, living nearby as a hermit, whom he visits in the hope of receiving some advice.

The hermit, it turns out, is one of Perceval's uncles, although Perceval does not know him. He learns that he sinned gravely by abandoning his mother when he set off in search of adventure. It is this, coupled with his failure to live a pious life, that led him to fail the Grail quest. He is informed the Fisher King is another of his uncles and that the Grail contains a consecrated 'host' that provides the one it serves with all he requires to sustain him. The one served from the Grail is, in fact, the father of the Fisher King, Perceval's grandfather. Perceval finally learns who the Grail serves, but before he can learn more he must first atone for his sins. This, his uncle informs him, will require a long penance. Perhaps, if he prays and attends church often enough, he might eventually be able to free himself from the stain of his past sins. Perceval agrees to follow his advice.

We are left to wonder whether Perceval will eventually become worthy of learning more, as Chrétien's tale leaves Perceval to focus on Gawain's exploits. However, whether he was ever able to find spiritual healing, or unlock the secrets of the Grail, we never find out from Chrétien. For, before Chrétien was able to tell us any more of Perceval or the Grail, he died leaving the tale unfinished. Thus, whatever ending Chrétien intended, we'll never know. The story ends unresolved, leaving behind it one of the most intriguing mysteries in the history of literature. Despite being unfinished, Chrétien's Grail legend became incredibly popular, so much so that several later writers attempted to complete the story.

These various continuations (of which there were eventually many) speculate as to the resolution of Chrétien's tale. Several postulate as to the holiness of the Grail and the lance. The lance is sometimes identified as the lance that pierced Christ's side during his crucifixion. Likewise, the Grail is identified as the cup used by Christ at the last supper. As such it is a holy relic infused with the power to sustain life and the key to healing and renewal. In Chrétien's original it is not entirely clear what, exactly, the Grail is or what makes it holy. Is it supposed to be holy in itself? Or is it holy because it carries the sacred host? Chrétien did not live long enough to tell us.

Both in Chrétien's tale and his continuations, the story unfolds in a world in which the boundaries between the natural and supernatural are blurred. The knights in these stories visit places like the Grail Castle, the Castle of Maidens, and the Proud Castle, all of which have a distinctly supernatural aura about them. In these places the visiting knights encounter items infused with enchantments or holy powers such as the Bed of Marvels, the White Lance that drips blood, or the Grail itself.

Sometimes, we might be forgiven for wondering if these places are located within the material world at all. They have a distinctly otherworldly feel to them, as if they were part of some elusive fairy realm or maybe located in a place where the material and supernatural worlds overlap. Such imagery is strongly reminiscent of Taliesin's poem of Arthur travelling to the otherworld of Annwfn, where he visits a series of similar mysteriously named castles. Of course, Chrétien's work drew, at least to some extent, on the same tradition of old Brittonic mythology as Taliesin. In Chrétien's case, the influence probably came mainly from the Bretons of north-west France who shared a cultural heritage with old Celtic Britain.

Within around a decade of Chrétien's work, another French poet by the name of Robert de Boron wrote *Joseph d'Arimathe.* It focused on the life of Joseph of Arimathea and the Holy Grail. It is Robert who did most to associate the Grail with Joseph and identify it as the cup from the last supper.[6] This same cup Joseph later uses to catch drops of blood as they fell from Christ during his crucifixion. It is Joseph, Boron tells us, who brings the Grail to Avalon, and this explains how it came to reside in Glastonbury at the time of Arthur. The link between Joseph of Arimathea and the Grail was now firmly established in Arthurian lore.

It was only a matter of time, of course, before the monks of Glastonbury Abbey began to capitalise on these stories. Legend has it that as early as 1191 the tomb of Arthur and Guinevere was supposedly discovered at Glastonbury.[7] Certainly, by the late thirteenth century, Glastonbury had become closely associated with Arthurian lore, Joseph of Arimathea, and the Grail. The enterprising Glastonbury monks would even claim their community had been founded by Joseph of Arimathea himself.

Naturally enough, it is Malory who gives us the definitive version of the Arthurian Grail legend. In Malory's version, the hero is not Perceval or Lancelot but Sir Galahad. Galahad was an addition to Arthurian lore who first appears in the Vulgate Cycle. He is the illegitimate son of Lancelot and Elaine of Corbenic. Elaine, also known as the Grail maiden, was the daughter of King Pelles, the Fisher King. Elaine becomes infatuated with Lancelot and, using enchantments to make him think she was Guinevere, seduces him. Galahad is the resulting child. For Malory, Galahad is more than just a knight; he is a paladin, for Galahad embodies values of Christian piety as well as chivalric prowess. He is equipped with a sword and a shield, both of which have considerable supernatural significance.

He draws his sword from a red stone, a feat only possible for the perfect and best knight. This sword, it transpires, was once wielded by Sir Balin, a man who could have been the greatest knight but went astray. Instead of achieving greatness, Balin delivered the infamous dolorous stroke that maimed the Fisher King. From that moment onwards, healing and renewal were only possible if the Grail quest was completed.

Of perhaps greater significance is Galahad's shield. This is a potent artefact originally fashioned by the son of Joseph of Arimathea for use in war against the Saracens. It is a white shield marked with a red cross – the symbol of the Knights Templar. As such it embodies the concept of the holy paladin; one of Pope Urban II's soldiers of Christ. Indeed, much in the character of Galahad channels late-twelfth and early thirteenth-century concepts of Christian mysticism as advocated by Bernard of Clairvaux, a co-founder of the Knights Templar. Only a pure and perfect knight can experience the inner mysteries of the Christian faith, as symbolised by the Grail.

To a significant degree, the Grail legend is very much a story of Christian mysticism. The Grail quest represents the quest of the Christian mystic. It is not a quest for knowledge that can be codified or explained through scholarship alone. It is a quest for a spiritual relationship with the divine that can only be achieved through living a life of pious purity, just as Saint Bernard taught. And that relationship is a mystical experience that offers spiritual wisdom in a form that cannot be described, understood or in any way codified in words.

At the beginning of Malory's Grail quest, the knights of the Round Table see a vision of the Grail. It appears floating in mid-air, suspended by a divine power, basking in a radiant holy light. However, it is shrouded in samite (a luxurious heavy silk veil), so it cannot be clearly seen. This inspires the knights to take a vow to embark on a quest for the Grail, and at least to be able to see it plainly, without its shroud.

The Knights of the Round Table are, of course, all good Christians. They have a good understanding of Christianity and, we can be sure, attend church, observe Christian festivals, and make confession. However, Bernard of Clairvaux's mysticism was all about going beyond this. An understanding and acceptance of the faith was, for Saint Bernard, just a starting point. A starting point for a spiritual journey to touch the divine. A journey he no doubt hoped his Knights Templars would pursue – just as the Knights of the Round Table pursued their quest for the Holy Grail.

In Malory's Grail quest, spiritual purity is essential for success. Gawain ultimately fails because of his unwillingness to do proper penance for his sins. Lancelot, for all his prowess, cannot succeed because of the sin of his adulterous affair with Guinevere. Only Galahad, the perfect, celibate, knight is pure enough to triumph. Malory is at pains to emphasise Galahad's purity, describing him as 'a clean virgin' whose pure and virtuous nature infuses his soul with 'the fire of the Holy Spirit'.[8]

In the end, it is only the pure Galahad who can fulfil the quest, to see the Grail and receive communion from it. It is he who ultimately unravels the mysteries and, taking the holy lance, he uses it to heal the Maimed King and undo the ills done by the dolorous stroke. Galahad makes one final great journey to the distant mystical land of Sarras. There he finally receives a divine revelation of the true significance of the Grail from Joseph of Arimathea himself. Having experienced the divine, he has no further desire for life in the mundane world and a multitude of Angels carry his soul up into heaven.

Malory ends his tale by telling us that a divine hand came down from the heavens, collecting the Grail and the lance, bearing them away never to be seen again. He, then, provides us with the ultimate medieval resolution to the tale begun by Chrétien. It brought a form of closure or, at least, completeness to the Grail legend. It seemingly answered the questions Chrétien left us with – what exactly is the Grail and what is its true significance? But for all its merit, we cannot ever know if Malory's answers were the answers Chrétien intended. And for that reason alone, the riddle of the Holy Grail has remained something of an unsolved mystery ever since. But, of course, that's what lies at the heart of its enduring appeal.

The Matter of England

Later in the Middle Ages, especially from the fourteenth century onwards, we see an increasingly number of chivalric tales appearing in English. Some of these, such as Malory and Gawain and the Green Knight, are firmly anchored in Arthurian mythology. However, these were not the only chivalric tales to become popular in medieval England. Another group of stories set in England emerged that increasingly found their way into Middle English verse. Later academics gave these the collective label of the 'Matter of England' (partly to distinguish them from the core narratives within the Matter of Britain).

How useful this term really is, is somewhat debatable. The primary common denominator behind these stories is simply that they are not (or are only very tangentially) related to Arthurian mythology. Aside from this, they are quite a mixed bag. It is probably just as accurate to describe them as 'other medieval English chivalric tales, not concerning Arthur'.

Keeping this thought in mind, a few common themes can be seen running through many of these stories:

- They start appearing in Middle English verse, mainly from the fourteenth century onwards. The earliest Middle English story of this sort appears to have been *King Horn*, which dates to the mid-to-late thirteenth century.[1]
- Although the popular later versions of these stories are written in Middle English, several of them are based on older versions that were originally written in French. In some cases, it is hard to know exactly when the earliest version of the tale first appeared.
- They deal with themes and stories that look back nostalgically to earlier English history. Many are set in pre-Norman England. However, some are not. For example, *Richard coeur de Lion* is essentially a dramatisation of the life of Richard the Lionheart.
- Themes of chivalric romance and/or *chanson de geste* feature to a greater or lesser extent in all these tales.

- The main characters in all these stories are from the upper echelons of medieval society. Typically, knights, nobles, kings, or the sons of such people.
- Sometimes the precise setting and even the precise period of history is difficult to pin down. As with the Arthurian stories, there is a significant amount of fictional license involved.
- Supernatural themes and fantasy elements are present in some but by no means all these stories.
- They are self-contained tales. They don't inter-relate with each other in terms of a shared mythological universe in the same way as the Matter of Britain.

Several of these stories are set in Anglo-Saxon England before the Norman conquest. Even many of the earliest versions of these stories (which are often in French) don't seem to have appeared much before the thirteenth century. By this time, the Norman conquest was a distant enough memory for the Anglo-Norman elite to have co-opted Anglo-Saxon history as part of their heritage. Certainly, by the fourteenth century, the distinction between Norman and Saxon was essentially defunct. It had been replaced by an emergent English identity.[2] And, with the advent of the Hundred Years' War, the distinction between 'English' and 'French' as nationalities became increasingly important.

The appearance of stories written in English would have made them accessible to a wider audience (within England itself). Like the earlier chivalric romances, these tales were produced with the intention they should be recited out aloud in public or semi-public settings by minstrels. Since many Englishmen understood little or no French (especially by the later Middle Ages), English versions were increasingly essential.

However, we should not get too carried away by the fact that these stories were able to reach an audience that included humbler commoners. These were still tales that focused on the lives and deeds of knights and nobles, just like Arthurian stories. That said, some had a slightly broader appeal and feature people who might be regarded as more peripheral to court circles than the Arthurian knights. In this sense, some of the Matter of England deals with people from a broader section of society.

The Matter of England is certainly less apt to focus on the grand sweep of British foundation mythology. The focus is often drawn more to the practical struggles and aspirations of the knights, lesser nobles, and gentry of England. But even stories that deal with lesser knights and country gentry are still stories of the ruling classes. There were only around 11,000–12,000 nobles, knights, and untitled manorial lords in fourteenth century England.[3] That's a very small, elite, minority. These are, ultimately, still the stories of the lords of the land and their families.

Tales of knights or noblemen who become disinherited feature in a few of these tales. Often their disinheritance is followed by a period in which they must re-build their reputation and prove their quality. On occasion, their disinheritance involves exile (perhaps because of the machinations of a wicked relative). Sometimes they might not even know they have been disinherited, growing up unaware of their true heritage.

Such scenarios may well reflect concerns that emerged in medieval England following the Anarchy of the twelfth century and the two major Barons Wars of the thirteenth. The social turmoil induced by these conflicts often resulted in the disinheritance of lesser nobles, knights, and gentry who backed the losing side. Occasionally, this disinheritance even led to outlawry. Examples of outlawry can be found in the *Romance of Foulke Fitzwarin* (based at least in part on a true story)[4] and in *The Tale of Gamelyn* (which is almost certainly fictional).

Nevertheless, many of these stories contain very similar ingredients to those found in the Three Matters. The tale of *Sir Bevis of Hampton* stands out as being an example of one that contains many such elements and proved to be enduringly popular beyond the Middle Ages. The fact that his story was re-produced in several different languages shows it also had appeal beyond England.[5] No fewer than six medieval English manuscripts survive (which is unusual). All are based on an earlier French language version of the tale and it is hard to say when the story first appeared, but the earliest surviving versions date to the early thirteenth century.[6]

What is especially interesting about the surviving English manuscripts is that they tell different versions of the same story. They also differ from earlier French versions. The core story remains the same but different incidents have been added depending on the version. This may reflect a series of creative changes introduced for different adaptations of the story. They might well have been introduced directly by the writers (whose identities are unknown). They may, however, reflect differences in the re-telling of the tale in oral tradition which different writers recorded. These stories were designed to be performed to an audience by minstrels after all. Differences may have resulted from a minstrel not being able to remember the original version and filling in any gaps with his own material. However, they could just as easily have resulted from deliberate creative changes. So, this may reflect individual minstrels setting out to place their own creative stamp on the story.

What we have in Sir Bevis then, is a series of snapshots of an evolving, living, story-telling tradition. Perhaps this was the norm for many medieval myths. Sir Bevis just so happens to be one of the few tales for which evidence of these creative transitions survives. Elsewhere, where perhaps just one manuscript survives, we can't see this process at work. But that does not mean it did not happen.

What made this story so popular we might ask? Why did this one warrant such frequent re-telling? Why was it translated into so many other languages? The answer may ultimately be a very simple and obvious one. It was a good story!

Sir Bevis is a tale of disinheritance and the ensuing struggle to recover a lost legacy. The story begins in Bevis' childhood. Whilst he is still a boy his father, now an ageing earl, is murdered by Bevis' mother's lover. Bevis avoids being slain but is sold to Saracen merchants and transported out to the Middle East. There he enters the service of the Muslim King Ermin and grows up to become an impressive young knight. His feats of bravery include slaying a ferocious wild boar and defeating one of Ermin's Muslim rivals in battle. These deeds win him the love of Ermin's daughter, Josian. However, Bevis is betrayed by Ermin's chamberlain and finds himself a captive, during which time Ermin marries Josian off to another lord.

Several years pass before Bevis finally escapes his prison and returns to rescue Josian. The couple then escape to Cologne in Germany, where Bevis' reputation is further enhanced by slaying a poisonous dragon.[7] After other adventures the couple finally marry and return to the East where Bevis' eventually overcomes his enemies in battle. Bevis and Josian become king and queen of Mombraunt and their son, Guy, inherits Ermin's kingdom. In time, Bevis miraculously converts his Middle Eastern Muslim subjects to Christianity.

This perhaps could have been the end of Bevis' story, but new adventures follow when he returns to England. He becomes embroiled with conflict there, culminating in a spectacular bloody battle in the streets of London. However, ultimately Bevis and Josian return to rule Mombraunt successfully for twenty years before they finally die and are buried in a lavish tomb.

Pinning down the story to a specific time is both easy and problematic. Superficially the story is set in pre-conquest times. King Edgar is named as the English king, which dates the events of the tale to the mid-to-late tenth century. However, the world described in the story contains numerous fictional and fantastic embellishments. It is not a world that especially reflects England, Europe, or the Middle East as they were during the tenth century. What we have here is a work of historical fiction. It may be set in pre-Norman times, but its characters and social values are very much of the later Middle Ages.

Its choice of pre-Norman England as a setting is partly down to romantic nostalgia. However, it also has the effect of placing the tale in an age distant from that of the intended audience. Distant enough to allow that audience to suspend disbelief and immerse themselves more fully in the world of Sir Bevis.

One of the more fascinating stories from the Matter of England is the *Tale of Gamelyn*. This tale stands out from others in so far as it takes us away from court life and the affairs of the nobility.[8] Gamelyn is one of three sons of a relatively minor country knight, Sir John of Boundis. Where and when exactly the story is supposed to be located is unclear. The language used shows it was written in the north-east Midlands. It is thought (but by no means known for certain) that it was written sometime in the mid-to-late fourteenth century. Aside from these clues, the story itself gives nothing specific away. Certainly, the action takes place somewhere in late thirteenth or early fourteenth century England but beyond that it is left to the reader to imagine where and when exactly.

The ageing Sir John dies, leaving provision in his will for his land to be divided between his three sons. Alas, the eldest son, Johan, proves to be a greedy and conniving individual who schemes to cheat his youngest brother, Gamelyn, out of his inheritance. These brothers are clearly not the refined paladins of Arthurian lore. They are rustic and coarse by comparison. Gamelyn, rather than seeking to prove his valour in a joust, tests himself in a wrestling contest with the locals. He mixes with the local yeoman and husbandmen quite happily. Clearly, he is a rural country lord, rather than a man of the court.

Gamelyn returns from his wrestling match with a group of locals with the intention of holding a feast in celebration of his wrestling triumphs. Unsettled by the rowdy mob, his brother locks him out. Taking the law into his own hands Gamelyn and the mob break in, forcing his brother to hide whilst they feast and make merry. However, his scheming brother bides his time until he can trick Gamelyn and clap him in irons. Johan keeps his brother in shackles whilst he feasts with the local abbot and other important clerical dignitaries. Gamelyn escapes with the aid of an old associate of his father's. He takes violent revenge by beating the clerics and making good his escape before the sheriff arrives.

The story shows Johan using trickery and corrupt local officials to dispossess and cheat his brother. Gamelyn is even forced to resort to outlawry and hide in the wild forest. Eventually, Gamelyn and his outlaw companions force their way into the local court and pass summary justice on its corrupt officers, hanging the lot. With the aid of his other brother Ote and following an appeal to the king, Gamelyn's fortunes are finally restored.

Ultimately Gamelyn is a tale of a minor member of the country gentry, cheated of his inheritance by corrupt local officials and a treacherous elder brother. The normal legal channels fail him, as they are simply too corrupt to deliver any kind of justice. In the end justice comes from outlaws and the eventual intervention of the king. It is a world away from the stories of Lancelot, Gawain, and Galahad and has much more to say about the mundane world of common folk and rural gentry. The story contains little to nothing by way of any romance and chivalry is mostly absent from the behaviour of its characters. In this sense, Gamelyn's tale is neither chivalric nor romance.

There is much about the story which was clearly written to appeal to a popular audience rather than a courtly elite. It deals with themes of injustice and corruption. It makes targets of the corrupt local officials and clerical landlords. Gamelyn becomes a champion of the ordinary folk. He treats them well when his brother treats them badly. He is loyal and generous to his servants and the local villagers. This is deliberately contrasted with the exploitation and corruption of the local sheriff, the court officers, and the senior clergy. Gamelyn, an outlawed minor member of the gentry, becomes the people's champion.

One notable feature of Gamelyn's story is that his response to injustice is a violent one. He beats the local clergy so badly that they must be carried away in carts. He kills a porter who gets in his way and throws his body down a well. We are treated to gleeful descriptions of broken bones as Gamelyn meets out his own style of violent vigilante justice to his enemies. This is a world away from the chivalrous jousts of Chrétien's Arthurian romances.

Gamelyn's story is far closer to being a genuine tale about the common folk of England. As it turns out, his tale reveals a violent and unjust world, not a world of chivalry and honour. Indeed, the language used in the composition shows that it was written with an eye to appealing to a common audience.[9] Yet, despite all this, we are still left with a story about the son of a knight.

So, at this point we might ask ourselves, what about the common folk of medieval England? The mostly illiterate majority who weren't nobles, knights, or gentry. What about their stories? What can we say, if anything at all, about the myths and tales that were important to them? Since, by definition, they left little by way of a written record, the answer is problematic. Gamelyn brings us close to their world, but can we get any closer? To do this we need to leave the legends of the lords of the land behind us and focus specifically on the folk traditions and stories of the wider population.

Folklore, Storytelling, and Community

The nobles, knights, and manorial lords of the Plantagenet world were able to share stories in ways that were unavailable to people of lowlier social rank. Most obviously, there was a high level of literacy amongst this section of society. Thus, the written chivalric romances and *chanson de geste* could be read by a large section of the intended audience. It was also the case that many lords employed professional minstrels within their households. So, even members of their households who were illiterate or only semi-literate could listen to a minstrel singing a *chanson* at a feast.

Indeed, the chivalric stories and songs were designed primarily for performance to an audience rather than private reading. A manorial hall was an ideal setting for a minstrel to regale the household with fantastic tales of knights and valorous deeds. And, because such halls were large, enclosed spaces, such stories could be enjoyed by an audience all year around regardless of the weather.

In our modern age we tend to think of minstrels as musicians. However, in the Middle Ages, the term was applied far more broadly. The profession included a wide variety of people with a wide variety of talents. The thirteenth-century troubadour, Giraud de Calanson, listed the qualities he believed it took to 'make it' in the business. This included a surprisingly long list of skills which encompassed virtually every conceivable performance art. Singing, storytelling, juggling, mastery of several musical instruments, puppetry, animal mimicry, and working with performing animals, were all part of the minstrel's repertoire.[1] Surely most were not this versatile, but Calanson's list shows just how widely the term 'minstrel' could apply. When it came to storytelling, many minstrels were as apt to recite a chivalric romance as poetic verse as they were to sing a chanson or play music.

A permanent position in the household of a nobleman or knight, represented the best paid and most secure work that a minstrel could find. Therefore, the best and most experienced minstrels would attach themselves to such a household rather than opt for a less secure, itinerant existence.

Away from the manorial halls, in the towns and villages, we find a very different audience. Literacy and semi-literacy extended to some members of the yeoman class, especially if their work required it. However, for these people, literacy was more likely to be limited to English, rather than French or Latin. Once we look beyond these people to the numerous husbandmen, labours, and villeins, literacy levels were poor to non-existent. Books, of course, were beyond the means of poor folk.

Most ordinary people, therefore, could not just sit down and read a story. However, if they worked at their lord's manor, they might still get to hear some of the stories performed by the lord's minstrel. When they went to church, they could hear stories from the Bible and the deeds of saints from their priest. They could also see pictures of Christian stories in the stained-glass windows of their parish church. They could also experience stories performed as plays. Hearing stories told, seeing stories performed or seeing them depicted in images, therefore, represented the primary means by which they were encountered.

People could share myths and folktales in the intimate privacy of their homes. But the homes of common folk were small and cramped, unlike the grand halls of the lords. Stories could not be transmitted to many people in such a confined setting, although families no doubt shared tales in this way.

Yet, despite these limitations, humble folk could share stories with each other in larger communal settings. However, for them, the lack of access to a private hall was an obvious limitation, especially in winter months when outside gatherings were impractical. As a result, larger gatherings, at which stories and songs could be communally shared, were mostly limited to the summer months. Summer festivals such as May Day and summer games were the key times when common folk could share folk tales and stories as a community.

Publicly performed plays and pageants provided one important means by which a large community could engage with stories. These could vary significantly in their nature. There were large, well organised, civic events like the Corpus Christi pageants of York. But, at the other end of the scale, there were also many informal plays and games, acted out in local village churchyards.

In medieval England performance art played an especially important role in religious storytelling. Nevertheless, despite depicting religious stories and themes, there was some unease amongst the senior clergy when it came to this form of entertainment. Sometimes considerable unease.

The most spectacular medieval dramas were the great civic pageants known (slightly misleadingly) as 'mystery plays'. To witness such a spectacle was a uniquely medieval communal experience. One of the more famous of these events was the York Corpus Christi pageant,[2] held annually in the early summer. The festival lasted an entire day, from dawn until dusk. The longer hours of daylight permitting a longer performance. The streets of the city were cordoned off to keep the pageant route clear. People from all over the city and the surrounding countryside flocked to witness the spectacle.

If you were lucky enough to get yourself a good place in the crowd at the start of the route, your day would begin when the first pageant wagon rolled into view. The wagon would be quite large and its platform (the stage) high off the ground. It might well be richly decorated. It sometimes featured several props (some of which might even take the form of moving mechanical contraptions).

On the stage, a small number of actors would perform the first play of the day. It would stop at the first station on its route and the play would begin. These plays were short affairs, perhaps lasting just 10 or 20 minutes, maybe 40 at the most. In York, the first play of the day would tell you the tale of the creation and the fall of Lucifer. These mobile, single act productions were produced by of the local guilds. In the case of the first play in the York Cycle, it would have been the bakers.

Once the play was done, the wagon would move along the street to the next 'station' and perform the same play again for a different audience. Over the course of the day, it would roll from station to station, playing the same act for a new audience each time. As it departed the first station, a new wagon would roll up to replace it. This one, produced by the plasterers, continues the creation story. It moves on to be replaced by the tale of Adam and Eve from the card makers. As the day proceeds the entire procession rolls past, each featuring a different play from a different guild. This continues until the entire biblical story of the world, from creation to the last judgement, has been played out before you.

The term 'mystery' play comes not from the fact that the subject matter is a mystery (indeed it is well-known to the audience). Rather, the term 'mystery' is an allusion to the trade guild that put on the play. The only mystery was to guess which trade put on the play. The guilds might have used the opportunity to showcase their crafts as part of their play. For example, the carpenters might have built some elaborate stage props to showcase their skill. Or perhaps the tailors might have provided their actors with some magnificent costumes in the hopes of catching the eye of some local dignitaries. All in all, it takes an entire day to see the whole production. That was a long watch, although you could wander off for a break if you chose.

The language used for these plays was Middle English of the local dialect. These were very much stories for the common folk. They could sometimes feature crude language and humour designed to engage a popular audience. For this very reason, some members of the clergy might have taken a dim view of the affair, preferring people to learn their religion from the pulpit. But, in general, the pageants had the approval and support of the ruling classes. They were a major civic event which the mayor and other city dignitaries would make a point of attending.

Not all plays were shown as such magnificent pageants. Some were staged outdoors, and others performed in halls. What survives is almost entirely religiously themed in nature. However, some religious plays could be quite crude in their language as well as incorporating humorous episodes. No doubt, the aim behind this was to successfully engage the common man and woman by speaking to them in a language they understood and found entertaining. In one Cornish drama, telling the tale of King David, the king's butler is given the following line (translated here in modern English):

> By my balls! Let no thief come,
> However big and tough the scum[3]

I think we can safely say this was not a passage lifted directly from the Bible. It is easy to see why senior clergymen might have been more than a little uneasy with such unorthodox methods of evangelism. Such plays and spectacles, nevertheless, serve as a reminder that religious stories formed a very common feature of medieval storytelling. Whatever the senior clergy thought, however, there is no denying that this form of communal religious storytelling was very popular and widely attended.

Of course, such spectacular pageants and staged plays were major occasions, not the sort of thing you'd see every day. However, there were other religious themed plays you might see on a less grand scale. These took the form of smaller local affairs, more informal and probably more improvised. They were typically performed by junior clerics in a local churchyard. We know only a little about these productions, often referred to as *miracula.* One of the few things we do know for certain was that they were strongly disapproved of by senior clerics.

Such productions were put on by junior local clerics with the specific aim of engaging with their local communities. They were designed for an audience of local villeins and husbandmen. They were simple, rustic, and unsophisticated affairs. They were also often crude and likely featured bawdy humour and raucous performances (or at least that was how the bishops tended to regard them). They were popular, that much is clear. However, the literate ruling classes record very little of their content, except to say that these performances were, quite often, regarded as shameful.

These plays sometimes involved masks and disguising, a surefire sign that disreputable happenings were afoot. One influential medieval friar bewailed the fact that so many people flocked to attend the 'latest shows' of these 'foolish clerics' but were often absent from the mass. Another document from 1220 gives us a hint of the kind of shenanigans that might accompany such performances. We are told of a play dealing with the Resurrection that, for one thing, was not shown at Easter. This alone was considered inappropriate. But this was not all that was wrong with it. For another thing it attracted a large mixed-gender crowd of common folk many of whom attended for no other reason than to indulge in personal pleasure. It hardly sounds like an edifying religious experience but there is no denying it sounds very interesting![4]

In addition to religious drama, there was a significant volume of secular drama produced by a variety of players for profit. These were also frowned upon by the powers that be. Consequently, very little by way of actual content survives. Again, much of what we know of such performances derives from the clerics who disapproved of them. In 1240, Bishop Walter of Worcester listed several such plays and entertainments that merited strong discouragement. These included 'King and Queen plays', 'ram-raisings', wrestling contests, and 'illicit guild-ales'.[5]

These events were frowned upon partly because they raised money for profit for those involved. Sometimes this was done by passing around the cap and sometimes by selling ale. A rare fragment of this material that survives is for a play called *Dame Sirith,* written in the West Midlands at some point in the late thirteenth century. The story is a simple one. A cunning old woman tricks a naïve young girl into having sex with a lusty young man. The audience no doubt found the bawdy goings-on highly amusing.

Aside from plays, stories were often heard in the form of ballads and rhymes performed by minstrels. In addition to minstrels who attached themselves to the service of lords, there were others who were itinerant. These players travelled the country, often following a seasonal itinerary, attending fairs, markets, and festivals. Here they would tell stories, play music, and sing popular ballads to make their living. Those who could not find regular employment with lords might alternatively make some money by offering their services to the wealthier yeoman. And, perhaps, a large crowd of relatively poor folk at a fair might collectively pay enough to make a good day's living.

Many ballads were learnt and transmitted purely by oral tradition, just as they had been in pre-Norman days. In the same manner, it is likely that many popular plays were similarly conceived. Often, such performances were delivered by people who were either unable (due to poor literacy) or simply did not bother to set down their work in writing. Unfortunately for us, most of what was recorded of these ballads has been filtered by what the literate (and hence largely elite) members of medieval society deemed meritorious. What tends to have been lost is anything which was deemed to be too crude, rustic, or 'shameful' (i.e., most of it).

Popular forms of minstrelsy and common plays often evoked the condemnation of the clergy. Indeed, few by way of any specifics survive regarding these, doubtless, highly popular forms of entertainment. Often,

Affix
stamp
here

Pen and Sword Books
c/o Casemate Publishers
1950 Lawrence Road
Havertown, PA 19083

all that survives is the indignant moralising of clerics such as Thomas de Chabham, writing in the early thirteenth century. The outraged de Chabham was especially critical of what he saw as the lowest form of entertainment: 'those who transform and transfigure their bodies with indecent dance and gesture, now indecently unclothing themselves, now putting on horrible masks'.[6]

Dancing minstrel troupes often dressed in masks and wore striking costumes. Generally, this appears to have been done for dramatic comic effect. Images of one troupe show a drummer, with other players dressed as monks and nuns (clearly included to send-up the holy orders). Another is dressed as a wild man or *woodwose*. The woodwose commonly appeared in such troupes (and was a recurring theme in medieval folklore to which we shall return). There were also characters dressed as devils and others wearing animal masks. One image even shows a masked player jauntily flashing a bare backside to the audience. The overall impression is one of brash, bawdy revelry. One can imagine such a colourful group featuring prominently in local fairs and street processions, much to the chagrin of the local bishop.[7]

Minstrels could, therefore, depict familiar folkloric characters in drama as well as tell stories and sing ballads about them. This conveyance of mythology and folklore through physical performance should not be underestimated. It was a critical way in which medieval commoners engaged with story-telling.

Amongst the named popular dramatic performances that attracted widespread disapproval were Robin Hood plays. Abbot Walter Bower, writing in 1440,despaired of the popular stories and plays featuring Robin Hood and Little John 'whom the foolish populace are so inordinately fond of celebrating both in tragedies and comedies'.[8] Such stories represent the kind of tales that were clearly popular with a wide section of the community. However, respectable men like Abbot Bower were hardly inclined to record details of what they no doubt considered to be frivolous and foolish tales. These were the tales of the 'foolish populace', not of respectable citizens.

This does not mean that stories of Robin Hood were not also popular with at least some people of standing. In a revealing letter of 1473, Sir John Paston informs us that he had employed a servant for three years to perform popular plays of Saint George and Robin Hood.[9] Robin would, therefore, appear to have had quite a broad appeal.

In the latter part of the fourteenth century, English literature was born. This was the time when our anonymous friend wrote his tale of *Sir Gawain and the Green Knight*. It was also the time when writers like Chaucer, Gower, and Langland created their literary masterpieces. But, they achieved more than simply giving us the first great works of English literature. In Chaucer's *Canterbury Tales* we find stories about people from all walks of life, most of whom are not knights or lords. William Langland's famous work, *Piers*

Plowman, features the eponymous farmer as one of its main characters. These stories move us away from the chivalric idealism of court circles to the world of millers and ploughmen.

It is in Langland's work that we see the earliest surviving reference to Robin Hood. In a section featuring the seven deadly sins, Langland has the character 'Sloth' tell us:

> I know not perfectly my Pater Noster
> As the priest would sing it,
> But I know ballads of Robin Hood
> And Randolf, Earl of Chester.[10]

The same character openly admits to idling away the day listening to frivolous tales and drinking ale. In this short section Langland presents us with a snapshot of the kind of stories that engaged a popular medieval audience. He also supplies us with a context: sharing an ale, perhaps in a tavern or at a summer festival. And it is to these stories, and to tales of Robin Hood in particular, to which we must now turn.

Robin Hood and the Greenwood

The earliest surviving stories of Robin Hood exist in the form of old minstrel's ballads dating back to the fifteenth century. We know, from sources such as John Paston, that Robin Hood plays were also popular at this time. Unfortunately, only fragments of one such play survives. As a result, we are largely reliant on the ballads for Robin's earliest stories.

A famous early ballad is the *Geste of Robin Hood.* The earliest surviving copies date to the early sixteenth century but the language used dates the story to the fifteenth. It is, like all the other ballads, written in English and almost certainly derived from older ballads that are now lost to us. Indeed, *Geste* is thought to combine themes from several shorter, earlier, ballads in a single epic narrative.[1] Typically, for a ballad of this period, it is written in a simple style with an emphasis on storyline rather than characterisation.

The tale opens with Robin and his outlaw band in the Greenwood, planning their next robbery. Robin's men go out in search of a likely victim and encounter a poor knight. They bring him back to Robin as a 'guest' for dinner but are surprised to discover that the poor fellow is virtually destitute. Robin learns that the knight has been forced to mortgage his land to a greedy abbot and is on the verge of losing everything. He is outraged and agrees to help the knight, lending him the money he needs to pay off the abbot. This the knight succeeds in doing, despite the abbot having bribed a local justice. When the knight's fortunes are restored, he proves a useful ally for Robin later in the tale. In the next section of *Geste*, Robin's men waylay a monk in much the same way. This guest is of somewhat different character to the knight. He is deceitful and pleads poverty despite being rich. As a result, Robin robs him of all he has.

Later in the tale, Little John travels to Nottingham and enters an archery contest. He so impresses everyone with his prowess that the sheriff asks to take him into his service. Little John agrees but gives the false name 'Reynold Greenleaf' to mask his outlaw identity. However, when Little John feels he is being cheated of his due maintenance he quickly reverts to crime. He steels from the sheriff and lures him into the greenwood with tall stories of good hunting. There the sheriff is ambushed by Robin and forced to agree to never seek to do Robin harm again.

Robin is rewarded for his earlier generosity to the poor knight in the next section of the tale. During another archery contest Robin wins but is betrayed to the sheriff as an outlaw. He and his men flee, barely escaping with their lives, to take refuge in the knight's castle. The castle is besieged, and the sheriff appeals to the king. Although Robin and his men escape to the forest, the sheriff returns to take the knight prisoner. Hearing the knight is in danger, Robin and his men stage a dramatic rescue, slaying the sheriff in the process.

The tale ends when the king is forced to travel north to set things in order. We are told he is 'King Edward', although it is not clear which one.[2] The king disguises himself as an abbot when he meets Robin. However, his royal bearing sets him apart from any abbot that Robin knows. The king is so impressed by Robin that he takes him into his service. However, Robin eventually gets bored with court life and, after a year, returns to his former life in the greenwood.

Another ballad from the period is the tale of *Robin Hood and the Monk*. In this story, Robin is worshipping in church when he is recognised and betrayed by a monk. As a result, he is captured, and the delighted sheriff sends the monk with a message to the king to inform him of the good news. En route the monk and his pageboy are ambushed and murdered by Little John and Much, the miller's son. The pair hide the bodies and assume their identities, taking the sheriff's letter to the king. In this way, they obtain a royal seal and are instructed to have Robin brought to the king. Of course, the royal seal is all they need to get into the castle where Robin is being held and stage a dramatic rescue.

Dramatic rescues, disguises, and assumed false identities are, as you may by now have guessed, a recurring theme in Robin Hood ballads. The tale of *Robin Hood and Guy of Gisborne* is no exception. Here Guy of Gisborne, a mercenary with an unpleasant reputation, sets out to deal with Robin for the sheriff. Like Robin himself, Guy is a yeoman of the forest. The stage is set for a dramatic confrontation between the two. Robin naturally triumphs in the end, cuts off Guy's head, and displays it impaled on his longbow. However, whilst this has been going on, Little John has been captured by the sheriff who is determined to execute him. Disguised as Guy, Robin shows up in the nick of time to stage a dramatic rescue. The hapless sheriff is shot dead by Little John whilst trying to escape.

Disguise and deception also feature in the tale of *Robin Hood and the Potter*. Robin and his men waylay a potter, but the potter proves a tough cookie, getting the better of Robin in a fight. Impressed, Robin befriends the potter and offers to sell his pots for him in Nottingham. Robin, as it turns out, knows little of the merchant's profession, and sells pots off at knock down prices (much to the bewilderment and amusement of other market traders). However, when he enters and wins an archery contest, people are more impressed. He disguises his identity from the sheriff but boasts that he was taught to shoot by Robin. The sheriff takes the bate when Robin offers to lead him to the outlaw. Naturally it is a trap. Robin and his men ambush the sheriff in the woods and steal his fine horse.

One final chapter of the original medieval story is played out in a ballad dealing with the death of Robin Hood. The only surviving copy is post-medieval, but it is thought to derive from an earlier medieval ballad.[3] Its details broadly match the ending of *Geste* and provides a shortened version of the tale. The ballad tells how Robin met his death at Kirklees Priory in West Yorkshire. Robin meets his demise when the prioress betrays him to her lover, Red Roger of Doncaster. Following a fierce fight, Roger is slain, and Robin mortally wounded. Robin's tales finally end as Little John lays him to rest somewhere near the priory.

The Paston letters demonstrate that there were also plays, featuring Robin Hood, being performed in the late Middle Ages. Only one fragment of such a play survives from 1475.[4] Its plot is very simple (indeed the entire work fits on a single scrap of paper) and largely action driven. The story is very similar to the tale of *Robin and Guy of Gisborne*. It features contests of wrestling, stone throwing, and archery as well as action packed fight scenes. The action appears to be the primary focus of the play. It would ideally have required space to perform and, as it featured archery, it would have been an ideal entertainment for summer games.

And this, in a nutshell, is all that survives of the original medieval Robin Hood legend. It shows us a man who is in some ways very familiar and in others quite different from his modern popular persona. What then can we say of Robin, based solely on these early tales?

First, we can say that the setting is always Nottingham, Sherwood Forest, or Barnsdale Forest (in South Yorkshire). These are all located within the same part of the world – the north-east Midlands and the southernmost part of north-east England. Secondly, in all the stories, Robin is identified as a yeoman of the Greenwood. In other words, he is clearly a commoner not a nobleman. He is not even a knight or a lesser member of the rural gentry. As such he is no Gamelyn. In social rank he is on a par with a man like Gamelyn's gamekeeper. In short, he is unmistakably portrayed as a man of the people.

Robin's natural habitat is the Greenwood. These early tales are full of references to life lived free in the depths of the woods. Part of this lifestyle clearly consists of living as a huntsman and, in Robin's case, as a poacher of the king's venison. We are never explicitly told why Robin was originally outlawed, simply that he was. However, there is little doubt that poaching, and highway robbery lie at the heart of his outlaw status.

One aspect of these early tales that might come as a shock to a modern audience is the violent nature of some of them. Robin not only kills Guy of Gisborne but displays his impaled head on his longbow. Little John and Much not only kill the treacherous monk but murder his page boy too, for no other reason than to leave no witness. It serves as a reminder, if any were needed, that the medieval world was a violent time in which such acts were not seen as especially out of place. Neither do they appear to have done anything to dint the undeniable popularity of these ballads.

The Robin Hood of these early stories does not rob from the rich to give to the poor. He is no social warrior fighting against the injustice of oppressive taxes. In general, he steels from the wealthiest members of society because they have the most money. He is, however, generally sympathetic to those who are poor or of a humbler social status. He even lends money to the poor knight and offers to sell the yeoman potter's pots. His main enemies and prime targets of his criminal activities are corrupt powerful men. Corrupt abbots, justices of the peace, greedy monks and, of course, the sheriff of Nottingham. Corruption within the system, not the system itself, are Robin's targets. Indeed, in *Geste*, Robin ultimately seeks and finds justice from the king.

In many ways, this reflects attitudes that were evident in the Peasants' Revolt of 1381 and Jack Cade's rebellion of 1450. In both cases, the primary complaints of the rebels centred around accusations of corrupt officials and bad royal advisors. In neither case did the mob seek to overthrow the entire system and depose the king. In fact, in both cases, the mob appealed to the king to intervene and restore justice to a system that they believed had become corrupted. In the case of the Peasants' Revolt, corrupt clerics were amongst the prime targets of the rebels. Indeed, their summary execution and mistreatment of clerics like Archbishop Sudbury precisely reflected the sentiments that we find running through these early Robin Hood stories.[5]

Placing these tales within a specific period of the Middle Ages is challenging. In general, most of these stories mention nothing specific about when they are supposed to be set. Only one mentions a King Edward. However, it does not tell us which one. It could potentially be any of the three Plantagenet King Edwards who reigned between 1272 and 1377. Nevertheless, many aspects of these stories are suggestive of a fourteenth- or fifteenth-century setting. The yeoman class, to which Robin belonged, became more prominent during this later medieval period. The constant references to archery contests reflect the obsession of the age of the longbowman – an age that only reached its zenith after the battle of Crecy in 1346.

However, we must beware. These tales may present us with a late-medieval setting simply because they were designed to appeal to a late-medieval audience. What survives are fifteenth-century versions of what were probably earlier ballads. But did the fifteenth-century minstrels modify their tales to include new elements to appeal to the tastes of the audience of their times? Probably. After all, the Arthurian romances present us with a setting that is clearly high medieval – a world of knights, chivalry, and courts. This was clearly done to engage the audience of the times when the romances were written. Such a world was radically different from the dark age, post-Roman world inhabited by any original Arthur.

Were there earlier, now lost, versions of these Robin Hood ballads, set in earlier centuries? Certainly, we know that Robin Hood ballads were popular decades before the creation of the earliest surviving copies we possess. Was King Edward mentioned in *Geste* because Robin really did live in the reign of a King Edward? Or was it simply that a King Edward happened to be on the throne when the minstrel concerned composed his ballad about Robin Hood meeting the king? This was popular entertainment after all. The goal was to engage an audience not to record history. There can be no question that dramatic license was at work. We just don't know to what extent that distorted earlier, now lost, versions of the story.

However, we can tell a lot from what these tales do not include as well as from what they do. In none of these early tales is there any reference to any kind of conflict between Saxons and Normans. There is not even a trace of it. It, therefore, seems highly unlikely that Robin Hood's story dates to a time when friction between Normans and Saxons was an issue. Robin is clearly identified as a commoner in all these early tales. His yeoman of the Greenwood identity is central to what makes him Robin Hood. We must, therefore, accept that the original Robin, if he existed at all, was not a nobleman or a knight, or even a member of the gentry. Stories about Robin being a disposed noblemen and stories of Robin championing Saxon rights against Norman oppression are, therefore, apocryphal. These elements were all added to the story in post-medieval times. They have nothing to do with the original tales of Robin Hood.

It is worth noting that, leaving archery aside, Robin and his companions fight with swords. Indeed, it is his skill with the sword, rather than the quarterstaff that is emphasised in these medieval tales.[6] Robin's quarterstaff is entirely absent from these early stories. Its addition to the legend is also post-medieval. By a similar token, Robin's companions in these stories are Little John, Will Scarlet, and Much, the miller's son. There is no Maid Marian or Alan-a-dale. These two are later, post-medieval additions.[7] Their addition is evidence of the process of accretion to which the legend was subjected over time.

Many folktales and myths are subject to the process of accretion. New elements are added to an original story as time passes. These often reflect popular fashions of the day or simple creative embellishments that happen to fit well with the original tale. The tales of Robin Hood are no exception. The best and clearest evidence for this process in action relates to Friar Tuck.

Friar Tuck does not appear in the early ballads, but he does appear in a surviving fragment from an early Robin Hood play. We meet Friar Tuck for the very first time in a Robin Hood verse play from around 1475. However, whilst Robin Hood himself is hard to pin down to a specific time or person, Friar Tuck is not.

Friar Tuck was a genuine outlaw, active in 1417. Like Robin Hood, Tuck appears to have engaged in the same kind of highway robberies. 'Friar Tuck' was a false name but, very tellingly, it was a name that seems to have been unfamiliar to the authorities before he became active.[8] Robin Hood stories were already in wide circulation well before 1417 (Langland tells us as much some four decades before). It may just be possible that the Friar Tuck of 1417 took his pseudonym from a character in a now lost Robin Hood ballad. However, if he had done, you'd have thought that his name would have been familiar to the authorities at the time, and it was not. The 1417 Tuck was, therefore, almost certainly the original Tuck; a later Greenwood outlaw who had nothing to do with the original Robin Hood. His addition to the legend by 1475 is a clear example of the process of accretion at work. He was added to the story because he was an interesting character who fitted the narrative well and added spice to the tale. It was as simple as that.

So, what of the real Robin Hood, if ever there was such a person? Was there ever such a thing as an historic Robin Hood? Well, if we start with what we know, the earliest reference to Robin from 1377 tells us that his ballads were already in wide circulation by this time. So, if there was a real Robin, he certainly must have lived before 1377. If we allow time for his legend to spread, it seems very unlikely that he can be dated to a period any later than the mid-fourteenth century. But what did people living in the Middle Ages think?

We have only two medieval sources that place a date on Robin Hood's life. Wyntoun, writing in 1420, tells us Robin was active in 1283. Bower, writing in 1440, tell gives a date of 1266 and associates Robin with the general period of lawlessness and upheaval that followed the Second Barons' War.[9] Both would, therefore, place Robin in the mid-to-late thirteenth century, during the final years of the reign of Henry III and the early years of his son Edward I. A King Edward is the only king mentioned in the earliest ballads. Is that simply a coincidence of accretion? It, nevertheless, appears to corroborate Bower and Wyntoun's claims.

In 1521, during the reign of Henry VIII, a fellow by the name of John Major dated Robin Hood to the period 1193–1194.[10] This was the time when Richard I was captive in Germany and his brother John was ruling England as regent. It was the first time that Robin had ever been associated with this early period.

Nothing in any medieval record or the surviving medieval story claims Robin lived at this time. Nevertheless, this was the view that would rapidly gain popularity during the sixteenth century. Later in the sixteenth century, another writer re-affirmed Major's claim and added, for the first time, a reference to Robin's supposed birthplace – Locksley. Then, in 1598 a playwright by the name of Anthony Munday produced a couple of very popular plays in which Robin Hood was presented as the disinherited Earl of Huntingdon. He also chose to follow Major's lead in setting his story in the time of Richard I and John.[11]

Munday's work had been intended as a work of historical fiction, loosely based around the original story. It was no more designed to serve as a serious history than Shakespeare's *Macbeth*. Despite this, it was destined to take on a life of its own. In later centuries the Earl of Huntingdon myth proved very popular. This was despite the fact that no one had ever mentioned this until several centuries after Robin's supposed death. More elements were added as the process of accretion collected further material like a tumble weed gathering detritus as it blows across a desert.

It would all reach a crescendo with Walter Scott's *Ivanhoe*, published in the early nineteenth century. Here, Robin is not only associated with the age of Richard the Lionheart, but he was also acting as a champion of the Saxons against Norman oppression. Never mind the fact that Robin's name would have been about as Norman as you could get in Richard I's time. Robin's story had, by this time, travelled a very long way from its roots. The plain fact is that none of this is based on anything written about Robin Hood during the Middle Ages. Indeed, the entire 'disposed nobleman' identity is directly contradicted by the original legend.

The truth is that more rigorous analysis of this vision of Robin, rooted as it was in post-medieval tradition, has found it wanting. The writers who advocated this narrative, from the sixteenth century onwards, were, in the words of medieval historian, J.C. Holt, 'at a loss to distinguish earlier evidence from later accretion, or historical record, however enigmatic, from poetic inventions'.[12]

Despite this, the Lionheart (or early Plantagenet) age version of Robin persists in the popular imagination even to this day. It was, nevertheless, a version of Robin that was increasingly being called into question, even as early as Victorian times.

In 1852, the historian Joseph Hunter attempted to apply a more rigorous approach to identifying an historic Robin. Looking through the historic record he found some fragments that appeared to match the oldest Robin Hood tales. Edward II was in Nottingham in 1323. By 1324, the king had a Robin Hood in his service as a porter. Earlier records showed that a certain Robin Hood had been a resident of Wakefield, very near Barnsdale forest, in 1316/17. Some residents of that area were dispossessed and outlawed following a failed rebellion during this period. Do these fragments point to the historic Robin Hood? Hunter thought they might.

However, Hunter's theory falls apart under detailed scrutiny. It turns out that what he found were no more than coincidences. The Robin Hood of Wakefield and the porter in Edward's service were almost certainly not the same person. The porter did not leave Edward's service to return to life in the Greenwood but appears to have retired due to old age. There is no evidence to show that Robin Hood of Wakefield was ever outlawed. In fact, if anything, the evidence suggests that he was not even dispossessed, let alone outlawed.[13] All Hunter had, in fact, found was a coincidence of names and places.

One of the big challenges we face in identifying a 'real' Robin Hood is his name. Robin is a diminutive form of the name 'Robert' – a very common name in the Middle Ages. The name 'Hood' or 'Hode' or variants thereof was not especially common but certainly not unknown. There were, therefore, many Robin Hoods in the Middle Ages. Finding one in the records is easy but finding the right one is like looking for a needle in a haystack. Hunter's co-incidence of names, therefore, gets us no closer to finding the right Robin.

However, one thing that Hunter's work did uncover is the fact that there was a Hood family present in Wakefield during the early fourteenth century. Further digging in the historic record reveals other Hood's cropping up in the area at around this time. Wakefield is only a few miles away from Barnsdale, one of Robin's traditional haunts. So, although the Robin Hunter identified doesn't fit the bill, he may well have been on the right track.

One further clue comes from a record dating to 1306. At this time, Edward I was sending prisoners south from Scotland and gave specific instructions for the guard to be strengthened. The reason given was that the prisoners would need to pass through Barnsdale, an area considered to be particularly notorious for its lawlessness at this time.[14] We, therefore, come back to Barnsdale forest during the reign of Edward I at a time when we know several people named Hood certainly lived in the area.

One last clue is the appearance of people in the historic record with the surname 'Robinhood'. This pops up from the very early fourteenth century onwards. It is an extremely rare and unusual surname, one that does not appear to have existed at all in earlier centuries. This might well suggest that Robin Hood's legend was already becoming popular as early as the start of the fourteenth century. This all points us back to Bower and Wyntoun's belief that Robin was active during the latter part of the thirteenth century. For my money, the balance of evidence points to this period, in the Barnsdale, Sherwood, and Nottingham area. But the man himself remains undeniably elusive.

But perhaps the precise identity of the historic Robin Hood doesn't really matter. What really matters is what the Robin Hood myth stood for in the eyes of a medieval audience. His appeal lay in the fact that he was just a common outlaw, a yeoman of the Greenwood. He had no heirs and graces and no ambition to do anything other than remain true to his roots. He even abandoned court life to live free in the forest. He was not a vindictive sheriff, corrupt justice, or avaricious abbot. He was no more, or less, than a common yet honest vagabond.

In short, Robin Hood, for all his criminality and violence, became a figure of hope in his own way. Hope that perhaps it was possible for a common scallywag, with a little cunning and a little luck, to 'get away with it' for once. A small win for the little man in a medieval world that appeared to favour powerful and corrupt men of rank so heavily. A blow against crooked, evil, councillors bent on twisting the king's laws to swindle good, honest folk.

So, if you want to find the real Robin Hood, don't bother looking in books, libraries, or archives. He isn't there. The real Robin lived in a wandering minstrel's ballad sung at a medieval summer fair or in a rustic play, performed for Sir John Paston's household. Or perhaps you might meet him at one of the intriguing sounding *illicit guild-ales* at the summer games. There you can hear about his exploits in idle tales at the ale, just as Langland's Sloth encountered him.

Of Earl Randolph and Other Folktales

One of the other popular ballads cited by Langland relates to Randolph, Earl of Chester. Unfortunately, no copies of any medieval *Randolph of Chester* ballads survive. Somewhat more fortunately, the identities of the earls of Chester are well-known, although there was more than one Earl Randolph.

Whatever this ballad was, it clearly held popular appeal. Two medieval Earl Randolphs stand out as providing material that might have appealed to minstrels.

The first candidate is Randolph II. This Randolph lived during the chaotic period of civil war between Stephen and Matilda known as the Anarchy (1138-1153). He began the war as a Stephen loyalist but, when royal decisions did not go his way, he had a habit of changing sides. Then, in his turn, he was betrayed by Stephen. As a result, he ended the war fighting for the Plantagenet faction. This earl was never 'outlawed' although he did rebel against an unpopular king who presided over a period of chaos. He also met a somewhat dramatic end when he was poisoned by William Peverel the Younger in 1153. Let's just say that there was certainly plenty of material there for a minstrel to work with.

The second prospect is Randolph III (1170–1232). However, this Randolph was never much of a rebel, let alone an outlaw. In fact, he was a staunch loyalist of the unpopular King John and later of his son, Henry III. Nevertheless, a peculiar incident in 1209/1210 would have supplied material for a great ballad. At the time, a Welsh army was threatening Rhuddlan Castle and Earl Randolph, tasked with its defence, found himself besieged, and desperately short of men.

In order to address this problem, a relief force was raised from a rag-tag band of minstrels, cobblers, and various dissolute commoners. This rabble apparently made such a din that the Welsh fled.[1] It is quite possible this tale was something of an exaggeration, but it is easy to imagine its appeal for minstrels. A story concerning a motley army of minstrels sounds like fertile soil from which a popular ballad might grow. Of course, it is entirely possible that the ballad itself exaggerated the role played by minstrels in the entire affair.

Perhaps the account of this event that has come down to us (which is not a contemporary one) owes more to this lost ballad than the actual history!

Another character whose tales attracted significant popularity was Saint George. Saint George became increasingly popular in England during the fourteenth century at the instigation of Edward III. He emerged as England's premier saint, replacing the more pacifistic Edward the Confessor and Edmund the Martyr. By the time of Henry V, George was firmly established as England's patron saint. As such, he supplied a martial role model better suited to the period of the Hundred Years' War. His name became a common war cry for English soldiers during this conflict and his aid was famously invoked by Henry V at Agincourt.[2]

It is little surprise to find Saint George appearing in pageants, miracula, and other now long-lost mummers' plays. The English mummers' plays were performed by troupes of masked players. Their performances originally appear to have consisted of visual displays, featuring a combination of dance and mime. These could sometimes be quite bawdy, and the mummers might even dice with their guests for money. However, as the form evolved, mummeries came to feature dialogue and more complex story-telling. Early Saint George plays of this sort probably drew their inspiration from the popular account of Saint George's life that appeared in *The Golden Legend*. However, over time, they became subject to popular creative embellishment.

Other characters were, at various times, added into the Saint George mummers' plays that had little to do with the original story. This led to a spectacle that became more akin to a pantomime than a religious drama. Eventually, such plays featured new characters like a quack doctor, who miraculously revives Saint George after he is slain. There was also a Turk (who provided the role of pantomime villain), and even Father Christmas made an appearance. However, the earliest reference we have to mummers' plays of this sort are eighteenth century.[3] We cannot, therefore, be sure whether any of these other characters appeared in the plays enjoyed by Sir John Paston in the 1470s. Some, and possibly all, of them might well have been later additions. We can be certain, for example, that the addition of Father Christmas was a post-medieval innovation.[4]

As it turns out, Robin Hood was not the only scoundrel to enjoy a popular following. Another outlaw ballad of the period is the tale *Adam Bell, Clym of Clough, and William of Cloudisley*. This ballad is thought to be fifteenth-century or, at the very latest, from the early sixteenth. It features a trio of common outlaws who, we are told, were active in Inglewood, in north-west England.[5]

The story displays so many similarities to the Robin Hood stories that they might be considered popular tropes of an outlaw ballad tradition. One of the three outlaws is betrayed to the authorities whilst visiting his wife in Carlisle. A local swineherd gets word to his companions that he has been taken by the law and scheduled for execution. His companions stage a daring midnight raid, slaying the gate porter, and infiltrating the city. They then hide and bide their time until the hour of the execution. At this point, they emerge from hiding, string their bows, and shoot the sheriff and the justice. A battle ensues during which the three outlaws make a daring get away. They then make a quick dash to the royal court and con their way into receiving a pardon before the king can learn the true extent of their crimes.

Such a tale could easily have served as a Robin Hood story. The *Adam Bell* ballad was written as a crowd pleaser, containing all the key elements that seem to have appealed to a later medieval audience. By the time *Adam Bell* was composed, his tale was woven into a well-established outlaw ballad tradition. It provides further evidence, if any were needed, that the myth of the outlaw antihero was, by this time, deeply embedded within popular medieval folklore.

Robin Hood and Adam Bell were not the only popular medieval rogue-come-tricksters. Another classic rogue of the period was French in origin and went by the name of Reynard. However, he was not a man but a fox! Stories featuring anthropomorphised animals long pre-date the Middle Ages. Such tales had been around since classical times (Aesop's fables being a great early example). However, in medieval France, from the twelfth century onwards, tales of Reynard the Fox began to circulate. His stories became so popular that his very name was adopted by the French as the name for all foxes. It was not long before Reynard's stories gained a significant audience in other countries, spreading to Holland, Germany, and England.

By the late fourteenth century, Reynard was well-known to English audiences. He is referred to in passing in *Sir Gawain and the Green Knight* and Chaucer based his 'Nun's Priest's Tale' on a classic Reynard story (although Reynard himself appears only as 'the fox'). Rather like Robin Hood, Reynard is a rogue who operates by guile and deception. Also, like Robin, he is cast in the role of a commoner in the mythical animal world he inhabits. Other, nobler, animals take on the roles of kings, aristocrats, and clergy in this world. The king, for example, is depicted as a lion. Also, like Robin, his escapades often result in his social betters being satirised and humiliated. Reynard is, in effect, another example of a kind of outlaw antihero. His popularity with an English audience is confirmed by the publication of a large volume of his tales, translated into English from Dutch, by Caxton in 1481.[6]

No doubt Sloth would have been happiest listening to a ballad of *Robin Hood*, or *Earl Randolph* with jar of ale in hand, at a summer festival. Such events were important communal gatherings, the ideal time for such stories to be shared amongst the commons. Such open-air performances afforded ample space for archery displays, wrestling matches and mock fights to entertain the crowd. They also allowed the whole community to gather to combine entertainment with participation in time honoured, folk traditions.

Some of these gatherings revolved around important Christian celebrations. The Corpus Christi pageants being a good example. Some were town fairs, essentially commercial gatherings, centred around famous annual markets. Yet others were folk celebrations, mostly unrelated to either Christianity or trade, their origins so ancient that they are now largely lost to us. It's now time to turn our attentions to the annual cycle of festivals, religious rites, and folk traditions that marked the medieval calendar. These events framed the medieval year, providing meaning to the rhythm of the agricultural seasons and the context in which stories could be shared.

Festivals, Rituals, and Folk Traditions

We are used to thinking of a year as starting on 1st January. This was indeed the case in Roman Britain. However, in medieval England the date for starting a new year was shifted to 25th March to coincide with the Feast of Annunciation. The feast celebrated the visit paid by the angel Gabriel to the Virgin Mary, to give her the good news that she had been chosen to give birth to the son of God. Nevertheless, January represented an important time of year in the medieval world, since this was the time when fields were ploughed, ready for the new growing season.

The first major festival after the Christmas period was Shrovetide in the early spring. In the Middle Ages, Shrovetide covered Shrove Sunday, Collop Monday, and Shrove Tuesday. It held particular significance because it represented the last opportunity for indulgence before the fasting period of Lent.[1] It was timed to align with Easter and, as such, can fall anytime between early-February and mid-March, six weeks before the Holy Week.

Medieval aristocratic accounts show that, aside from Christmas, Shrovetide was the main time of year for feasting and merrymaking. Shrove Sunday would be marked by a religious service to herald in the festivities. Collop Monday would be a time for feasting and an opportunity to consume all the types of food that would be banned during Lent. The word 'collop' signifies a cut of meat, reflecting the fact that a lot of meat was consumed at this time.

Shrove Tuesday would be given over to sports. For the common folk, three sports were especially popular at this time. All three were exceptionally violent. The first was football. That would be medieval football, not modern football. At this time football had no real rules. You had two teams consisting of as many people as you could muster. Then you set up two goals at either end of the village. These might simply consist of two posts. Then all you had to do was touch the opposing team's goal with the ball. No rules. Brawling was considered a legitimate and even expected part of the game. If you did not fancy football, you could spend the day betting on cock fights or perhaps try your hand at the sadistic sport of cock threshing. In this latter 'game' a cock or hen was tied to a post and the players took it in turns to throw sticks at it. The player who managed to kill the cock wins. All three games serve as a grim reminder to the violence inherent to medieval society.

Shrove Tuesday was followed by Ash Wednesday, an altogether more sober experience. Villagers would attend church to be anointed with ash by the priest. The priest would intone a Latin admonition, reminding the faithful of their mortality and marking the start of Lent. The priest would then cover the altar, the church cross and images of the saints with special cloths.

During Lent, for the next six weeks, the faithful would avoid eating meat, cheese, milk, butter, or eggs. The more devout would also remain celibate. It was a time for privation and to contemplate the weight of your sins. It was a good time of year to avoid celebrations, as it was a busy time for farmers. Pastoral farmers would be busy with lambing and calving, whilst arable farmers were occupied with crop sowing.

The date of Christ's crucifixion, unlike the date of his birth, is recorded in the Bible. According to the gospels, he was crucified at the time of Jewish Passover. In the early church, attempts were made to stick to this date but since the Jewish and Julian calendars did not align, this was problematic. By Plantagenet times, the date for Easter was fixed on the first Sunday after the first full moon of the spring equinox. This placed it at around the same time as Passover, although the two festivals only rarely coincided.

In most of Western Christendom, Easter came to be referred to by a variation on the Greek name for this festival – *Pascha*. However, in England and Germany it was called Easter or (in Germany) *Ôstara*. The Venerable Bede, writing in Anglo-Saxon times, tells us this is because Christ's crucifixion coincided with the spring festivities of an old pagan Saxon goddess, Eostre. Aside from Bede, there is little in the historic record to verify this. More importantly, there is no indication of what rituals may have been performed as part of pagan Eostre's feast (beyond, obviously, a feast). The folklorist Ronald Hutton points out that we cannot even be certain that there was a goddess of this name.[2] The term might refer to the time of year or perhaps the name of a pagan festival rather than the goddess. Also, by the time Bede wrote, the old pagan Anglo-Saxon beliefs had been replaced by Christianity.

The approach of medieval Easter was marked with the Palm Sunday service, held on the Sunday before Easter. It celebrated Christ's arrival in Jerusalem on a donkey and the scattering of palm fronds before him as he rode through its streets. It was celebrated by a religious procession, culminating in the service. Of course, palm trees are thin on the ground in England, so the faithful brought tree branches and other foliage to the service instead.

Palm Sunday was the first of a series of religious processions that marked the medieval spring and early summer. Each of these would feature their own religious liturgy and be led by the clergy. A total of seven religious processions were held at this time of year. In addition to Palm Sunday these were: Saint Mark's Day (25th April); the Monday, Tuesday, and Wednesday of Rogation Week (the sixth week after Easter); Ascension Day (the Thursday of Rogation Week); and Corpus Christi.[3]

In the week following Palm Sunday, Maundy Thursday celebrated the Last Supper. The Lenten cloths, which had covered the devotional objects in churches were officially uncovered at this time. Since early Plantagenet times, the monarch traditionally distributed alms in the form of 'maundy money' to the poor after the Maundy Thursday service.

Good Friday was a sombre affair, a time to mourn Christ's passion and crucifixion and contemplate the weight of earthly sins. The congregation would kneel barefoot and be invited to crawl to the foot of an image of the cross and kiss it. All the while, the priest would remind them of their unworthiness in the sight of God. Once this service had been completed, all church candles and lights would be extinguished, to signify the death of Christ.

Easter Sunday would be marked by another major service but one far more celebratory in nature than that of Good Friday. Church attendance would be at its highest for the Easter service, the most important service of the year.[4] Candles would be re-lit and sweet-smelling incense and herbs liberally used. This was a popular time for baptisms, signifying, as it did, a time of renewal and re-birth. After the religious rituals were completed, the celebrations could begin. A full week's holiday traditionally followed medieval Easter. These celebrations featured three important medieval Easter traditions: pace eggs, Morris dances, and mystery plays.[5]

Pace eggs took their name from the common European name for the Easter period (variations on *Pasche*). Pace eggs were hardboiled eggs, lavishly decorated with paints and dyes. Edward I had 450 of these eggs ordered for his Easter festivities on one occasion. Painted eggs were an innovation that dates all the way back to the classical world. Eastern Christians may have originally adopted them from the Persian festival of Nowruz, held at around the same time of year. The Nowruz egg reflected the Zoroastrian belief that the spring equinox marked the time of year when the world was first created. Their popularity in Western Christendom was greatly heightened by the fact that eggs were prohibited during Lent. For poor people, who could rarely afford meat, eggs were a real treat. As a result, being deprived of eggs for six weeks prior to Easter was a big deal. The thought of an Easter egg would have been something to really look forward to.

The Morris dance was a medieval innovation; however, it began life as a dance popular with the aristocracy. As such, you'd be more likely to see it performed at court than on village greens. In its original form, it consisted of a troupe of colourfully dressed, bell-bedecked, male dancers, an attendant fool and one (and occasionally more than one) ladies. The dance was based around the idea of the troupe of dancing men attempting to court the lady. The 'joke' being that she spurned their advances in favour of the fool. Later, the part of the 'lady' would be played by men in drag or dropped entirely. However, the original Morris dance required the participation of women. What began life as a fashionable courtly entertainment was eventually adopted as a folk dance during the Early Modern period.[6]

A third popular entertainment was provided in the form of mystery plays. These would be of the same sort you might see at the York Pageant at Corpus Christi. Given the time of year, it is quite likely that many of these would have featured Easter themed stories.

Easter Monday was a time for fairs and for indulging in sports such as archery and wrestling or, if you were from the ruling elite, jousting and hunting. The British weather improved at this time of year, making it easier for large outdoor gatherings to occur. It might well represent the first good opportunity, since wintertime, for common folk to gather in large numbers to share stories and listen to ballads.

Many manorial lords traditionally held a feast for their entire household at this time of year. If you were a 'good' lord, you would feel duty bound to ensure that even the humblest of your servants was well fed at your banquet table. Feasts could provide an ideal opportunity for such households to hear minstrels play, listen to ballads, and share stories. Perhaps, if your lord was Sir John Paston, he might organise a Robin Hood play for you.

The holiday period finally came to an end after Hocktide. Hocktide spanned the Monday and Tuesday in the week after the holiday week. These two days were still holidays and were given over to 'misrule'. During this time gangs of young women would 'kidnap' young men or, more rarely, a gang of young men would kidnap a local girl. The abducted person would then be held in 'hock' for ransom. The ransom money could be used for a charitable purpose but was often used to buy ale. It was a practice much frowned upon by the church but very popular with the people. In addition to the fact that money raised was often spent on frivolity and merry making, the practice clearly facilitated lascivious behaviour.[7]

Shortly after the easter festivities (and occasionally overlapping them), was Saint George's Day, on 23 April. His popularity reached new heights during the period of the Hundred Years' War, where he was increasingly viewed as the patron of the common soldier. His feast day would have been a good time on which to see a play featuring the saint. During the late fourteenth and early fifteenth centuries, a significant number of religious guilds dedicated themselves to organising annual 'ridings' of Saint George. These 'ridings' took the form of a street procession in honour of the saint. The first recorded riding occurred in Norwich in 1420.[8] As time went by, these events became more elaborate and spectacular. Such parades would feature someone playing the role of Saint George himself but might also feature Saint Margaret (another famous dragon slayer). They were typically accompanied by an entourage of colourfully dressed attendants and some ridings even featured model dragons fashioned from timber and canvas.

Most medieval ritual festivities up to this point in the year had a strong Christian dimension. This changes when we come to the celebrations associated with May Day, a day that had no specific Christian association at all.

An early medieval Irish document known as *Sanas Chromaic*, written in around 900 AD, provides us with the earliest reference to 'Beltane'. This was the ancient pagan Celtic celebration of the start of summer, held on 1 May. This document tells us that Beltane literally meant 'lucky fire', a possible reflection of an old druidic ritual that gave it its name. It is postulated that on 1 May, druids would light two fires and that cattle would be ritually driven between them. The druids would recite incantations to protect the cattle from disease and predation prior to their being put out to pasture.[9]

Evidence of these old fire rituals (minus the druids) were observed in Ireland right up to the nineteenth century. Evidence from the sixteenth and eighteenth centuries shows observance in parts of Scotland and they were also practiced in Cumbria up until the late eighteenth century, in south-west England up to a similar time, and in Wales until the nineteenth.[10] All these areas represent parts of the British Isles that retained their Celtic culture the longest. Common themes can be seen running through these rituals. They often centred upon blessing livestock as they were put out to pasture on 1 May. They all involved fire (often but not necessarily two fires). Lastly, they sometimes involved scapegoating, where one of the young men present was selected by lot to be pelted with eggs or made to jump over the fire.[11]

However, these rituals, though undeniably ancient, may not have originally been Celtic. It is possible they reflect a tradition from an even older culture. Evidence of these rituals can be found all over Europe where pastoral farming is common, many areas of which have no historic connection to the Celts. The connection lies with the needs and concerns of pastoral farmers, almost regardless of culture.

Such observances are not in evidence elsewhere in England. Instead, 'the May' was 'brought in' with flowers and garlands. Sometimes this might have involved a procession. Sometimes a structure would be erected on which garlands and fresh foliage collected from woods and meadows could be displayed. In medieval times, a ritual visit to a wood or meadow to collect flowers and foliage appears to have been a key feature of the celebration.

May Day is described by Malory in book nineteen of *Le Morte D'Arthur*. The first chapter, he tells us, how Queen Guinevere 'rode on Maying'. The queen and her court, clad in green, ride out into the woods and fields and, once there, they 'were bedashed with herbs, mosses and flowers, in the best manner and the freshest'.[12]

The earliest references to maypoles are late-medieval. During the period 1350–1400, they became a firmly established feature of 'Maying'. Originally, these poles appear to have simply been used to hang May garlands from and they may also have been decorated with ribbons. However, as far as we know, the famous ribbon dances were a post-medieval practice. People danced around the poles but not with ribbons. Sometimes young women were elected as Queens of the May (occasionally a young man might be elected king) and hold a mock summer court.

If you were to see a May Day celebration today, you might catch sight of a dancer covered in a framework decked out with foliage. This is the famous Jack-in-the-Green. Some have suggested this figure is a vestige left over from ancient pagan fertility rites. However, the Jack-in-the-Green does not enjoy such an ancient heritage and certainly was never part of the medieval tradition. Sadly, Jack did not feature in May celebrations until the seventeenth century.[13]

The practice of using fresh summer foliage to celebrate the May nevertheless appears to have been at the core of these early summer rituals. The practice is particularly strong in areas of arable farming, where crops, rather than livestock, are the staple produce. So, as with the Beltane fires, these rituals connect with the land and, in this case, specifically with the need for crop fertility.

This raises the question, if these rituals (or variants thereof) are pre-Celtic, how old can they be? Delving back into pre-history there is no easy way to tell. However, since they are linked to the needs and fears of an agricultural society, they cannot pre-date the adoption of farming. The transformation of Europe to an farming society was largely complete by 4000 BC.[14] It is possible that these ancient May traditions date back this far, well before the emergence of the Celts.

May Day marked the start of summer. By this time of year, the English climate was pleasant enough to accommodate large outdoor gatherings. The summer, therefore, was the primary time of year when common folk could gather, celebrate communal traditions, and share folk stories.

The medieval calendar features three major religious dates. Aside from Easter and Christmas, the third key date is Pentecost (or Whit Sunday). Pentecost falls on the seventh Sunday after Easter. Aside from Easter and Christmas, Pentecost in the Middle Ages was the most highly attended religious service of the year.[15] It featured a religious procession and a service in celebration of the day on which the disciples received the Holy Spirit.

May Day and Pentecost would herald the start of the season of summer festivities, held at different times by different communities over the course of the season. These were variously known as summer games, summer ales, summer plays, or feasts (which collectively provide a good flavour of the activities they encompassed).

As with May Day itself, a 'Summer Queen' (and perhaps a Summer King) might be elected to preside. Such a practice possibly related to the 'King and Queen plays' that so horrified the clergy. These games certainly had a reputation for drunkenness and licentiousness. As the disapproving Robert Brunne wrote in 1303:

> Dances, cards, summer games,
> Of many such come many shames.[16]

It was at such events that you might see a Robin Hood play. Alternatively, you might participate in a local archery or wrestling contest, such as those described in the Robin Hood ballads.

The next significant summer Christian festival was Corpus Christi, held sixty days after Easter (which placed it anytime between late May and mid-summer). Although it had its roots in the thirteenth century, it was only formally instituted by the church in 1317. Its aim was to celebrate the potency of the Eucharist. To begin with, communities began celebrating it with parades in which the symbolism of the Eucharist featured prominently. However, by the mid-fourteenth century, this had evolved into the grand spectacle of the pageant plays, such as the ones at York.[17]

A medieval mid-summer was the occasion of a traditional fire festival. This appears to have consisted of people setting a wheel alight and rolling it down a hill, lighting a bonfire, and/or organising torchlit processions. The official religious occasion was Saint John's feast day (as in John the Baptist). But one might well ask, what does John the Baptist, a man who baptised people with water, have to do with fire?

Our thirteenth-century friend Jacobus de Voragine sought to explain the connection by noting that 'John was a burning and a shining torch'.[18] However, de Voragine also recorded a connection to earlier pagan rituals. He tells us that in pagan times people burnt animal bones on bonfires at midsummer to ward off dragons and the pestilence brought by their poisonous breath. More specifically, the smoke from such fires were supposed to drive away these monsters. This may seem like bizarre superstition but in fact in makes a lot of sense. Rotting animal bones are a potential health hazard. Burning them, therefore, would indeed have served to ward off pestilence. De Voragine goes on to provide us with a description of the mid-summer bonfire rituals of his day (around 1260): 'Lighted torches are also carried around this bonfire...and a wheel is spun because the sun then begins to lower its cycle.'[19]

The corporation of London issued instructions for watchmen to be on the lookout for 'disorder' on mid-summer night in 1378, indicating the celebrations could be rowdy (not to mention a fire hazard). There was an attempt to bring the occasion under closer civic control at this time by organising a procession led by civic dignitaries. Participants were instructed to make sure they carried their fires in cressets (pails hung from poles).[20] Heaven only knows what kind of chaos this missive was designed to reign in!

The late summer and early autumn represented a critical time in the agricultural calendar. The first day of the harvest time (at the start of August) was known as Lammas Day and was marked with a ritual dating back to Anglo-Saxon times. A loaf of bread was baked using the first grains harvested and blessed in the local church. The aim, of course, was to seek God's blessing on the harvest to come.

The harvest period itself was the busiest and most labour-intensive time of year. Very little free time was available until it had been successfully brought in. Much of the hard work would have occurred throughout the month of August. Often, entire families would spend every daylight hour toiling in the fields. Only once crops were successfully gathered in would people have time to relax and celebrate with a hearty meal and a few drinks.

As the year moved into the autumn, we encounter medieval Allhallowtide at the end of October. The time we now call Halloween.

Halloween as we know it today is a mix of the Irish pagan festival of Samhain and the Christian observance of Allhallowtide. However, the fact that the two fall at the same time of year is purely an accident of history. Samhain was a key festival for the Irish Celts. It marked the turning of the year, the time when life was dying off and winter fast approaching. It was a time for feasting and coming together, it was also a chance to share stories around a fire, and for discussing and resolving issues within the local community. It may have been a pagan Irish New Year's celebration, although we cannot be certain of this. The early Irish tale of *The Wasting Sickness of Cú Chulaind* tells us that the men of Ulster came together for a seven-day period centred on Samhain for meetings, games, amusements, and feasting. The reason for the festival, according to this early source 'was to give every warrior the opportunity to boast of his valour and exhibit his triumphs'.[21]

There is some debate as to whether, and to what extent, ritual bonfires may have been a feature of Samhain. Now, since Samhain featured feasting, one might expect a bonfire to be present (if for no other reason than to use for cooking and warmth in the autumn). There is patchy evidence for bonfire traditions at this time of year in parts of Celtic Britain (in parts of Ireland,

Wales, Scotland, and the Isle of Man). However, it was far from widespread enough to be certain that it was originally a central feature of this festival or that it necessarily held any ritual significance.[22]

There is some evidence to suggest Samhain had some supernatural associations in parts of the Celtic world. Folklorists have recorded that some fires were used for divination with stones, and some were said to keep away fairy folk or ward off some fearful spirit. However, such beliefs are recorded in post-medieval times. Do they date back to earlier times? We cannot be sure.

Unfortunately, there is limited evidence to suggest that Samhain held any pagan religious significance. For all we know, this could have been a purely secular affair. In medieval Wales, although the date was marked in the calendar, it does not appear to have held any pagan religious or mythological significance. And a careful study of the Coligny Calendar indicates that the Celtic Gauls celebrated May Day with a feast but not Samhain. For the Gauls, May, not November, appears more likely to have marked their New Year.[23] As the folklorist Ronald Hutton observed, there is nothing in any medieval record to suggest that Samhain was ever a major pan-Celtic festival. Indeed, even where it was celebrated, there is no firm evidence of associated religious ceremonies.[24]

Any associations that Samhain had with supernatural forces (and it appears to have had some) were reinforced and shaped by medieval Christianity. Indeed, Halloween became associated with ghosts and spirits because of Christian rather than pagan belief. To fully understand the origins of Halloween as we know it today, it is to medieval Christian belief to which we must turn.

All-Saints Day was originally inaugurated to celebrate all the minor saints who did not have a dedicated feast day in the Christian calendar. The problem was that there were more saints than days in the year, making it impossible to celebrate them all individually. Initially, the church set the date for an All-Saints Day in mid-May. It was moved to 1 November, by Gregory III in 844. He did this for no other reason than to align it with the day on which he planned to consecrate a new chapel in Saint Peter's. Gregory himself was a Syrian who almost certainly knew nothing of any Celtic traditions, let alone Samhain.

Later in the Middle Ages, a three-day observance called Allhallowtide evolved around All-Saints Day. This began on All-Hallows Eve (31 October) with an evening mass and a vigil for the saints. All-Hallows itself was set aside as a day of feasting and celebration. Then, in the tenth century a French Benedictine abbot added All Souls Day (2 November). This was a day set aside to pray for the souls of the departed; to ease their suffering in purgatory and speed their passing into heaven. *The Golden Legend* tells us that the abbot was inspired to inaugurate All Souls Day because he had learnt:

> that voices and howls of demons had been heard near a volcano in Sicily, and that the souls of the dead were being snatched from the demons' grasp by the power of alms and prayer.[25]

By the fourteenth century, All Souls had become a well-established fixture of Allhallowtide. It made perfect sense, therefore, for the spirits of the dead to contact the living prior to All Souls Day to petition their aid. It is this element of Allhallows that created a link between Halloween and ghosts.

Later (long after medieval times), the Samhain and Allhallows traditions would blend. It was only by sheer chance, that they happened to fall at the same time of year. However, it is from the Christian, rather than the pagan, festival that the association with ghosts derives. We only need look at the Mexican Day of the Dead, to see how the All-Souls tradition inspired a festival of ghosts, even in the absence of any Irish connection.

Christmas, aside from Easter, represented the most important celebration in the Christian calendar. However, if you read the Bible, you'll quickly realise that we are not told when exactly Jesus was born. The 25 December was picked during Roman times to align with several Roman pagan festivals. The Romans already celebrated Saturnalia, which began on 17 December and ran for up to seven days. They also celebrated a sun festival on 25 December. And then, of course, there was the Roman new year on 1 January. Since this time of year was widely regarded as a holiday period across the Roman Empire, it made sense to hold a mass to celebrate the birth of Christ at this time. In any agricultural society this period represents a good time of year for a holiday. The hours of daylight available for outdoor work are at their most limited. It is also a time of year when the amount of work required is minimal.

By the high Middle Ages, preparation for Christmas began with the period of Advent. Advent began with a Sunday church service to mark the occasion. This was followed by a four-week period of fasting and penitence in the run up to Christmas. Christmas Eve would be subject to a particularly restrictive fast; no meat, eggs or cheese were permitted.

Christmas Day featured no fewer than three masses. After these were performed, a chorister would sing the genealogy of Christ from Saint Matthew's gospel from the church rood loft. The rood loft, and the church more generally, would be decorated with candles and tapers. Once the serious religious observances were done with, the festivities could commence – the famous twelve days of Christmas, running until the epiphany on 6 January.

Each of the days of this period were eventually marked by a different Christian festival. The twenty-sixth became the feast of Saint Stephen, the first Christian martyr. The twenty-seventh was set aside for Saint John the Evangelist, and the twenty-eighth marked the day of the Holy Innocents (the day on which the infants slaughtered on Herod's orders were commemorated). In England, the twenty-ninth was set aside for Saint Thomas Becket. The thirtieth, depending on the year, was marked by a feast of the Holy Family.

Most of these days were celebrated with feasting. The local lord would lay on feasts and entertainments for his tenants. A more lavish and generous feast would enhance the lord's prestige and reputation. A more meagre affair would be taken by the lord's peers as a sign of poverty and reduced status. Minstrels would be kept busy at this time of year, providing a good opportunity for people to hear ballads and stories. The Christmas toast, with wassail bowls, reached a height of fashion by the fourteenth century. At this time, particularly elaborate and expensive examples of wassail bowls were in vogue.[26]

The carol was originally a ring dance accompanying a song. It would be performed by a ring of singers, dancing whilst holding hands. For most of the Middle Ages carolling had no direct religious association. A carol could just as easily have a bawdy lyric as convey any religious sentiment.[27] From the 1300s onwards, more religious themed carols start appearing. By the 1500s, the singing was separated from the dance and Christmas carolling began taking on an increasingly religious character.

For a long time, present gifting was more closely linked with 1st January than Christmas. However, during the fifteenth century, the gifting of Christmas presents started becoming popular. There was no Santa in medieval times and the image of Santa Claus as we know him today, evolved after the Middle Ages. Only in the late fifteenth century do we see the very earliest signs of the concept of a Father Christmas beginning to take shape. At this time he was simply known as 'Sir Christmas' and associated with general seasonal good cheer rather than gift giving.

Entertainment formed an important part of medieval Christmas festivities. This was a time of year for people to indulge in games and for minstrels, jesters, acrobats, and players of all kinds to ply their trade. The late-medieval Christmas also featured something known as 'Hognel time'. This lasted into January and was undertaken by Hogglers. We do not know what this involved, except that the Hogglers raised money for their parish funds.[28]

This was also a good time of year for 'disguisings', a practice that became popularly known as mumming. Over the Christmas period, mummers might sing songs, make speeches, organise games, or even put on plays. They could (and often did) elicit money in exchange for their performance. Sometimes this could be raised for a genuinely good cause but often it was just a way for poor folk to make some coin. The practice had its dubious side since criminals sometimes used mumming as a cover for illegal activity. In some towns mumming was banned for this very reason.

At Christmas 1347, Edward III was entertained by a large troupe of over 80 mummers. These people wore a selection of impressive masks, some simply wore masks of men or women, but some came as angels, dragons, peacocks, or swans.

These days we might associate hobby horses with summer dances and May Day. However, in the late Middle Ages, hobby horses were more commonly associated with Christmas festivities. The earliest reference to hobby horses is from the latter part of the fourteenth century, where they are described as being a relatively 'recent' English innovation. This makes sense since the word itself is thought to be fourteenth-century in origin – 'hobby' being a term used for a small horse.[29] Medieval hobby horses often featured in dances and mummer's plays. It is likely that they were originally conceived to represent knight's horses in mock jousts.

Misrule, featuring pranks and tomfoolery, was very much associated with medieval Christmas. Hijinks of this kind were especially common on 1 January, so much so that it became known as the 'Feast of Fools'. The worst offenders were the junior clergy. Silly pranks, irreverent gesticulations, mudslinging, and even mock sermons in praise of demons were all part of the fun.

Exeter Cathedral was plagued by silly behaviour during the 1320s when one stuffy senior cleric complained of 'disorderly laughter and illicit mirth'.[30] In 1390, the archbishop of Canterbury visited Lincoln Cathedral and was most outraged at what he found. Apparently, some of the junior priests decided it would be a hoot to dress up as members of the laity and interrupt the service with rude songs and silly games. There was a clampdown on misrule, especially amongst the junior clergy, during the fifteenth century. However, it was never entirely stamped out and clearly remains part of our modern Christmas revelries.

Once the twelve days of Christmas were done with, the first significant communal ritual of the medieval agricultural year was speeding the plough. Early January was time for rural communities to begin ploughing the land, ready for the new growing season. It was a significant event in a society that was so dependent on a good harvest.

The first day's ploughing was often marked by medieval folk ritual. In late thirteenth-century Nottinghamshire, there are records of a plough race being held every 7 January. In the early fifteenth century, there are records of a ritual in which a plough was led around a fire, prior to ploughing the first furrow of the new year. These rituals were eventually focused on 'Plough Monday', typically the first Monday after twelfth night. And so, with the first furrow ploughed, a new agricultural year began.

Woodwose, Giants, and Beast-men of the Wild

If you were fortunate enough to have been entertained by a mummers' play at Christmas, you would have, no doubt, witnessed a variety of different disguises. One character you might have seen would have been a naked, hairy, beast-man, frantically running about with foliage in his hair. This character is a familiar sight in the Middle Ages; he is a wild man of the woods, otherwise known as the woodwose. He frequently appears in illustrations, carvings, mummers' plays and literature. But who were these mysterious wild men?

The woodwose came to be commonly presented as a naked man, covered in a thick coat of black or grey hair. Usually only his knees and elbows were hairless, or, in the case of wild women, her breasts might also be hairless. These creatures were half-man, half-beast; neither entirely human nor, strictly speaking, animal. They dwelt only in remote, wild places, deep in the heart of the woods or roaming remote moorlands. They made their homes in caves or perhaps in crude burrows beneath the roots of trees. They knew nothing of civilisation, living only in the wilderness, in places normally considered unfit for human habitation.[1]

The idea of beast-men was not new to medieval times, of course. Entities such as centaurs and satyrs, both literally half-beasts, date all the way back to classical antiquity. The book of Daniel tells us that the Babylonian King Nebuchadnezzar was driven mad by God as punishment for his arrogance. As a result of his insanity, Nebuchadnezzar was forced to live as a savage wild man amongst the beasts. The medieval woodwose borrows much from these earlier examples. However, he nevertheless stands out as a distinctively medieval mythical concept.

Whilst the woodwose had the form of a man (aside from his hirsute appearance), in many respects, he was a primitive beast. He was often presented as lacking anything resembling human intelligence, relying instead on feral, animal instinct. He was usually portrayed as being unable to speak, only capable of grunts and growls like a wild animal. He was utterly ignorant of civilised ways; unable to build anything more sophisticated than a crude hovel, largely ignorant of clothing and unable to make any but the most rudimentary tools. Perhaps most important of all, he was ignorant of God. It was not that he did not believe in God or that he believed in some pagan God. The fact was he was utterly ignorant of God just like any other wild beast.

In all respects he was a savage. If he used weapons at all, it was rarely anything more than a crude club. However, no one doubted that he was incredibly strong. What he lacked in intelligence and artifice he made up for in sheer brute strength and savage ferocity. In many ways, he was no different to a wild boar or a bear. He was just another wild animal of the forest. Indeed, in one medieval illustration woodwose are shown in a feral mob, accompanied by raging wild boars, attacking a band of knights.[2]

The savagery and ignorance of the woodwose could be taken as a sign of a form of madness. In medieval eyes, madness typically had three causes. You could be sent mad by God to test your faith. Or perhaps, like Nebuchadnezzar, you had sinned and were driven mad as a punishment from God. If your sins were not too grave, the madness would pass after a time. If, however, your sins were so grave as to be unforgivable, you might remain permanently deranged. The woodwose was a man, but clearly a man who had lost his wits, compelling him to live as a wild beast. And, since he could not know God, his damnation seemed assured.

Certainly, the woodwose was often depicted as a slave to his animal instincts. Like a wild boar he would attack ferociously if startled. Driven by animal lust, if he saw a fair maid, he might drag her off into the forest to have his way with her. There were even stories of woodwose abducting children to raise as their own in the wild. In his bestial, feral state, he might have even resorted to cannibalism. He was, in effect, a bogeyman to be feared; a monster to scare children at summer games.

In many ways, the wild woodwose displayed many of the traits associated with giants and ogres in the Middle Ages. Brutish and savage, ignorant of God and the ways of civilised Christendom. The monstrous Grendel, from the story of Beowulf, encapsulated many of these traits. Brutish, savage, and so strong and violent that he would rip men apart with his bare hands. Grendel is monstrous in no small part because he was a descendant of the Biblical Cain, the first murderer. His witless savagery was the product of inherited sin of the darkest kind. This was how many viewed the woodwose. He was a witless beast man, doomed never to know God and to lead a wretched existence as a savage beast. The woodwose was, in almost every respect, the epitome of everything a refined medieval man feared becoming. A man divorced from both civilised society and from God. In that sense, the woodwose recalled how many saw the ancient pagan world – a world of savagery, wilderness, and godlessness.

The woodwose was thought to dwell in remote locations, far from the villages and towns of men. In the tale of *Sir Gawain and the Green Knight*, it is in the wilderness, whilst searching for the Green Chapel, that Gawain encounters wild beasts. These include dragons, wolves, bears, boars, ogres, and wild men.[3] Of course, the 'wilderness' is a dangerous, godless place. When Gawain finally locates the Green Chapel, he instinctively feels it is an evil place, a place where diabolic rituals are performed. These feelings arise from the fact that the chapel is an old pagan barrow, located in the wild. This is not to say that nature and wild places were always represented negatively in medieval times. They were sometimes even celebrated, as they are when Malory tells us of Guinevere seeking flowers from the woods to bring in the May. However, the natural world was also seen as dangerous. Dangerous in so far as it is wild and untamed; hence potentially violent and brutal. Dangerous, also, in so far as it is associated with ancient pagan superstitions. Both such dangers are clearly implied in the medieval depiction of the woodwose.

Culturally, the woodwose reached the height of his popularly in literature and art from the fourteenth to the sixteenth century. Thereafter, the old medieval bogeyman gradually fades from history. In the early modern world, many of the medieval concepts underpinning the idea of the woodwose were questioned. And, as man explored his world, so the regions of true wilderness diminished. Exotic places such as India, once thought to have been home to many wild men, became increasingly familiar. As the world was explored, no hairy wild men were found and so it was that the woodwose faded from cultural relevance. He was doomed to disappear along with the old medieval world he'd inhabited.

Like the woodwose, giants were frequently viewed as violent and savage creatures, ignorant of God. Indeed, earlier in the Middle Ages, woodwose were sometimes depicted as a type of giant. It was only later that representations of them shrink down to human proportions. Chrétien depicts a giant herdsman in his tale of Yvain who might be regarded as something of a hybrid between giant and woodwose. He is presented as a large primitive man, wielding a club, and dressed in ox-hides. When he stands upon a stump, we are told he is fully 17 feet tall. His ugliness and brutishness make the knight who encounters him (Sir Calogrenant) suspect that he may not even know how to speak. However, it transpires that the herdsman can speak. He is clearly ignorant of civilised ways and clearly a creature of nature, however. He even claims to act as herdsman to the wild animals of the forest.[4] This mysterious herdsman directs the knight to a fountain that has the power to unleash a great storm. To test himself the knight (rather foolishly) activates this magic against the advice of the herdsman. Sure enough a violent tempest is unleashed.

In Chrétien's *Yvain*, the giant herdsman and the fountain both represent powerful natural forces. Here, they are not evil as such, but they are clearly powerful, and both exist outside of the structured boundaries of the civilised world. They are forces of nature, powerful and perhaps dangerous, indifferent to chivalrous society and order.

However, giants, unlike the woodwose, were not necessarily always regarded as stupid, mindless beasts. In the Norse stories, and likely also in Anglo-Saxon, giants were portrayed as possessing an intelligence and society not too dissimilar from Gods or men. They made weapons, lived in their own houses and halls, sometimes accumulated great wealth, and even had their own kings. They were, nevertheless, regarded as dangerous and, ultimately, as enemies of the gods.

But, at the other extreme, giants could be depicted as crude, savage, brutes. Chrétien's herdsman may be primitive and uncultured, but he is ultimately presented as a largely benign creature of nature. A far more savage example can be found in Geoffrey of Monmouth's *History of the Kings of Britain*, in the form of the giant of Mont-Saint-Michel. This creature, Geoffrey tells us, emerged from somewhere in Spain. Driven by base lust, he kidnaps the niece of a duke and takes refuge on the summit of Mont-Saint-Michel. Arthur and his knights seek to stage a rescue and slay the giant, knowing that other knights tried and failed, meeting a grisly fate. Those who were not slain outright were taken captive and eaten alive.

When the giant is first encountered, he is described in the most lurid terms. We are left in no doubt that this giant is an inhumane monster rather than simply a large, powerful, man: 'His face was smeared with the clotted blood of a number of pigs at which he had been gnawing.'[5] When he fights, he wields a crude club, so large that even two men could not lift it. Arthur eventually succeeds in killing the monster after a tough fight. However, even the great Arthur is forced to concede that he had not fought so fierce and strong a foe for a very long time.

Another giant mentioned in Geoffrey's history is named Gogmagog. Gog and Magog are named in the book of Revelation as allies of Satan who must be vanquished at the end of days. The association of this biblical reference with a giant clearly shows that this monster represented diabolical forces. Gogmagog is not simply ignorant of God but openly in league with Satan. The medieval giant is often savage, brutish, and cannibalistic; a warning as to what life divorced from God and Christendom represented in the medieval mind.

The famous phrase 'Fee-fi-fo-fum' would later be placed in the mouths of giants seeking the blood of Englishmen. It has become a famous refrain, associated with the desire of giants to feast on human flesh. It recalls the horrific appetites of the Mont-Saint-Michel giant and might well have been known during the Middle Ages. However, the earliest written record of this phrase is from the late sixteenth century. Although it had already been in use for some time by this date, it is impossible to trace it back any further.

Other types of wild, beast-man hybrids that held a place in the medieval consciousness were inherited from the classical world. These creatures were known of through old classical tales, as well as appearing in medieval bestiaries and as illustrations in other medieval manuscripts. One such creature was the centaur, whose history dates to early classical antiquity.

The medieval world took its lead from the classics when it came to portraying the centaur. Like the woodwose or the giant, these creatures were very much 'of the wild' rather than creatures of civilisation. The typical centaur was seen as drunken, promiscuous, and savage and shunned permanent settlements in favour of more remote, wilder environments. The Parthenon frieze shows centaurs infamously gatecrashing a royal wedding feast to kidnap the female guests to have their wicked ways with them. Similarly, Heracles had to rescue his wife from the clutches of the lustful centaur, Nessos.[6]

However, whilst centaurs were generally depicted as lustful savages, not all were necessarily so crude. The immortal Chiron, who became the tutor of Achilles, was more cultured and refined. He was skilled in the use of a bow, unlike other more primitive centaurs. He was also famed for his skill in the use of healing herbs. When he was fatally wounded, Chiron experienced an apotheosis, becoming the constellation of Sagittarius. He appears in some medieval manuscripts, either with his bow or bearing his healing herbs. Chiron, as the offspring of a Titan, is, however, an exceptional centaur.[7]

In the medieval tale of *Saint Paul the Hermit*, Paul flees from civilisation to take refuge in the remote wilderness. There, he exists on a diet of bread sent to him by God, born by wild creatures. To find him, Saint Anthony must seek directions from such wild creatures as a centaur and a satyr.[8]

Rather like the centaur, the satyr was a beast from classical antiquity. With the upper body of men and the lower body of goats, these creatures also had a reputation for drunkenness and lustful excess and were, too, inhabitants of the wild and remote places of the world. In *The Golden Legend* we are informed that in ancient times pagans used to mistakenly believe that satyrs were forest gods.[9] However, although they were closely associated with such entities as Dionysus (the Greek god of wine and revelry), they were not actually regarded as gods. It was an easy mistake to make, since the Greek God Pan, who was the god of forests and wild places, had an appearance much like a satyr.

We might ask to what extent medieval people believed such creatures were real, or whether they were regarded as purely mythological. Such a question is difficult to answer. Some no doubt regarded most such beasts as largely mythical, others regarded at least some of them as real. During the Middle Ages, books known as 'bestiaries' became very popular. These books might best be described as encyclopaedias of the animal kingdom. They typically feature a series of short entries for each animal, noting interesting facts relating to their physical appearance, behaviour, and habitat. Sometimes they might even feature short anecdotes and famous myths. These bestiaries often contain a mix of real and mythical creatures within the same volume, showing no real distinction between the two.

Of course, people in medieval England would never have seen satyrs, centaurs, or woodwose. But, then again, very few (if any) of them would have ever seen an elephant or a giraffe. It would have been easy enough to believe that such creatures did exist in the more remote places of the world, in the depths of the woods or in an empty wilderness. The medieval world had far more wild and unexplored places in which such creatures might be hiding. The limitations of medieval knowledge made the existence of such creatures a possibility that could not easily be dismissed.

Beast-men and primitive giants existed in the wilderness, in a world of nature that sat outside the ordered harmony of medieval society. They also clearly sat outside the communion of Holy Mother Church. This could result in such entities being viewed in a variety of ways. On the one hand, the natural world and the wilderness were undeniably God's creation. Since these creatures were beasts of a sort, they were like the other wild beasts in the world. In this sense, they were potentially no different from wild boars, bears, or wolves. Dangerous and savage but nevertheless part of God's creation. Saints like Paul the Hermit sought refuge in the wilderness to escape the corruption and temptations of urban communities. They preferred the company of wild beasts to the company of men and were clearly sustained and supported by God in this choice.

In this context, wild creatures such as the centaur or woodwose, though wild and beastlike, at least had the merit of being liberated from the worldly corruption of urban life. On the other hand, they had no knowledge of God or civilisation. Like the wild beasts who shared their wilderness domain, they were slaves to their lusts and savage urges. This made them dangerous and unpredictable but not necessarily evil.

At their most extreme, such creatures carried a dark association with ancient paganism. Wild, savage, brutal, and potentially either deceived by Satan or even openly in league with Satan. The savage Grendel and the terrifying Gogmagog are both overtly linked with unforgivable sin and Satan. And the cannibalism of the woodwose and man-eating habits of giants testifies to the horrific savagery to which such creatures could descend. At best, then, such creatures were potentially dangerous and unpredictable, like a wild boar. At their worst, they could become nothing less than a diabolic manifestation of the evils of ancient paganism.

The Perilous Fairy

Fairy folk, like the beast-men of the wilds, had a dangerous reputation in the Middle Ages. However, their nature was distinctly supernatural. Not only were they magical in make-up, they also inhabited an enchanted 'otherworld' only partially connected to our world. They were beings who appeared to draw their power from wild and mysterious forces. And, whether malign or benevolent, they had their roots in the ancient pagan world. If we attempt to define how, exactly, medieval society regarded fairies we quickly encounter a complex and bewildering picture. In some ways, defining who the fairy folk were and their place in medieval cosmology can prove as enigmatic and elusive as one of their enchantments.

The word 'fairy' or 'fay' came to be applied to otherworldly beings whose identity evolved from a variety of different pagan traditions. These different traditions had both similarities and differences in the ways in which they chose to depict fairies. Part of our difficulty in understanding the history of them lies in the fact that they cannot be pinned down to any one specific pagan folk tradition. We cannot say fairies were originally Irish, or even Celtic. Neither can we locate their origins specifically in Norse or Ango-Saxon tradition, nor are they creatures of the classical world. Indeed, their medieval identity was shaped by all these traditions, not by any one alone.

From the classical world, medieval culture inherited stories of such creatures as nymphs and dryads. They were nature spirits. Whilst they might be considered minor divinities, they were not gods of the same order as the Olympians. They held supernatural powers and were blessed with considerable longevity but were not truly immortal. Neither were they worshipped by name in the same way as a true god like Zeus or Athena. Instead, if they were honoured at all, they were typically venerated collectively at a shrine. These entities dwelt in the natural world rather than on Mount Olympus. They inhabited the rivers and woodlands that reflected their supernatural powers.

Norse and Anglo-Saxon mythology spoke of elves, another supernatural race. Norse mythology categorises them into elves of light and elves of the dark.

Some dwelt high in the heavens in a realm of great beauty, others in a dark, cold, underworld. Both were capable of magic and of fashioning marvellous items. They could be malevolent and dangerous and some early medieval medical books, from the Anglo-Saxon period, identify elves as a source of disease.[1] The Saxons believed elves were able to cause maladies through enchantments, hauntings, possessions, or with 'shot' (a kind of supernatural dart or spear) and Saxon medical manuals speak of certain physical or psychological maladies as 'elf-shot'. The recommended remedy for such maladies often took the form of a potion and a spell. One remedy was a salve, which would be applied if one happened to be plagued with elves or other night spirts.[2] The kind of maladies caused by elves could also be caused by evil witches and other malign spirits. These entities were, therefore, perceived to be causing harm in much the same way (and hence the same remedy was often deemed appropriate).

The otherworldly realm of Annwfn from pagan British mythology was a place that mortals could visit. It was possible to cross the boundary between the material world and Annwfn, sometimes accidentally. You could sail there by ship or, perhaps, wander unwittingly into Annwfn whilst walking deep in the forest. The beings who lived there held supernatural powers such as shapeshifting and enchantment. Their magic was to be feared. Their otherworld was like the mortal world but different. Alike in so far as its people had a king and lived in a society not unlike the mortal world. They even often appeared in a form much like mortal men and women. Different in so far as these were clearly a race of supernatural entities, capable of shapeshifting and magical enchantments. And their king could command terrifying forces if you were foolish enough to offend him.

The Tuatha Dé Danann of Irish mythology were similar to the denizens of Brittonic Annwfn. They, too, often appeared in human forms. They, too, held supernatural powers and the ability to shapeshift. It is possible, but by no means certain, that some of these entities might even have been regarded as deities by the pagan Irish. Certainly, there is no denying the considerable powers wielded by some of their number, such as the Morrigan. They also dwelt in an otherworld that is set apart from the world of men. However, their otherworld was concealed underground, hidden beneath ancient barrows.

These diverse depictions of supernatural beings, originally from different traditions, merged in a cultural melting pot. It was within this context that the medieval concept of the fairy was forged. However, none of these creatures sat easily with the pervading Christian cosmology of the time. They were set apart from the mundane world whilst also being able to somehow interact with it. That said, they certainly weren't residents of heaven or hell, or even purgatory. They were associated with the old superstitions of the pagan world, so they were clearly not creatures of God. Equally, however, they were not wholly or obviously of creatures of Satan. Such an identity rendered them enigmatic, even intriguing, but clearly problematic and potentially perilous. As mentioned, in early medieval England, such entities appear to have been commonly referred to as 'elves', following old Anglo-Saxon and Norse traditions. However, Celtic and classical ideas were also present.

To make matters even less clear, many medieval stories about these mysterious entities would not even attempt to name or classify them. The word 'fairy' was of Old French origin and only began to spread to the British Isles in the high Middle Ages. By the late Middle Ages, it had become a widely used term. Medieval writers also used the word 'fay', derived from the same root. Whilst these terms could be applied to fairy creatures themselves, they could also be used to describe their magic. Almost any mysterious magical effect, even if originating from humans, could potentially be described as 'fay'. This was especially true if it was magic associated with ancient pagan forces or wild places.

From the perspective of the medieval church, fairies were something of a conundrum. In theological terms, belief in such creatures was generally viewed as a hangover from pagan times. To many churchmen, they were no more than foolish superstition. Some believed that if such entities existed at all then they were nothing less than demons, sent to deceive fools. Augustine of Hippo, writing during the late fourth and early fifth century, taught that Celtic tales of woodland spirits who supposedly mated with human women were clearly demonic Incubi.[3] Some forms of medieval exorcism could be directed specifically against elves, implying that were viewed in a similar way to demons.[4] Yet other churchmen saw such fairies as lower ranking fiends, unlikely to pose a significant threat to men but fiends, nevertheless.[5]

Nevertheless, fairies were not usually regarded as demonic. Indeed, some churchmen were quite happy to promulgate stories of fairies. Gerald of Wales (as he is popularly known) was chaplain to Henry II and a royal clerk. He wrote extensively on a variety of subjects during the 1180s and 1190s. And one of the subjects he touched upon was the nature of fairies.

In a work of 1191, Gerald related the tale of another priest Elidyr. It is a tale which, he claims, happened sometime in the past (although he does not clarify when). When this Elidyr was a boy of 12, he became sick of the harsh discipline of his schooling and ran away. Hiding by a riverbank he encountered two small men, the size of pygmies, who invited him into their enchanted realm. There, they promised, he could play and lead a carefree life. He entered their lands through a concealed tunnel by the riverbank and found their realm to be beautiful and agreeable (if somewhat dark). He even befriended the king of their land. Elidyr found the inhabitants of this otherworld to be honest if somewhat scornful of the ways of mankind. However, they treated him well for as long as he held their trust.

Unfortunately for Elidyr, he made the mistake of telling his mother about this mysterious otherworld. In particular, he let slip that gold was very common there. His mother, being only human, encouraged him to bring some gold back to her. To his shame, he stole a golden ball from the king's son. The little people were greatly offended by this. They pursued him and snatched back the ball. Feeling guilty, he eventually returned to the riverbank to apologise but could never again find a way to access the mysterious fairy realm.[6]

Gerald himself did not know for sure what these strange little men were exactly. He speculates that perhaps they were descendants of ancient settlers in Britain (he picks up on Geoffrey of Monmouth's writing, suggesting there might be an ancient Trojan connection). He does not ultimately reach any firm conclusions on these little folk. Were these pygmy folk fairies? Or something else?

Another early Plantagenet writer of fairy tales was yet another cleric. This one was Walter Map, Archdeacon of Oxford, and a courtier of Henry II. Map, like Gerald, was a man with Welsh connections. He originally hailed from the Welsh Marches, although he spent most of his adult life in England and France (especially whilst travelling with the itinerant Plantagenet court).

Map's story is set in the days of old Briton, before the coming of the Saxons. It is the tale of the British King Herla who receives a visit from a pygmy-king. This strange creature is described as no larger than a monkey and having the appearance of a faun. More specifically, he is described as having the visage of the ancient Greek god Pan. The faun-king offers to attend King Herla's wedding in return for inviting him to a wedding to be held at his own fairy-court. A bargain is struck, and the two kings attend each other's weddings. To reach the faun-king's realm, Herla and his courtiers must pass through a cave into an underworld kingdom. It is not, however, an unpleasant place. It is a beautiful and wealthy land, brightly illuminated with many lamps.

After the wedding, Herla departs with many gifts. The faun-king gives him one last gift, a small bloodhound who jumps into Herla's arms. The faun-king warns Herla that his party should not dismount until the little bloodhound has first alighted. However, when the royal party returns to Britain, they find that 200 years have passed. The old British kingdoms have gone, and the Saxons now rule the land. A few courtiers dismount, forgetting the faun-king's warning, and are instantly transformed to dust. Herla reminds his companions that they must first wait for the dog to alight. But it does not. As a result, Herla and his companions find themselves doomed to wandering the land as spectral riders. They do so for several centuries before finally disappearing in the reign of Henry II.[7]

Both Gerald and Walter Map's tales have a fair bit in common. They are both told by Welshmen serving in Henry II's court. They both speak of a pygmy-like fay folk, dwelling in an underground realm. In both cases, these entities possess strange supernatural powers. Both realms are described as beautiful and both are fabulously wealthy.

However, there are also some differences. In Map's case, his description of Herla and his spectral riders supply us with an early English example of the Wild Hunt legend. This Wild Hunt was dubbed 'the household of Herlethingus' by Map and in Old English, the king would have been called 'Herla Cyning' (King Herla). This is not that unlike the French 'herlequin' who led a French version of the Wild Hunt in earlier French stories. There are also phonetic similarities with Herne the hunter, first mentioned in connection with a Wild Hunt by Shakespeare. Map's story, however, is one of the earliest versions of the Wild Hunt tale in England.

Medieval scholar Jean-Claude Schmitt suggests that Map's faun-king is in fact supposed to be the king of the dead.[8] The fact that Herla and his court end up condemned to spectral wanderings would seem to provide some support for this theory. They also dwell in an underground realm: perhaps suggestive of the classical underworld. However, Walter Map himself does not suggest such a connection. Indeed, his description of the people of this strange otherworld as being diminutive fauns seems an unlikely fit to a realm of the dead. Map also indicates there is a historic connection between the faun-king's people and the Britons. The faun-king claims the king of the Britons is connected to him by land and descent.[9]

Indeed, the second important feature of Map's tale is that his pygmies are described as faun-like. Map explicitly compares the faun-king with Pan, the classical god of the wild and not Pluto, the god of the dead. These, then, are a people more closely associated with the wild forces of ancient paganism than with a land of the dead.

The idea that these fay folk (in the case of both tales) exist in an underground realm has several possible pagan precedents. The Irish Tuatha Dé Danann dwell underground, albeit generally beneath ancient barrows. In the old Irish story of *Conle the Redhaired*, Conle is tempted by an alluring fairy to accompany her to her realm beneath a Fairy Hill. There he finds an enchanted place of everlasting feasts, no cares, and no death.[10] However, since north European elves could also dwell underground, we cannot necessarily assume a purely Celtic influence for Gerald and Walter's fairy tales.

In both of these early fairy tales, the fairy folk are described as a pygmy race and neither the Tuatha Dé Danann, nor the people of Annwfn were generally described in such terms. In both instances, the general picture is of a supernatural race of similar stature to mankind (although both have shapeshifting powers).

So, from where do we get this race of pygmy fairies? And how might we square this with Map's claim that they are somehow related to the Britons?

The answer might lie in Brittonic mythology. The old Welsh Triad titled 'Three Oppressions that Came to this Island, and Not One of them Went Back', mentions three races that once oppressed the Britons. These included the Saxons and the Picts. However, the first 'oppressor' is described as 'Cor(y) aniaid', who supposedly came to Briton from Arabia.[11]

It is a tale of invasion and migration reminiscent of that found in Irish mythology (the Tuatha Dé Danann supposedly migrated to Ireland from Spain). Perhaps, in both cases, such tales dimly record old stories of the migrations of Celtic and other ancient peoples in pre-Roman Europe. What is particularly interesting about the Coryaniaid is the fact that the name implies a race of dwarfish or stunted folk or, to put it another way, a race of pygmies. It is a word that might relate to the Breton word 'Korriganead', which was also used to denote a race of fairies.[12] If this is so, Gerald and Walter may be drawing on the same old Brittonic folk tradition, a tradition that had its roots in ancient Britain and Brittany. This would square with Map's claim that these fairy folk enjoyed a shared history with the Britons.

However, other stories of fairy folk bear a closer affinity to the Irish barrow dwelling fairies. William of Newbury, writing at the end of the twelfth century, recorded a story concerning a farmer's mysterious experience at Willy Howe (a barrow in Humberside). The farmer, drunk, returned home late at night when he heard singing coming from the barrow. When he went to investigate, he found a company of mysterious people banqueting within. They even offered him a cup, but, fearful of their fay enchantments, he flung away the contents and fled. The goblet itself was said to have been made from some strange, otherworldly material.[13] In this case, the fairies concerned are humanlike and dwell within a barrow, far closer to the kind of fairy you'd find in pagan Irish stories.

Over time a range of different names emerged, denoting different kinds of fairy beings. This inevitably reflects the different cultural influences at work in the evolution of fairy lore. Goblins originated in the twelfth century, probably in the French/Spanish border area. At the time the terms used would have been the Old French *gobelin* or Latin *gobelinus*. By the fourteenth century, the English term 'goblin' was born. In England, this became associated with the term 'hob' (the first attested use of the term 'hobgoblin' is sixteenth-century, although it may have been in use during the fifteenth).[14] The goblin became identified with diminutive mischievous sprites that appear to have assumed some of the malign characteristics of the old Anglo-Saxon elves. As a result, they assumed a generally ugly or sinister appearance in folkloric imagination and a reputation for thievery and general mischief.

Wayland (known in Norse mythology as Völund) is the most prominent named elf character to feature in Norse/Saxon mythology. Wayland appears human, despite his magical crafting talents. However, Norse elves were shape changers and, as such, could theoretically assume a diminutive form. In this sense, the physical description of such a creature, capable of assuming a wide variety of forms, is somewhat secondary. We also have some evidence to suggest that the Anglo-Saxons regarded elves as diminutive creatures, at least in some situations. One Anglo-Saxon spell against the malady of elf-shot includes the phrase 'Out little spear, if you are in here!', which implies the archer was also 'little'.[15]

In time, the folkloric character Puck became associated with a hobgoblin persona. However, Puck was originally an old English word from the early Middle Ages. At this time, it had a linguistic association with the word for pox, thereby linking this entity with the malady inflicting power of the elves. The term Puck was in use long before the term goblin or hobgoblin arrived in England. Puck would later (during the sixteenth century) acquire a new nickname in the form of 'Robin Goodfellow'. What we appear to have, then, is an evolving identity that emerges over time rather than a fixed categorisation rooted in a specific pagan tradition. The goblin of British folklore is a composite of several different earlier identities. He is an elf, he is puck, he is a hob, and he is the French gobelin and later still he acquires the name Robin Goodfellow. He is, in essence, an evolving cultural fusion. He draws on earlier pagan superstitions, but he is not a creature of the pagan world. The fairy and the goblin are essentially medieval creations whose identities becomes increasingly fleshed out during the early modern period.

However, this depiction of fairies as diminutive creatures such as goblins, 'pygmies', or coryaniaids was by no means a consistent theme in Plantagenet times. Geoffrey of Monmouth's references to the mysterious ladies of Avalon and Morgan le Fay provide an alternative example of how fay-like beings were often viewed. Like the Tuatha Dé Danann or the otherworldly subjects of Annwfn, the medieval fairy could also be seen as being a supernatural being of humanlike size and appearance.

Fairies of this sort featured increasingly in chivalric romances. They could sometimes appear as beguiling maidens, dancing late at night in the woods, seducing any wanderer who might happen upon them. They might also supply mortals with gifts, often of wonderous magical items. The romance of *Escanor* describes an entire fairy castle filled with magical wonders.[16] The ability to fashion and supply magical marvels are strongly rooted in both Celtic and Germanic traditions and both fed into these medieval tales.

Medieval fairy tales often tell of fairy folk beguiling and seducing mortals. However, the love of a fairy could be fickle, and they often ended up abandoning mortal lovers to return to their own world. The fairy folk remained creatures of wild places to be encountered in a wood or by a stream, or perhaps near an old barrow. In this regard, they retained an association with old paganism and that which remained wild and untamed. They may not have been evil, but they always remained capricious and potentially dangerous. Increasingly, fairy and fay powers became associated with the colour green, most clearly illustrated by the fay magic that transformed the Green Knight in Sir Gawain's tale. However, this was green magic rather than black. Like the fairies themselves, it was not generally regarded as overtly demonic. It was, however, dangerous, and untamed.

The perilous nature of fairies is most evident in their habit of abducting human children and replacing them with changelings. However, stories of changeling children, although popular on the Continent, do not appear in the British Isles during the Middle Ages. The earliest English record of such behaviour dates to 1519.[17]

Fairies remain elusive, magical, and potentially perilous through most medieval tales. In the main, they appear as beings of human stature rather than as pygmies or dwarves. And it is this vision of them, as powerful humanlike supernatural beings, that can be found in one of the most famous of all medieval fairy tales – the tale of Sir Orfeo.

Sir Orfeo was written by an anonymous English author at some time in the thirteenth or early fourteenth century. The version that survives is written in Middle English, although it claims to be a translated version of an older Breton lay. No older French/Breton version survives, however. It is loosely based on the classical myth of Orpheus and Eurydice, except that the role of Greek gods from the original story are taken by fairies. That, along with other creative changes, renders the story of Sir Orfeo quite different from the Greek myth that inspired it.

Sir Orfeo is a mythical English king who is happily wedded to the beautiful Queen Heurodis. Whilst the queen is sleeping under a tree in an orchard, she receives a disturbing dream. In it, an otherworldly king tells her that he will come to bear her away the following day. The court is distraught and despite every effort to mount a strong guard to prevent any such abduction, the queen is spirited away by sorcery. Orfeo, heartbroken, surrenders care of his kingdom to his steward and leaves to wander in the wilds as a hermit. His only comfort in this self-imposed exile is his harp.

For years, Orfeo wanders in the wilds, scratching out a pitiful existence on a meagre diet of berries, herbs, and roots. Then, one day, he sees a regal host riding through the forest. He recognises his wife riding amongst them and sets off in pursuit. He follows the riders as they leave the forest and ride into the heart of a rock. The party passes through into the rock, travelling for fully 3 miles until they finally emerge into the fairy king's realm. And what a land it is! We are told that it is a land as bright as summer sunshine.[18] In the heart of the fairy-king's realm lies a magnificent crystal castle, lavishly decorated with gold, gemstones, and beautiful carvings. It is so wonderous that it seems to Orfeo as if he is looking upon the court of Paradise.

Orfeo enters the crystal palace by offering to sing for the fairy-king. Once inside, he witnesses a most bizarre sight. The halls are filled with a great crowd of mortals whom, he is told, were drawn to the fairy realm at the very moment of their death. And yet, we are informed, none of them are yet dead.[19] These unfortunate souls are mortals caught in the moment between life a death; suspended forever in this strange fairy never neverland. They include women caught at the instant of death in childbirth, others who'd received fatal wounds frozen in their final death throes and so on. It is a most sinister and disturbing scene. And, amongst this crowd, was Orfeo's queen, suspended like the others, asleep beneath an orchard tree.

Orfeo is finally admitted to the presence of the fairy king and his court. His appearance is both otherworldly and awe inspiring. His crown shines with such a brilliant radiance that it is impossible to look at it directly. The king is surprised even to see him, remarking that no mortal has ever dared to voluntarily come to his court before. He nevertheless agrees to hear Orfeo's performance. Orfeo's music proves to be so captivating that the king is most impressed. He rewards Orfeo by granting him anything that is in his power to grant. Naturally enough, Orfeo asks for the return of his queen. The fairy king, though reluctant, is true to his word and returns Heurodis to him.

Here, there is no hint of pygmies. The fairies of this tale are clearly of human stature. However, once again, the fairy realm is described as a place of supernatural beauty, so beautiful that it appears to be a paradise to mortal eyes. The fairy king is much closer in description and nature to the king of Annwfn or to one of the Tuatha Dé Danann, radiant and regal, like their King Lugh.

Interestingly, the fairy realm described in Orfeo is a place that appears to exist in a nether world between our world and the afterlife. The people held there are not dead but are close to death, caught in the last moment of their mortal existence. For that reason, they are not yet in heaven, hell, or purgatory but neither are they in the land of the living. This diverges considerably from the original Greek myth.

In the tale of Orpheus, he must visit the underworld to rescue Eurydice. Such a place, however, cannot exist within the context of medieval Christian cosmology. As a result, the writer of the *Sir Orfeo* draws on old tales of otherworldly beings to create a world that exists between life and afterlife, neither one nor the other. It is a vision of a fairy realm that is a uniquely medieval creation, drawing on past traditions but also adapting them to fit a Christian worldview. This 'in-between' existence of fairies reflects the unease with which such creatures were viewed. Although graced with impressive supernatural powers, they could certainly not be classed as angelic. And, whilst some churchmen taught that they were demons, attempting to deceive men, this view was not universally held.

Some Christian writers, unable to class fairies as either demonic or angelic, struggled to find another way to make sense of them. One answer can be found in the thirteenth-century work entitled *The South England Legendary*. The anonymous writer suggests that perhaps 'elves' were angels who had remained neutral in the struggle between God and Satan. They were not damned to hell, like demons, but neither were they permitted to remain in heaven. As a result, they were banished to dwell within their own otherworld.[20] It is this 'in-between' condition that we find reflected in Orfeo. It has a certain logic to it, although it is impossible to say just how widely accepted this view of fairies became. *The South England Legendary* claims that fairies could adopt the form of beautiful women and could be found dancing deep in the forest. They would willingly make love with mortal men who crossed their paths, but such liaisons were potentially perilous.

The fact that the *Legendary* classifies fairies as a form of angel tells us a lot concerning how its writer regarded the physical appearance of such creatures. A fairy of this kind might assume the form of beautiful women, but the truth was that they had no fixed physical form. This was because they were fundamentally a type of angel or demon. In medieval theology it was held that angels and demons could only assume a physical appearance by manipulating vapours in the atmosphere. This 'airy' substance coalesced into a visible, tangible, physical form but it was ultimately only conjured by the angel. In many ways it was an illusion, it was not really the true essence of the angel itself.[21] Such forms were, therefore, simply a method of manifestation to allow fairies to interact with men. Fairies, like angels and demons, were spiritual entities who had no true physical form.

Fairies, then, were generally not regarded as wholly evil, but neither were they regarded as good. They could be fair, friendly, and generous, but they could also be dangerous and potentially deceitful. They could be capricious, and their motives were often inscrutable. They had their own agendas which, sometimes, caused harm and hardship to mortals unfortunate enough to cross their paths. That they possessed wonderous powers and were capable of works of great beauty was beyond doubt. But, behind this beauty and cordiality, lay potential peril. Ultimately, it was this ambiguity and the fact that their stories drew on a variety of older, pagan superstitions, that made them so feared. The concept of the fairy that had evolved by the end of the Middle Ages was neither wholly Celtic, Anglo-Saxon, Norse, or classical. It was a blend of all these traditions. In addition, and perhaps most importantly, it was also a product of medieval Christian cosmology.

The Medieval Bestiary

If you visit a medieval church, read a medieval manuscript, or peruse a medieval map you'd quickly notice images of fantastic creatures. Whether it be gargoyles adorning a church roofline, sea serpents on a map, or unicorns in the margins of a manuscript, medieval art is replete with them. When faced with such images you may well wonder what myths and stories lie behind them. Whilst some of these creatures appear in classical or medieval literature, many feature only incidentally, if at all, in any tale.

So, where and how were all these marvellous creatures conceived? And what did they signify in the mind of a medieval observer? Many had their origins in the classical world. Some, of course, were associated with specific myths, such as Medusa, the minotaur, the fire-breathing chimera, or the many-headed hydra. Anyone with a good classical education (which included most of the medieval elite) would have been familiar with these stories.

However, not all mythical creatures were associated with specific myths and fables, even if they originated in the classical world. The Roman writer Lucan, in his epic poem *Pharsalia* relates the story of the civil war that ended the Republic. Part of the narrative deals with the march that Cato the Younger and his army embarked on in the North African desert. There, he describes how the army was plagued by all manner of poisonous serpents. One of these was the dreaded amphisbaena, a most bizarre creature, a serpent with a head at each end of its body.

Here, the fantastic (in the form of the amphisbaena) is presented as if it is just another serpent in the Libyan desert. For Lucan, it was a real animal, encountered by Cato's soldiers along with all the other desert snakes. It is in contexts such as this that we often encounter fantastic creatures in classical and medieval culture. Not in fables or myths, but in supposedly factual accounts, presented as if they were as real as other exotic beasts. As far as many people were concerned griffins, unicorns and phoenix birds were every bit as real and credible as crocodiles, giraffes, and hippopotami.

The famous fourteenth century world map, known as the Mappa Mundi, contains illustrations of a wide variety of exotic and mythical creatures.

In Africa, we find the rhino, seeming living alongside the basilisk and the unicorn. In Egypt, we see crocodiles and the phoenix. In Scythia, there are griffins. In the seas we find mermaids swimming alongside fish. In Sri Lanka, dragons.[1]

As far as the artist who originally drew these illustrations was concerned, these were all strange creatures that lived in distant exotic places. Places about which he had, no doubt, heard mysterious tales but had never visited. Of course, neither he, nor anyone he knew, could ever have seen a unicorn or a dragon. But, then again, they'd be extremely unlikely to have ever seen a crocodile or a rhino either. Most medieval illustrations of creatures like crocodiles or giraffes were clearly drawn by artists who'd never seen their subjects in real life.

Knowledge of exotic beasts and mythical creatures was primarily transmitted from the classical world into medieval culture via the medium of the bestiary. These books were created as works of natural history or encyclopaedias. The earliest date back to classical antiquity. These were added to and elaborated on during the Middle Ages. Two especially influential works were *Physiologus* and *The Etymologies* of Isidore of Saville.

Physiologus was written in Alexandria during late-Roman times (quite likely at some point during the third century). Its author is unknown. It is essentially a collection of descriptions of animals, plants, rocks, and fantastic creatures. No real distinction is made between creatures we regard as mythical today and real animals. Pelicans, hedgehogs, and foxes appear alongside entries related to the phoenix, sirens, and unicorns.

The Etymologies consists of an extensive encyclopaedia, spanning twenty volumes. It was written in the early seventh century by Isidore, the bishop of Saville. One of the volumes deals with animals and it is in this volume where we find several fantastic mythological creatures interspersed with entries relating to real animals. Here we can read about griffins, in an entry between elephants and the lynx. We can also find entries for basilisks, amphisbaena, the phoenix, and many other creatures we'd consider mythical.

In some cases, Isidore raises the question as to whether certain exotic beasts, such the chimera or centaur, exist or not. He appears agnostic on the subject. Perhaps such exotic creatures exist. Do they appear plausible? Has anyone seen them? Could those who reported them have mistaken them for something else? These are all questions Isidore thinks to raise. In some cases, he expresses scepticism. He may express scepticism about the existence of sirens but accepts the reality of the phoenix as if it were no more likely to be a myth than the elephant or the crocodile. He does not supply his readers with a definitive judgement in every case.[2]

The unicorn is recorded in several classical works. In these early stories, it is always shown living in distant, exotic lands. Perhaps these creatures dwelt in the wilds of India, or maybe Ethiopia. In the Mappa Mundi, they are shown dwelling in Africa. They were fierce, wild beasts, and their single horn could be wielded as a dangerous weapon. In some early accounts, unicorn-like creatures were variously referred to as *cartazons* or *monoceros*. For the Roman writer, Aelian, these beasts dwelt in the remote wilderness of India, sported a spiral black horn, and had an aggressive temperament. An ancient Greek source also mentions the Indian *cartazon* and notes that it was famous for its loud bellowing cries.[3] However, there were no significant Greek or Roman tales of unicorns. As far as the ancient world was concerned, the unicorn was no more than another exotic wild animal, dwelling in remote, mysterious lands.

During the Middle Ages, the unicorn acquired a much greater cultural significance. Indeed, it is medieval unicorn folklore that largely shapes our view of unicorns today. Unicorn mythology evolved to new heights in three key areas: mysticism, heraldry, and medicine. It is no exaggeration to say that the golden age of the unicorn fell between the twelfth and fifteenth centuries. What began the period as no more than an exotic, wild beast became a creature of great symbolic significance. And an important reason why this happened was down to an accident of mistranslation.

As the Jewish diaspora and later Christianity spread across the classical world, there was an increasing need to make scripture more accessible. The Old Testament books were all originally in ancient Hebrew, so these had to be translated, first into Greek and later into Latin. As the translators worked their way through scripture, they encountered a dilemma: how should they translate the creature known as a *re'em*? If you were a Hebrew scholar of the time, you pretty much knew what a *re'em* was (it was probably some kind of ancient wild oxen). But how do you translate that into Greek? And, having done that, how does a later translator go about translating that into Latin?

The result of this was that the Latin Vulgate Bible, which was used throughout the Middle Ages, translated re'em into *unicornis* and, thus, the unicorn became a biblical beast.[4] Indeed, this interpretation even persisted in early modern English bibles. And so it came to pass that the King James version of Job 39: 9-10, reads: 'Will the unicorn be willing to serve thee, or abide by thy crib? Canst thou bind the unicorn with his band in the furrow? Or will he harrow the valleys after thee?' The image of the unicorn as a wild, untameable beast was now confirmed by scripture.

In time, a whole new mythology evolved around the unicorn, a mythology that fed into the growing movement of Christian mysticism. How can anything tame a wild beast such as a unicorn? In the age of relics, saints, and miracles, of course, anything is possible by God's grace. From relatively early on the idea that the normally ferocious unicorn could be pacified by a chaste, virgin took root.

The image of a unicorn laying its head in the lap of a maiden is a common theme in medieval art. After a time, this image evolved to place the pair in a woodland scene, with hunters lurking amongst the trees in the background. In such imagery the unicorn came to symbolise Christ submitting to enter the virgin's womb to save mankind. For this reason, the unicorn is sometimes depicted with its horn pointed at the girl's belly. The hunters took on their own mystical significance, as sinners seeking salvation.

Influenced by Christian mysticism, the imagery used in such scenes became increasingly elaborate. Symbols of purity, such as fountains, or of God's promise of salvation, such as Gideon's fleece could be added to provide additional layers of meaning. In one image, a woman is depicted placing a collar on the unicorn, attaching it by a leash to a pomegranate tree. An educated medieval audience would have understood this as visual metaphors for love, fidelity, and eternal life.[5]

In addition to its growing role in religious mysticism, the unicorn had secular significance in the field of heraldry. The unicorn's reputation as a fierce beast (except when pacified by a virgin) endured. In some bestiary accounts it is even portrayed as strong and aggressive enough to fight the mighty elephant. Medieval imagery of a lion and a unicorn fighting appears as early as the ninth century. Clearly, a beast of such bravery and ferocity had significant appeal for the martial, chivalric culture of medieval Europe. An early fifteenth-century Scottish coin bears the image of a unicorn sporting a crown about its neck.[6] By the middle of that century it had become part of Scotland's royal coat of arms.

The unicorn also held medicinal significance. More specifically, its horn was said to have marvellous curative properties. It was an idea that dated all the way back to antiquity. Physiologus reported that the unicorn could purify water poisoned by serpents by making the sign of the cross.[7] Philostratus, writing in the second century, claimed that some people of his day strongly believed in the curative powers of unicorn horns. It was thought that goblets made from unicorn horns could protect the drinker from poisons, disease, fire, and injury.[8]

Of course, the fact that physical unicorn horns apparently existed made the reality of these creatures seem quite plausible. Such horns were owned by several aristocrats across Europe in the fourteenth and fifteenth centuries.[9] Some were even fashioned into goblets, presumably to harness their medicinal and protective powers. These horns were actually the teeth of an arctic whale we now know as a narwhal. Nevertheless, the fact that these horns were physical objects of convincing appearance lent significant credence to the acceptance of unicorns as real creatures.

If the unicorn was famed for its healing powers, other creatures were infamous for the toxicity of their poisons. This was especially the case with snakes (either real or mythical). One especially venomous creature was the basilisk which we can find dwelling in Africa, along with the unicorn, on the Mappa Mundi. *The Etymologies* informs us that the basilisk is the king of snakes. It was considered so venomous that even its odour could kill. Indeed, it could infamously slay a man just by looking at him. The only thing the basilisk feared was apparently the weasel: the only creature capable of hunting down and slaying such a terrible serpent.[10]

Some sources describe the creature as possessing crownlike markings on its head, which would tie in with its title as king of snakes. Although perhaps this may have been a crude description of a cobra's hood.[11] Certainly, there are highly venomous cobras present in both Africa and India, some varieties of which can spit their venom, causing blindness. Could travellers' tales of these dangerous snakes have inspired tales of basilisks? And, if so, is its vulnerability to weasels an allusion to the cobra-killing mongoose?

Another highly toxic creature that is sometimes confused with the basilisk is the cockatrice. This beast is a monstrous hybrid animal that combines the features of a serpent with those of a cockerel. It is often depicted with a serpentine body but with the head, legs, and wings of a cockerel. The cockatrice is supposedly hatched from a cock's egg incubated by a serpent, clearly a most unnatural creature. As lethal as the basilisk and seemingly sharing in its vulnerability to the dreaded weasel, the two were sometimes confused with each other in medieval as well as more modern times.[12]

Casting an eye across the Mappa Mundi, we find another mythical creature, the phoenix, dwelling in Egypt, not too far from the African unicorns and basilisks. The phoenix also had its origins in classical times. One of the most detailed early accounts comes from the ancient Greek historian, Herodotus, writing in the fifth century BC. He also places the phoenix in Egypt but explains that it is thought to be a very rare bird, visiting the land only once every five centuries on the death of its parent. Herodotus describes it as having red and golden plumage, but otherwise having the appearance of an eagle.[13]

What made the phoenix most notable was, of course, its supernatural cycle of death and renewal. In Herodotus' early version of the tale, this element is absent from the story. The bird does, however, have a most fantastic burial ritual. When the parent bird dies, its offspring embalms the body in myrrh and brings it to the temple of the sun in Egypt.[14]

At some point, tales of ritual embalming in the temple of the Sun became tales of ritual re-birth. By Ovid's time, writing at the beginning of the first century, the legend of the phoenix had developed. In Ovid's version, the phoenix builds itself a nest of rare spices and embalming agents after living five centuries. It then expires in the perfumes of this nest. The offspring is then born from the body of the old phoenix, before transporting its dead parent, complete with the nest, to the city of the sun.[15]

By the early Middle Ages, this birthing ritual had developed further. The legend had finally evolved into a form close to that which we're familiar with today. Isidore provides a description in *The Etymologies* that reflects the early medieval understanding of the creature. Here, the phoenix is presented as having scarlet plumage and living for over five centuries. As the time of its death approaches, it constructs a bier from aromatic twigs. These are ignited by the sun's rays, consuming the phoenix in flames before the bird can rise again, renewed, from the ashes.[16]

Naturally enough, the medieval world was able to read mystical significance into this imagery. The act of immolation and renewal served as an allegory for death and re-birth of the faithful in the kingdom of God. And the aromatic twigs could be taken as signifying the good works of the righteous.[17]

In another remote corner of the Mappa Mundi, we can see an image of a griffin, fighting with people in the wilds of Scythia (situated in modern day Ukraine and the region lying between the Black and Caspian Seas). Images of griffins appear frequently in medieval bestiaries, artworks, and heraldry. However, its history dates back far earlier. Indeed, these fierce lion-eagle hybrids have truly ancient antecedents.

Images of griffin-like creatures appear in Egyptian and Mesopotamian art as early as 3000 BC.[18] The ancient Minoan palace at Knossos features a famous frieze of griffins (albeit wingless ones) in the throne room. For the Minoans, the griffin imagery may have held a religious significance, with the griffins serving as guardians to a priestess-queen (since the throne they guard seems designed for a woman). Although this interpretation is disputed by some, the presence of the griffin in a throne room is telling. These beasts were, therefore, associated with royalty or, perhaps, religious authority, as early as 1500 BC.[19]

In Greek mythology, the griffin was said to have dwelled in Scythia (as the Mappa Mundi shows). There, they served as guardians for a gold, rich land. Although sceptical, Herodotus reported that the mysterious one-eyed Armaspians of this region often stole gold from the griffins, thereby incurring their wrath.[20]

Isidore, writing in early medieval times, reports griffins living in Hyperborean mountains (a region supposedly to the north of Scythia, perhaps the Urals). He confirms the ferocity of these creatures and their ferocious attacks on both horses and humans.[21] The griffin appears in a few medieval tales as well as featuring in bestiaries and artwork. In the *Romance of Alexander*, they are harnessed to act as steeds for a flying contraption fashioned by the king. In another *chanson de geste*, the hero slays a griffin and presents its claw to Charlemagne. A griffin even appears in Dante's *Divine Comedy*, transporting Beatrice to paradise on its back.[22]

In the seas of the Mappa Mundi, we see illustrations of fish but also of a mermaid. Illustrations of these mysterious marine creatures became common during the Middle Ages. The medieval mermaid represented an evolution from the classical Nereids: the attendants of Neptune the sea god. In antiquity, the Nereids were benevolent lesser goddesses of the ocean, the fifty daughters of Neureus, according to Hesiod. They were beautiful sea nymphs, although they were generally not depicted as having fish tails (indeed, Hesiod describes the Nereid Amphitrite as having trim ankles).[23]

In classical times, the siren represented another mythical creature with close ties to the sea. Unlike the Nereids, the sirens were of a more malevolent sort. These creatures haunted the islands around Sicily and were originally envisaged as winged, bird-like, women whose singing lured mariners to their deaths. As with the Nereids, sirens were not classically depicted with any fish-like features.

The earliest known depiction of a mermaid type figure comes from the second century AD. The classical writer Lucan came across such an image in relation to the Semitic moon and fertility goddess, Atargatis. For the Greeks, this goddess was associated with their Aphrodite, the goddess of love and passion and her Roman counterpart, Venus.[24]

During the early Middle Ages, the image of the fish-tailed mermaid gradually emerged, drawing on these earlier archetypes. From the Nereids, they acquired their beauty and close connection with the oceans. From the classical siren, they acquired more malevolent characteristics, sometimes taking on the role of a capricious temptress.[25] And, from the early images of Atargatis, they acquired their association with passion and carnal desires. The tendency to associate such entities with temptation is more clearly in evidence in *The Etymologies*. Here, Isidore claims that the sirens were not originally bird-women at all but rather harlots leading men to ruin.[26]

It is not certain at what point the term 'mermaid' or 'merfolk' came into popular use. However, images of such creatures appear in medieval art before the term itself was invented. The earliest attestable use of the word 'mermaid' is found in Chaucer's 'Nun's Priest's Tale' of c. 1386.[27]

The medieval imagery of fish-tailed mermaids increasingly adopted the symbolism of temptation and danger with illustrations showing mermaids with combs and mirrors, signifying the sin of pride. Mermaids with musical instruments are an allegory for temptation and those holding fish are indicating that they are in the grip of sin. An illustration of a mermaid with a monkey on her tail is symbolic of the bestial side of man's nature.[28] A fifteenth-century carving on a wooden bench at the Zennor Church in Cornwall, shows a mermaid with a comb and mirror; classic symbols of pride. Local folklore speaks of a young chorister who was seduced by a mermaid and disappeared with her to her watery home beneath the waves.[29] Whether this local legend inspired the fifteenth-century carving, or whether it was itself inspired by the carving, is impossible to say for certain.

The medieval mermaid was often depicted in literature of the period as a kind of fay creature of the sea. Potentially dangerous and a source of wild temptation, there was something of the pagan about her. Sometimes she could be benevolent but, very often, any love match between a man and a mermaid would end badly. However, much like the fairy, the mermaid could also be benevolent. She might provide helpful warnings of impending bad weather at sea or aid her human friends with gifts.

In 1403 in Holland, following a fierce storm, a group of young women discovered a 'mermaid', washed ashore. They took her in and taught her to weave and wear clothes. She integrated with their community as best she was able but never learnt to speak. It is not clear from this account if this mysterious woman had a fishtail or not.[30] Perhaps she was simply a shipwrecked foreigner.

Not all merfolk were female, however, although this is how they are mostly depicted in medieval art. One story of a merman comes from Sicily in the thirteenth century. The merman in question was a fellow known as Colá Pesce ('Nick the fish'), who was such a skilled diver that people believed he was a merman. Colá, it was said, had a supernatural bond with the ocean and was most reluctant to be away from it for any length of time. When he was brought for an audience at the king's court the unfortunate Colá died, since he was unable to survive away from the sea.[31]

Another strange creature associated with water was Mélusine, whose story was most famously told in the *Tale of Mélusine*, written by John d'Arras in the late fourteenth century. In this tale, Mélusine is clearly identified as being of fairy stock. She is the beautiful daughter of an Albanian king. This king married a fay woman by the name of Pressine whom he encountered by a mysterious woodland fountain.

Although Pressine and the king had three beautiful daughters together, their relationship is doomed. She agreed to marry him on condition that he never enter her bedchamber when she birthed or bathed their children. Of course, the king tragically forgets his promise and, as a result, Pressine leaves him. She takes her daughters and returns to the mysterious Isle of Avalon.

Years later, Raymond of Poitou encounters Mélusine by a fountain in the French forests. Just like the Albanian king many years before, he is stricken by Mélusine's great beauty and marries her. Once again, their marriage comes with the condition that he should never enter her chamber whilst she bathes. Of course, the time inevitably comes when he breaks his word. When he sees Mélusine bathing he witnesses her in her true form. The upper part of his wife is indeed a beautiful woman, but the lower part is that of a serpent.

Though deeply shaken by this revelation, Raymond remains true to Mélusine and does not reveal that he knows her secret. But when one of their sons later proves to be a murder, Raymond, in the heat of the moment, blames

Mélusine's serpent blood. Mélusine then realises Raymond has broken his promise. She transmutes herself into a flying serpent before departing, never to be seen by Raymond again. As was often the case, love between a mortal and a fay woman was ultimately doomed. When Mélusine adopts the form of a flying serpent, she becomes almost dragon-like. Despite this, we know (since d'Arras has already informed us) that Mélusine is a fairy creature and not a dragon.

Another medieval beast with dragon-like features is the gargoyle, whose image appears so commonly on medieval churches. These creatures were originally inspired by the legend of a beast known as La Gargouille who was, in fact, a dragon. This particular dragon reputedly ravaged the area around Rouen in France. Its reign of terror finally ended when it was slain by Saint Romanus, the local archbishop.[32] Since this time gargoyles were placed on the side of churches as a symbol of this vanquished beast to ward off evil.

Of course, dragons had a significant role to play in medieval mythology. And, rather like the other exotic creatures on the Mappa Mundi, we can find a dragon lurking in a remote part of the world. This time, in the distant exotic land of Sri Lanka. And it is to these magnificent yet terrifying beasts to which we must turn next.

The Great Dragon

Of all the mythological creatures that feature in medieval art and literature the dragon is surely the most iconic. It appeared in stories throughout the Middle Ages and illustrations of dragons, of a wide variety of types, liberally grace numerous manuscripts.

Dragons, appear in the stories of many different cultures all around the world and their history dates all the way back to the misty dawn of antiquity. They featured in the mythology of ancient Mesopotamia as the terrifying goddess Tiamat. Greek mythology contains tales of several dragon-like creatures such as the many-headed-hydra that guarded the golden fleece and the fearful Typhon.

Medieval England inherited images and stories of dragons from the classical world, Anglo-Saxon, and Norse mythology as well as from the Celts. Some conformed to the common popular image of a dragon: flying, four-legged, fire-breathing reptiles of great size and power. Others were more serpent-like. Many lacked wings, while some were many-headed. Whilst some breathed fire, others spewed forth poisonous vapours. Though they came in a wide variety of different forms, they were very often regarded as manifestations of malevolence and evil.

Dragons feature prominently in the mythology of many different cultures. In Chinese culture they are regarded as auspicious creatures and often seen as benevolent bringers of good fortune. However, Western medieval Christendom evolved a very different concept of dragons. We are often presented with a vision of a terrifying beast, admired for its strength and ferocity but also feared and vilified for its evil nature.

One of the main reasons for the dragon's dark reputation stems from the Bible and perhaps the most famous dragon of all – Satan. In the book of Revelation, Satan is described not simply as a dragon but as *the* great dragon. At the end of days, we are told that the dragon (Satan) will be bound for a millennium. At the end of that time, he will be unleashed and gather his armies for the final Battle of the Apocalypse. It is a story that most people in medieval Europe would have been familiar with. Not only was the great dragon evil, he was the very epitome of evil.

A slightly different type of dragon, well-known in medieval times, was the beast that battled with Cadmus in Ovid's *Metamorphoses*. The dragon slain by Cadmus was a powerful and terrible enemy indeed. This beast appears to have been a great serpent, so powerful that it did not even flinch when Cadmus hurled a millstone at it. It is described as crested, with azure, iridescent scales, three forked tongs, and three rows of razor-sharp teeth. Identified as the servant of Mars, the god of war, it hisses like a serpent and breaths a venomous vapour.

This dragon lurked in a gloomy cavern, beside a beautiful stream in an ancient grove and Cadmus' companions made the mistake of disturbing the monster when they sought to draw water from the stream. The beast emerged from its lair and slaughtered them. Some were slain by its poisonous breath, others by its venomous sting, while some were crushed within its coils. In the end, Cadmus overcame the monster by driving his spear deep into the creature's throat.[1] This image of a dragon is very serpentine, even down to its venomous sting and ability to constrict its prey. It is also notable for its poisonous breath, which would come to be a characteristic of many medieval dragons.

The association with poisonous breath could sometimes be extended to an even more insidious power. The dragon slain by Saint George not only slew people with its poisonous breath but was also plague-bearing. This dragon demanded tribute by way of food from the town it terrorised. Initially this took the form of sheep but, when the livestock ran out, the dragon demanded human meals. It was when a maiden was sent to feed the beast that Saint George stepped in and vanquished the monster. It is a classic example of rescuing a damsel in distress from the evil dragon. It would be a theme that would recur in other medieval (and later) dragon tales. In this case, the dragon is slain by Saint George. However, its power is broken in no small part because the townsfolk agree to be baptised. Following the conversion of the people and the death of the dragon, a church is built that housed a wonderous spring with incredible healing powers.[2]

In Saint George's dragon slaying story, we can see a powerful allegorical struggle between good and evil played out in the saint's life. The dragon is not only evil but a bearer of pestilence; an impure creature, clearly one of Satan's servants. It is defeated by the valour of a knight, the innocence of a maiden and the Christian faith of the townsfolk. In place of a plague-bearing dragon, the town now possesses a church and a healing spring. The message is clear – as God triumphs over Satan, so shall healing and faith triumph over pestilence and paganism.

The identification of dragons as the embodiment of evil is a recurring theme in *The Golden Legend*. These creatures are the servants of Satan, fiendish foes of the saints and martyrs. The medieval religious processions of Rogation Week of Salisbury Cathedral featured a dragon effigy and a lion banner. The dragon symbolised Satan and the lion banner symbolised Christ, made manifest as the lion of Judah.[3]

Dragons also featured prominently in North European mythology (whether Anglo-Saxon, German, or Norse). These dragons sometimes appear as serpents, as is the case for the immense, world embracing, Midgard Serpent of Norse mythology. Viking raiding ships frequently had dragonheads affixed to the prows to terrify their enemies, perhaps an allusion to the dreaded Midgard Serpent. As these peoples were pagan, dragons had no association with Satan for them. However, dragons were closely associated with serpents (and often depicted as such) and serpents generally had an evil reputation. After Ragnarök, Norse mythology tells us that oath-breakers and murderers will be sent to dwell in Nastrandir. Nastrandir is described as a hall built from the spines of snakes. The interior walls are covered in the heads of snakes, spitting venom at the damned within.[4]

One of the most famous dragons from the Northern pagan traditions is Fafnir, although he began his tale as the human son of a sorcerer. When Fafnir's father comes into possession of a ransom paid in gold, the hoard includes the cursed ring Andvaranaut. The cursed ring brought death to any who possessed it and so it would prove with Fafnir's father. Fafnir and his brother, out of greed, collude to slay their father and take the gold. However, once their father dies, they soon fall out. Fafnir is determined to keep the entire hoard for himself and transforms himself into a terrible dragon in serpent form. He then proceeds to make a lair on Gnita-Heath where he lay down upon the golden hoard to guard it. Naturally enough, Andvaranaut brings about Fafnir's downfall since it is not long before the greedy dragon is slain by the heroic Sigurd.[5]

Fafnir is another example of a serpent-like dragon. In this tale he famously sits on top of his golden hoard, jealously guarding it from all comers. The image of a dragon guarding its hoard of gold has roots in the avaricious Germanic dragons, of whom Fafnir was a prime example. Another example comes in the form of the terrifying beast that mortally wounded Beowulf in his final adventure. This Anglo-Saxon dragon displays many similarities with Fafnir, especially when it came to hording gold. However, Beowulf's dragon displays two particularly distinctive characteristics – he is a firebreather and he can fly. In this sense, he conforms more closely to the 'classic' image of a dragon we have today.

Another firebreather appears in the Arthurian tale of *The Knight with the Lion.* Here the beast is encountered by the story's hero, Sir Yvain, deep in the heart of a forest. When Yvain first sees the creature, it is locked in mortal combat with a lion. This dragon grips the lion coiled in its tail whilst its fiery breath engulfs the hapless feline. We are told that its bite was venomous and breath spews flames precisely because 'it was so full of wickedness'.[6] So intense is the heat from its fiery breath that its gaping maw is compared to a cauldron. Sir Yvain intervenes of course. Using his shield to protect himself from the fierce flames he slays the dragon, slicing it up into tiny pieces. He thereby saves the lion, who rewards him by becoming his faithful companion. Once again, we are left in no doubt that the dragon is an agent of evil and wickedness.

Sightings of dragons and visions of dragons could be taken as a sign of impending doom or oncoming war. An entry from the *Anglo-Saxon Chronicle* in 793 speaks of terrible portents in Northumbria. These portents included violent thunderstorms and the sighting of a fiery dragon flying across the sky.[7] Of course, 793 was indeed a fateful year, as later that year a Viking raiding party infamously sacked the monastery of Lindisfarne.

Later in the Middle Ages, Geoffrey of Monmouth, tells us of the prophecy of two dragons, given by Merlin to the British King Vortigern. When King Vortigern excavates the foundations of a castle on Merlin's advice, two dragons are released. One is red and one is white. As soon as they are unleashed the two creatures fight each other. On witnessing this fierce supernatural battle, King Vortigern commands Merlin to explain its meaning. Merlin explains that the red dragon represents the Britons, and the white, the Saxons. The fight between the two is, of course, a portent of war. It is a prophecy of the impending cataclysmic struggle between the Britons and the Saxons that was about to engulf Vortigern's kingdom.[8]

The idea of dragons as a portent of war between peoples echoes Ovid's identification of Cadmus' dragon as a servant of Mars, the god of war. Monmouth's use of dragons in prophecy and of dragon symbolism in general departs somewhat from the concept of dragons as agents of pure evil. In Monmouth, we find the image of battling dragons used to symbolise war or impending strife.

Another of Monmouth's dragon prophecies concerns Uther Pendragon. It relates to a vision seen in the sky above Winchester just before he becomes king. A brilliant star shot out a ball of fire that took the form of a dragon. This dragon extended its tongue from which two rays of light shone. One ray pointed to Gaul and the other to the Irish Sea, where it divided into seven small rays.

Uther naturally sought the council of Merlin to explain this vision. Merlin explained that the star and the dragon signified Uther himself. The beam of light reaching out to Gaul signified his unborn son, Arthur, who was destined for greatness. The second signified Uther's daughter, whose descendants would be kings of Britain.[9] In honour of this prophecy, Uther had two golden dragons made and assumed the name 'Pendragon' (which Geoffrey tells us meant 'dragon's head'). This symbolism would later be assumed by King Arthur himself, who, according to Geoffrey, wore a dragon-crested helmet.

Here, the image of the dragon is employed as a portent of greatness, especially in terms of war and conquest. The assumption of dragon symbols by both Uther and Arthur is designed to convey a sense of destiny. As such, it is adopted as the symbol of a powerful king, destined for glory and, in Arthur's case, a conqueror.

The image of the two battling dragons in Vortigern's vision appear elsewhere in Welsh mythology. In the tale of 'Lludd and Llefelys', in the *Mabinogion*, one of the three plagues afflicting the Britons is caused by two dragons fighting. This plague took the form of a supernatural scream that was heard across the land on May-eve. This scream caused men to be weakened, and women to become infertile. The screaming was found to emanate from a dragon, locked in mortal combat with another of its kind. This dragon, we are told, was a dragon of the Britons, being assailed by the dragon of another people (the Saxons). In this case, both dragons are of the flying variety, since their battling occurs in the sky. Only by pacifying both dragons and sending them to sleep, can the plague be lifted, and balance restored.[10] As with the battling red and white dragons in Vortigern's vision, the battle dragons of the second plague represent turmoil and strife. Only once the fighting stops is balance restored, ending the plague.

Dragon imagery of this kind seems to have some connection with Ovid's representation of a dragon as a servant of the god of war. This would certainly explain an association with war, conflict, and conquest. However, it is also the case that 'dragon pair' imagery dates to pagan Celtic culture. Some Celtic scabbards and swords from the pre-Roman period show images of a coiled pair of dragons facing each other. One such example was found in the Thames near Battersea and Hammersmith.[11] This demonstrates that the connection between dragons and battle prowess and/or war was certainly present in Celtic pagan culture.

The dragon pairs appearing in the *Mabinogion* and in Geoffrey's *History* draw their inspiration from this old pagan symbolism. Hence, Arthur adopting the dragon head crest signalled his status as a great conqueror and war leader. It also seems to be the case that, for the pagan Celts, a dragon pair in conflict signified war. A dragon pair pacified would, therefore, indicate a society in balance/at peace.

Some pagan Celtic war trumpets (carnyx) were dragon headed. An example of a dragon-headed carnyx can be found illustrated on Trajan's Column in Rome and on the emperor Augustus' breastplate. Only a few examples of Celtic carnyx survive. Parts of seven were discovered in Corrèze in southern France; in this case most appear to have been boar headed and one was serpentine. Roman depictions of Celtic carnyx dragons appear to show them as crested, rather like the dragon described in Ovid's *Metamorphoses*.

Thus, on the one hand, the dragon could be seen as a fierce but noble beast, an allegory for martial prowess and conquest. On the other, it was often regarded as an evil creature, an agent of Satan. In most medieval dragon stories, dragon slayers are usually knights, war leaders, or saints. However, in at least one English dragon tale, the dragon slayer comes from humbler stock.

There is a pool located near Lyminster Church in Sussex that is reputed to be bottomless (it is actually 30 feet deep). Known as the Knucker Hole, it was supposedly named after a dragon who dwelt there in medieval times. Nineteenth-century writers reported that the dragon was supposedly slain by a medieval knight. Local folklore attributes the demise of the eponymous Knucker to the guile of a local village lad by the name of Jim Pulk. Jim Pulk defeated his dragon by baking a poisoned pie and feeding it to the beast. When the monster succumbed to the poison, Pulk severed its head with his scythe just to make sure. However, Pulk did not live long to celebrate his triumph. Tragically, he accidently consumed a few drops of his own poison when wiping his mouth on his sleeve after quaffing a celebratory ale.[12]

Knucker's tale was not recorded before relatively modern times, so we might legitimately question whether it genuinely dates to the Middle Ages. One detail suggests that it might. The name 'Knucker' derives from Old English, which suggests an Anglo-Saxon origin. However, the idea that the beast was slain by someone other than a knight, saint, or heroic Saxon warrior, seems sadly more likely to be a post-medieval invention. If Jim Pulk's tale is medieval, it is more likely to have originated during the fourteenth or fifteenth centuries. Tales concerning commoner folk start to become more prominent during this later period and it is only from around this time that we start seeing stories of millers and ploughmen from the likes of Chaucer and Langland.

Whether Pulk's story is medieval or later is impossible to pin down. That said, the tale of Knucker himself, is more likely to be of medieval origin. Knucker was not alone as being associated with a particular feature in the English landscape. Saint George's dragon, perhaps the most famous of medieval dragons, also came to be associated with the English landscape. Indeed, unusual or striking features in the English countryside often attracted their own myths and legends in medieval times. And it is to these fascinating mysteries in our landscape to which we turn next.

Mysteries in the Landscape

The image of Saint George locked in combat with the dragon became especially prominent in the later Middle Ages. From the time when he became England's patron saint, the cult of Saint George the dragon slayer captured popular imagination.

If you happen to visit Uffington in Berkshire, you'll find a hill there, known locally as Dragon Hill. It is a natural hill, remarkable only for the fact that it has a flat top, devoid of grass, exposing the natural white chalk soil. Local folklore has it that Saint George slew his dragon upon this very hill and the reason the hilltop is bare is because the dragon's blood poisoned the earth, preventing anything from growing.[1] Whether this tale goes all the way back to medieval times is impossible to say for sure, although it was certainly recorded as being in circulation during the eighteenth century.

Dragon Hill itself lies next to another curious feature in the landscape, the famous Uffington White horse. England features a number of these hill carvings – images carved into the sides of chalk hills. The age of other famous examples such as the Long Man of Wilmington are disputed. Indeed, there are some who would argue for a relatively modern date for these carvings. The White Horse and Cerne Abbas Giant are exceptions. The Cerne Abbas Giant has recently been dated to the late Saxon period and might be a depiction of Heracles. The Uffington Horse is even older. Scientific tests of the Uffington Horse date it to 1000 BC. Its stylist design is in keeping with early Celtic art.[2] If you visited the Dragon Hill in medieval times, you would have had a good view of the horse. The presence of the nearby white horse may well have encouraged an association with Saint George (who is usually depicted riding a white horse in medieval art). If the Dragon Hill story is indeed of medieval origin, it most likely dates to the period between 1350 and 1550; the time when the saint's popularity was at its height.

If you travel across England, you can find many locations that have old stories associated with them, just like Dragon Hill. Antiquarians and folklorists began collecting and reporting on these stories during modern times, especially from the nineteenth century onwards. At the time they were recorded, many of these tales were already old, often many generations old. However, if the earliest written record of a tale appears only in the eighteenth or nineteenth century, it is hard to know when exactly that tale originated (even if it claims to have a medieval origin).

The English landscape has many striking natural features and ancient ruins. It has ancient neolithic barrows and standing stones. It also has many features and landmarks that hold a haunting natural beauty. Places like the impressive Wookey Hole caves and the eerie standing stones of Stonehenge were all present in the medieval landscape. These were places to which people have always attributed a special significance. So, in the Middle Ages, it is no surprise to find such places attracting myths to explain their origins and add colour to their history.

There is a megalithic tomb in a Berkshire hillside, that has been known as Wayland's Smithy since Anglo-Saxon times (when it was recorded as having the name *Welande smithe*). As we have seen, Wayland Smith was famed for his talent in fashioning wonderous objects. An early eighteenth-century account reports that the local people believed that a fairy dwelt within the smithy. It was said that if you left a shoeless horse and some money outside the smithy, he would shoe the horse for you.[3] This particular folktale may not date all the way back to medieval times, but the place was certainly associated with the famous elf smith throughout the Middle Ages.

One of the most impressive megalithic landmarks in England is surely Stonehenge. Its name is Anglo-Saxon which, if literally translated, means 'stone gallows'.[4] This would imply a somewhat sinister reputation in the pagan Anglo-Saxon mind. However, the most famous medieval myth associated with Stonehenge, is found in the work of Geoffrey of Monmouth.

According to Monmouth and his *History*, Stonehenge was constructed because Aurelius Ambrosius wanted a monument to commemorate the British heroes who fell fighting the Saxons. In his search for a suitable memorial, Aurelius consulted Merlin. Merlin advised him that he might find what he was looking for in Ireland. There, according to the seer, was a great stone ring, known as the Giant's Ring, on Mount Killaraus. This great stone ring had been crafted by giants, who had brought the stones with them from Africa and imbued them with certain supernatural properties. Merlin claimed the monument had the power to cure the sick if you bathed at the foot of one of its stones. By pouring water over a stone and mixing it with an herbal infusion it was possible to create a potion capable of healing any wound.[5] And so it was that with Merlin's aid Aurelius brought the Giant's Ring from Ireland and set it up at Stonehenge.

There are several locations across England (some natural and some man-made) that carry the name 'grim'. These places often have supernatural associations. Examples include several Grim's Ditches (such as exist in Berkshire, Buckinghamshire, and elsewhere) and Grimspound (the remains of an old Bronze Age settlement). The name 'grim' could be associated with the devil during the Middle Ages, but also had older pagan significance.[6] In Norse (and most likely also in pagan Anglo-Saxon) mythology the word 'grim' was associated with the concept of a masked avatar of Odin (or, for the Anglo-Saxons, Woden).

The original context is most clearly illustrated by the Old Norse poem, *Grimnismal*. In this poem, Odin appears as 'Grimnir' (the cloaked one or Shadow-Face). This enigmatic Shadow-Face visits a king to test his hospitality. However, the king, fearful of Shadow-Face's powers, has him taken and held captive between two bonfires. It is a scene vaguely reminiscent of the old May-eve bonfire rituals (some of which involved the lighting of twin bonfires).[7] There, Shadow-Face is tortured and deprived of food or drink for eight days in order for the king to learn his identity. However, Shadow-Face reveals nothing. Finally, one of the king's sons brings Shadow-Face food and drink and shows him some kindness. Only then does Grim impart mythical knowledge of his identity and role within the supernatural world. He declares the king's son to be the new king and foretells the death of the old one. Sure enough, no sooner does he make this pronouncement and reveal his identity than the old king trips and falls on his sword. Odin, as Grim, imparts great mystical knowledge but, also foretells a terrible doom for those who fail to offer him proper hospitality.[8]

In the late seventeenth century, a traveller in the Hebrides recorded that the locals had an old proverb 'he is between two Bel fires' relating to old May-eve bonfire traditions.[9] We might wonder who 'he' is. During much of the early and high Middle Ages the Hebrides were occupied by Norwegian settlers (and indeed became part of the kingdom of Norway). One of the Hebridean Islands even bears the name Grimsay (which would have meant 'Grim's Island' in Old Norse). Could the 'he' between the Hebridean Beltane fires be a reference to Odin? Early medieval Norwegian settlers would no doubt have been familiar with the *Grimnismal* story. If they witnessed the local Celts lighting twin fires at Beltane, the connection with 'Grim' would have been obvious for them. *Grimnismal* ends with Odin imparting knowledge of his many names to the king's son. By means of this twin fire ritual, in which the god himself fasts for a week and is tormented with flames, the names of the pagan god were learnt.

References to places such as Grim's Ditch or Grimspound, therefore, carried with them echoes of old pagan Anglo-Saxon and Norse belief. For the medieval Christian, these old pagan associations represented a reminder of ancient ignorance and godlessness. It is easy enough to see how Odin's/ Woden's avatar of 'Grim' might later come to be associated with Satan or, at least, with a dangerous supernatural power.

Wookey Hole, in the heart of Somerset, is a series of limestone caverns that feature several spectacular stalagmite and stalactite formations. One of these formations is known as the Witch of Wookey Hole. An old legend, associated with these caves, claims that they were once the lair of a witch. This witch supposedly plagued the region until she was turned to stone by a monk from Glastonbury Abbey. Sometimes this monk is named as Father Bernard and the general assumption is that these events occurred in the Middle Ages.

In 2007 a search of the Wookey Hole caves revealed several 'witch marks' in the third chamber, in the vicinity of a feature known as the witch's chimney.[10] These markings are protective wards, designed to drive away malign supernatural forces. They appear to have been in common use between around 1550 and 1750, during the height of the early modern witch-hunts. Therein, lies the clue to the true origins of the story of the witch of Wookey Hole. An examination of the historic record shows that the earliest reference to the witch dates to 1628.[11] Prior to this, there is no record of any association between witches and Wookey Hole. The popular legend, as it turns out, appears early modern in origin.

In 1480, Wookey Hole caves were visited by William of Worcester, who provides us with a detailed account of his visit. In doing so he gives us an insight into the local traditions associated with them at this time. He tells us that at the entrance of the caves was a rock known as the 'Porter'. Apparently, it was the local custom that one should ask permission of the Porter before entering the cave. The rock formation that became known as the witch during the Early Modern period was described by William as a figure of a woman, spinning with a distaff. William also notes that a well in one of the inner caves contained holy water.[12] So, as it turns out, medieval folk tradition associated the caves with a holy well rather than a witch or evil magic. The figure that was later called a witch was simply a woman at work with her spinning in medieval eyes. Wookey Hole's more sinister reputation is, therefore, the product of the early modern world, not the medieval one. It is a good example of a place that appears to have a medieval story associated with it, but which was actually regarded quite differently in medieval times.

One famous mystery of the English landscape does not relate to any tangible feature in the landscape at all, natural or man-made. This is the myth of the lost land of Lyonesse. This land is one of the many kingdoms mentioned in Arthurian lore whose identity and precise location are clouded in uncertainty. Rather like the Isle of Avalon, we can only speculate as to whether it referred to a real place and, if so, which place it referred to. Lyonesse features in the tale of Tristan and Isoude. Sir Tristan is a knight who hails from the land of Liones (Lyonesse). The tale itself tells us little of this land, save for its close association with Cornwall. By implication, we might assume that it lay somewhere near to Cornwall.

In the fifteenth century, William of Worcester wrote in his *Itinerary* that between Saint Michael's Mount (just off the south Cornish coast) and the Isles of Scilly there had once been land. This land had contained woods and fields and no fewer than 140 parish churches.[13] In 1584, the topographer John Norton made the explicit connection between this mysterious sunken land and Lyonesse. Lyonesse was, therefore, identified as a lost land, sunken beneath the seas off the west Cornish coast.

Cornish folk tradition holds that this lost land was called Lethowsow. When it sank beneath the sea, only a single man escaped the cataclysm, galloping to safety on a white horse. This fellow was named Trevillian, and this apocryphal tale is represented in the Trevillian coat of arms (which features a white horse rearing up out of the sea). How many of these tales of lost Lyonesse can be traced back to the Middle Ages is questionable. However, stories about a strange lost land off the Cornish coast were certainly in circulation in the late Middle Ages.

Many of the myths and stories concerning the English landscape have their origins in medieval or even earlier times. However, stories of this sort are of an ever evolving, living nature. Over time these tales are added to and, in many cases new stories are created. The tales associated with Wookey Hole are a classic example. Here, the myths that grew up about the witch were presented as medieval but were in fact early modern in origin. On the other hand, genuine medieval tales of a holy well did not survive in folk tradition. The myths linked with the English landscape are not a fixed set of traditional narratives handed down from generation to generation. Instead, it is probably better to regard them as an ongoing dialogue between the land and its people.

On Bosworth Field

On 22 August 1485, Richard III lay dead on Bosworth field. A triumphant Henry Tudor was proclaimed king on Crown Hill that very day. But Henry VII (as he became) was a new kind of king, different from his predecessors. Richard III shared one thing in common with every other English king of the previous three centuries. Richard could trace his ancestry, through the male line, all the way back to Henry II, the very first Plantagenet king. Not so, Henry VII. He was not a Plantagenet. He was not even a member of the York or Lancastrian cadet branches of the Plantagenet family. He was a Tudor. As a new Tudor age dawned, it not only spelt the end of the Plantagenets but also the Middle Ages.

As we come to the end of our journey through the world of medieval myths and legends, it is a good opportunity to reflect. What exactly came to an end in 1485? The myths and supernatural beliefs of the Plantagenet world had been truly unique. Certainly, they built on what had come before. They drew inspiration from older stories from pagan times, from the classical world, and from the early Middle Ages. They were born of a fusion of Celtic traditions from Wales, Ireland, and Brittany; from the old pagan stories of the classical world; and from the Northern European traditions of Germany and Scandinavia.

However, it would be wrong of us to imagine that these stories were nothing more than simple re-imaginings of older traditions. It was much more than that. What we have is not simply the survival of old, pagan beliefs, sanitised and re-packaged for the Christian age. Of course, some old stories were appropriated. Most obviously, this occurred with many of the old classical myths. But, the Plantagenet age also witnessed the creation of genuinely new myths and beliefs.

Arthurian lore reached its creative zenith during the reign of the Plantagenets. Prior to the twelfth century, stories of Arthur had existed only in fragmentary form. Starting with Geoffrey of Monmouth, what began as a few passing references and the odd heroic poem evolved into a rich foundation mythology of the origins of Britain. The chivalric culture of Camelot could not have been conceived of in earlier times.

Robin Hood, the free yeoman of the forest, emerged as a true folk hero of the people in the late Middle Ages. He was a character who had no noble blood, was not a knight and, indeed, was not even a member of the gentry. Earlier times would have struggled to produce such a rich storytelling tradition around someone of such a lowly social status. There were, of course, limits. Robin Hood was a rebel, but he was no revolutionary. He was not a class hero advocating the overthrow of an unjust system. He was an outlaw seeking to expose corruption and hypocrisy within a system that he never fundamentally questioned.

Even the way society regarded magic changed fundamentally during the period. Old pagan beliefs served as a starting point but no more. The way magic was practiced and regarded changed radically, absorbing significant new ideas from the Arab world and, critically, from Christianity itself. Ritual necromancy required medieval Christian theology to function. Indeed, it relied far more on the church ritual of exorcism than it did on any earlier pagan understanding of magic. Most magic practiced during the medieval period was deeply infused with Christian liturgy, frequently borrowed from well-known prayers, bible passages, and rituals.

The Plantagenet period evolved its own unique myths and legends for two key reasons. The first was the multi-cultural nature of the Plantagenet realm itself. It was founded on a cultural melting pot of Celtic, Anglo-Saxon, Norse, Roman, and French. It was the influence of all these traditions working in combination, rather than any one of them on its own, that was so important. Together, they created something uniquely Plantagenet, something that could not have existed if any one of these influences had been absent.

The second key reason was medieval Christianity. Medieval Christianity was more than simply the religion of the Bible. It was an evolving, living source of its own unique mythology. The cult of saints, the miraculous power of relics, tales of marvels and miracles, and the evolution of Christian mysticism all feature prominently. These beliefs both informed and transformed the mythology of the age to the extent that its influence became all pervading. Everything from how people conceived of ghosts and fairies, to the tales of Arthurian knights, drew extensively on the wellspring of medieval Christian cosmology. Christian inspired mythology was not simply static nor was it interpreted with reference to rigid, unchanging biblical canon. It evolved and grew. New saints were added. New relics were discovered. New tales of miracles and marvels emerged. And, as Christian mysticism evolved, so too did the rich language of symbolism and imagery that accompanied it.

Many of these beliefs were, of course, uniquely medieval. The fantastic worldview of *The Golden Legend*, with its marvels and miracles, has not survived into the modern age. Over the century that followed Bosworth, *The*

Golden Legend was just one of many old certainties that were swept away. Protestantism toppled medieval Catholicism from its dominant position in the cultural life of Europe. The old hegemony, with its saints, relics, miracles, and mysticism did not survive the maelstrom of the Reformation. Puritanism stripped Christianity back to its basics. More than that, it actively set out to dismantle what it saw as a misguided medieval legacy of superstition and false teaching.

As beliefs changed, so too did the world itself. The age of pike and shot rendered the old age of knights and castles obsolete. As the sun set on Bosworth field, the old stories, myths, and folk practices of the medieval world became part of the past. They belonged to a world that was passing. Throughout the Middle Ages, Arthur and his knights may have been regarded as mythical figures, but they remained relevant. War, throughout the period, was still fought by knights on horseback. Men just like Sir Lancelot continued to lead armies into battle. Knights continued to fight in much the same way as their mythical forebears had supposedly done. This happened at Bosworth too. But Bosworth also featured artillery pieces and men using early handguns. The world was changing. In the age of black powder that followed, the knight would lose his military relevance.

In an age of religious reform and puritanism, there would be little room for the old stories. Saint George and his dragon were increasingly out of step with a Tudor regime that frowned on saints and the world of *The Golden Legend*. Tales of Robin Hood, the master archer, certainly held a special relevance in the age of Crecy and Agincourt but not in the age of the musket. The idea that one might find dragons lurking in the remote corners of the world became increasingly untenable as more and more of the world was explored. And a belief in magic would gradually wither and die under the cold light of science.

Living, breathing, medieval mythology came to an end with advent of the early modern age. The world around which its stories had been woven was disappearing.

Now it is long gone. But it is by no means forgotten.

Knights may no longer ride out to do battle, but we remain intrigued by tales of their valour and their chivalrous ideals. We no longer use longbows, but we still warm to the idea of Robin Hood, the people's champion. We know dragons are not real, but we remain fascinated by them. The old medieval world, complete with its own unique myths and legends is long gone. But the memory of it remains with us as part of our identity today. In our modern age, we create our own stories but, be in no doubt, these stories continue to draw inspiration from our medieval past.

Notes

The Plantagenet World

1. York had a population of 12,100, Bristol 10,600. Only five other urban centres had populations exceeding 5,000 – Coventry, Norwich, Lincoln, Salisbury, and Lynn. Mortimer, *The Time Travellers Guide to Medieval England*, p. 10.
2. Orme, *Going to Church in Medieval England*, pp. 141-142.
3. Mortimer, *The Time Travellers Guide to Medieval England*, p. 46.
4. Mortimer, *The Time Travellers Guide to Medieval England*, p. 46-47.
5. Mortimer, *The Time Travellers Guide to Medieval England*, p. 39.
6. Borough ordinances of Worcester, cited in Mortimer, *The Time Travellers Guide to Medieval England*, Article 34, p. 231 and Article 68, p. 232.
7. Mortimer, *The Time Travellers Guide to Medieval England*, p. 256.
8. Weir, *Lancaster and York*, p. 288.
9. Friar Clyn, states that he wrote his account of the Black Death in Ireland just in case there were any survivors. By implication, the friar was clearly uncertain as to whether there would be any. There would be survivors. However, the good friar would not be among them. Gummer, *The Scourging Angel*, p. 92.
10. Kieckhefer, *Magic in the Middle Ages*, p. 67.

The Legacy of Classical Antiquity

1. Charlemagne's reforms triggered a renaissance in Latin literature. Without it, it is quite possible that many classical works would have been lost. Over 9,000 Latin manuscripts survive from this period: the entire surviving corpus of classical literature. Heather, *The Restoration of Rome*, pp. 339-340.
2. Mortimer, *The Fears of Henry IV*, pp. 45-46.
3. Ovid, *Metamorphoses,* Book 1, p. 29.
4. Nennius, *Historia Brittonum*, pp. 7 and 17.
5. Wood, *In Search of the Dark Ages*, pp. 10-11.
6. Wetherbee, 'Statius', in *Classical Reception in English Literature*, p. 227.
7. Minnis, *Other Worlds*, pp. 425-426.

Tales of the Druid Bard

1. Jones and Jones, *The Mabinogion*, p. ix.
2. Many of the triads are older than thirteenth century. However, they also include some that are late medieval (fourteenth and fifteenth century). Some were not recorded until even later. Some fragments can be dated all the way back to the nineth century. Bromwich, *Trioedd Ynys Prydein*, pp. xvi-lii.
3. Bromwich, *Trioedd Ynys Prydein*, p. 228.
4. Lewis and Williams, *The Book of Taliesin*, pp. xxxii-xxxiii.
5. Lewis and Williams, *The Book of Taliesin*, pp. 59-60.
6. Skene, *The Four Ancient Books of Wales*, p. 277.
7. Lewis and Williams, *The Book of Taliesin*, p. xxvii.
8. Lewis and Williams, *The Book of Taliesin*, p. 214.
9. Jones and Jones, *The Mabinogion*, pp. 3-5.
10. Lewis and Williams, *The Book of Taliesin*, pp. 98-101.
11. Lewis and Williams, *The Book of Taliesin*, p. 55.
12. Lewis and Williams, *The Book of Taliesin*, p. 99.
13. Lewis and Williams, *The Book of Taliesin*, p. 13.

The Mead Hall of Beowulf

1. Bede identifies the conversion of the Isle of Wight, in 686, as the time when Britain finally became wholly Christian. Bede, *Ecclesiastical History of the English People*, pp. 230-231.
2. Brondsted, *The Vikings*, p. 276.
3. Alexander, *Beowulf*, p. 11.
4. Wood, *In Search of the Dark Ages*, pp. 74-75.
5. Alexander, *Beowulf*, p. 56.
6. Alexander, *Beowulf*, p. 65.
7. Westwood and Simpson, *The Lore of the Land*, p. 25.
8. Crawford, *The Poetic Edda*, p. 126.
9. Giles and Ingram, *The Anglo-Saxon Chronicle*, AD 793.

Skalds of the North

1. Hutton, *The Stations of the Sun*, p. 7.
2. Brondsted, *The Vikings*, pp. 194-209.
3. By Sturluson's time (the early thirteenth century), most well-educated Christians in Western Europe would have been very familiar with classical stories concerning Troy via Ovid and Virgil. Sturluson is no exception. For him, myths concerning the old Norse gods could be explained by presenting them as culturally superior Trojan lords, natural masters of a more primitive pagan society. After having provided this context in his Prologue, Troy is hardly mentioned again in the main narratives and the stories generally avoid further Christian references.

4. Crawford, *The Poetic Edda*, p. xxi.
5. Crawford, *The Poetic Edda*, pp. 42-43.
6. Sturluson, *The Prose Edda*, p. 36.
7. Sturluson, *The Prose Edda*, p. 39.
8. Sturluson, *The Prose Edda*, p. 12.
9. Sturluson, *The Prose Edda*, p. 39.
10. Sturluson, *The Prose Edda*, p. 26.
11. Sturluson, *The Prose Edda*, p. xxv.
12. Sturluson, *The Prose Edda*, p. 71.
13. Sturluson, *The Prose Edda*, p. 77.

Tales from the Island of Destiny

1. Jones, *The Plantagenets*, pp. 79-80.
2. Lindahl, McNamara, and Lindow, *Medieval Folklore*, pp. 214-215.
3. Gantz, *Early Irish Myths and Sagas*, p. 170.
4. Gantz, *Early Irish Myths and Sagas*, p. 86.
5. Lindahl, McNamara, and Lindow, *Medieval Folklore*, pp. 63-64.
6. Lindahl, McNamara, and Lindow, *Medieval Folklore*, p. 64.
7. In the *Cattle Raid of Cooley*, she manifests as a crow, a beautiful maiden, an old woman, a wolf, and even an eel.
8. Gray, *Cath Maige Tuired.*
9. Gantz, *Early Irish Myths and Sagas*, p. 58.
10. Gantz, *Early Irish Myths and Sagas*, pp. 251-255.
11. Gantz, *Early Irish Myths and Sagas*, p. 45.
12. Gantz, *Early Irish Myths and Sagas*, p. 11.

Conversion and Transformation

1. Orme, *Going to Church in Medieval England*, p. 204.
2. Orme, *Going to Church in Medieval England*, pp. 203-204.
3. Orme, *Going to Church in Medieval England*, pp. 53-55.
4. Bede, *Ecclesiastical History of the English People*, p. 77.
5. The early medieval account given by Bede, in the eighth century, mentions nothing of this story. Bede simply states that Augustine performed miracles that helped prove the truth of the Christian message to the pagan locals. The first mention of this particular tale dates to Goscelin and William of Malmsbury in the early twelfth century. Westwood and Simpson, *The Lore of the Land*, p. 212.
6. Revell, *Religious and Ritual Practices in the Western Provinces*, pp. 219-222.
7. Bede, *Ecclesiastical History of the English People*, pp. 91-92.
8. Orme, *Going to Church in Medieval England*, p. 12-13.

Saints and Martyrs

1. Bede, *Ecclesiastical History of the English People*, p. 152.
2. Bede, *Ecclesiastical History of the English People*, p. 152.
3. De Voragine, *The Golden Legend*, p. 277.
4. De Voragine, *The Golden Legend*, p. 102.
5. De Voragine, *The Golden Legend*, p. 103.
6. Mortimer, *The Perfect King*, p. 278.
7. De Voragine, *The Golden Legend*, pp. 238-242.
8. De Voragine, *The Golden Legend*, p. 392.
9. De Voragine, *The Golden Legend*, p. 409.
10. De Voragine, *The Golden Legend*, p. 369.
11. De Voragine, *The Golden Legend*, pp. 650-651.
12. Barker *Agincourt*, pp. 283-284.

Relics and Holy Sites

1. Freeman, *Holy Bones*, p. 51.
2. Freeman, *Holy Bones*, p. 26.
3. Bishop Vitricius, quoted in Freeman, *Holy Bones*, p. 13.
4. Freeman, *Holy Bones*, p. 13.
5. Freeman, *Holy Bones*, pp. 209-210.
6. Freeman, *Holy Bones*, p. 208.
7. Mortimer, *The Fears of Henry IV*, pp. 111-112.
8. Mortimer, *The Time Travellers Guide to Medieval England*, pp. 266-267.
9. Mortimer, *The Time Travellers Guide to Medieval England*, p. 269.
10. De Voragine, *The Golden Legend*, p. 282.
11. Gummer, *The Scourging Angel*, p. 88

Visions, Prophecy, and Mysticism

1. The full version of this story is found in Chapter 12 of Bede's *Ecclesiastical History of Britain*, pp. 284-287.
2. Runciman, *A History of the Crusades, 1 The First Crusade*, pp. 236-249.
3. Runciman, *A History of the Crusades, 2 The Kingdom of Jerusalem*, pp. 252 -253.
4. Coulton, *Medieval Panorama*, Vol. 2: *The Horizons of Thought*, p. 167.
5. Meister Eckhart, quoted in Coulton, *Medieval Panorama*, p. 161.
6. Hildegard of Bingen, quoted in Maddocks, *Hildegard of Bingen*, p. 55.
7. Constant, *Concepts of Prophecy in the Middle Ages*, pp. 36-38.
8. Constant, *Concepts of Prophecy in the Middle Ages*, p. 75.
9. Constant, *Concepts of Prophecy in the Middle Ages*, pp. 240-244.

Magic in the Middle Ages

1. Henry IV introduced the first legal sanctions against heresy in 1401. These measures were introduced to combat the Lollardy (an early form of proto-Protestantism). Mortimer, *The Fears of Henry IV*, pp. 235-236.
2. Kieckhefer, *Magic in the Middle Ages*, p. 10.
3. Kieckhefer, *Magic in the Middle Ages*, pp. 49-50.
4. Kieckhefer, *Magic in the Middle Ages*, p. 30.
5. Levak, *The Witch-Hunt in Early Modern Europe*, p. 45.
6. Kieckhefer, *Magic in the Middle Ages*, p. 12.

Common or Folk Magic

1. Kieckhefer, *Magic in the Middle Ages*, pp. 57-90.
2. Kieckhefer, *Magic in the Middle Ages*, p. 65.
3. Anglo-Saxon spells are usually directed against maladies caused by elves. In some cases, the spell suggests these maladies were caused by small darts or arrows, known as 'elf-shot'. In the main, horses and cattle appear to have been considered most at risk from elven darts. Storms, *Anglo-Saxon Magic*, p. 24.
4. Kieckhefer, *Magic in the Middle Ages*, p. 71.
5. Kieckhefer, *Magic in the Middle Ages*, p. 77.
6. Bennett, *Richard II and the Revolution of 1399*, p. 112.
7. Kieckhefer, *Magic in the Middle Ages*, p. 59.
8. Kieckhefer, *Magic in the Middle Ages*, pp. 3-5.

Learned Magic

1. The scholar Marsilio Ficino was commissioned to undertake the translation on behalf of Florentine banker, Cosimo de' Medici. Kieckhefer, *Magic in the Middle Ages*, p. 145.
2. Plautus, '*Amphitro*', 1-25, quoted in Beard, North, and Price, *Religions of Rome*, p. 29.
3. Translation by Issac Newton, Keynes MS 28, 2.
4. Kieckhefer, *Magic in the Middle Ages*, p. 13.
5. *Picatrix* is the Latin name for this book. The original Arabic name is *Ghāyat al-Ḥakīm* (The Goal of the Wise). It was most likely compiled by Maslama ibn Ahmad al-Majriti, an Andalusian mathematician working in the late tenth and early eleventh century. However, this attribution is contested.

Necromancy and Demons

1. Kieckhefer, *Magic in the Middle Ages*, p. 6-8.
2. Ruys, *Demons in the Middle Ages*, pp. 93-94.
3. Kieckhefer, *Magic in the Middle Ages*, p. 158.

4. Ruys, *Demons in the Middle Ages*, pp. 5-6.
5. *The Latin Vulgate New Testament Translation*, Chapter 12, Verse 9.
6. Ruys, *Demons in the Middle Ages*, p. 39.
7. Ruys, *Demons in the Middle Ages*, pp. 42-43.

Heresy and Witchcraft

1. Freeman, *Holy Bones*, p. 85.
2. Costen, *The Cathars and the Albigensian Crusade*, pp. 73-74.
3. Barber, *The Trial of the Templars*, pp. 248-249.
4. Mortimer, *The Fears of Henry IV*, p. 235.
5. Kieckhefer, *Magic in the Middle Ages*, pp 198-199.
6. Johnson, *The Shadow King*, pp. 173-176.
7. Levak, *The Witch-Hunt in Early Modern Europe*, pp. 54-55.

Ghosts and the Walking Dead

1. Englander, Norman, O'Day, and Owens, *Culture and Belief in Europe*, pp. 16-17.
2. Englander, Norman, O'Day, and Owens, *Culture and Belief in Europe*, p. 18.
3. Gordon, *The Walking Dead in Medieval England*, pp. 85-88.
4. William of Newburgh, quoted in Gordon, *The Walking Dead in Medieval England*, p. 108.
5. Gordon, *The Walking Dead in Medieval England*, pp. 213-215.
6. Schmitt, *Ghosts in the Middle Ages*, pp. 82-83.
7. Schmitt, *Ghosts in the Middle Ages*, p. 82.
8. Pálsson and Edwards, *Eyrbyggja Saga*, p. 95.
9. Based on Giles & Ingram, *The Anglo-Saxon Chronicle*, AD 1127.
10. See Schmitt, *Ghosts in the Middle Ages*, pp. 93-121 for a fuller discussion of this phenomena.
11. Englander, Norman, O'Day and Owens, *Culture and Belief in Europe*, p. 17.
12. Malory, *Le Morte D'Arthur*, Vol. 2, p. 511.

Chivalric Mythology

1. Keen, *Chivalry*, p. 52.
2. Southworth, *The English Medieval Minstrel*, p. 39.
3. Keen, *Chivalry*, p. 51.
4. Keen, *Chivalry*, p. 103.
5. Freeman, *Holy Bones, Holy Dust*, pp. 117-118.
6. Southworth, *The English Medieval Minstrel*, p. 33.
7. Keen, *Chivalry*, p. 48.
8. Keen, *Chivalry*, p. 47.
9. Copeland, *Classical Reception in English Literature*, p. 256.
10. Keen, *Chivalry*, p. 116.

11. Keen, *Chivalry*, p. 102.
12. Keen, *Chivalry*, pp. 121-123.

Arthurian Lore

1. Wood, *In Search of the Dark Ages*, p. 53.
2. Monmouth, *The History of the Kings of Britain*, p. 51.
3. Wood, *In Search of the Dark Ages*, pp. 44-45.
4. Monmouth, *The History of the Kings of Britain*, p. 217.
5. Monmouth, *The History of the Kings of Britain*, p. 282.
6. Monmouth, *The Life of Merlin*, pp. 6-7.
7. De Troyes, *Arthurian Romances*, p. 1.
8. There were probably at least a couple of dozen female troubadours (or, more accurately, *trobairitz*) active during the period between the mid-twelfth and mid-thirteenth century. These women mainly worked in southern French courts and wrote in the Occitan language. Like their male counterparts, the theme of their music was courtly love.
9. De Troyes, *Arthurian Romances*, p. 207.
10. Lupak, *An Oxford Guide to Arthurian Legend and Literature*, pp. 104-108.
11. Malory, *Le Morte D'Arthur*, Book 21, Chapter VII.

Knights of the Round Table

1. De Troyes, *Arthurian Romances*, p. 265.
2. The theme of adulterous love was taken to a shocking extreme in this story. Amorous adoration of a dashing knight for a powerful lady was a common theme in courtly romances of the time. It was not unusual for these ladies to be married to a powerful lord and, therefore, be of social rank significantly higher than their knight. However, courtly love was typically portrayed as a chaste love, romantic, pure, and unconsummated. At the very least, it was a love that had to be kept secret. However, Lancelot and Guinevere's love in this tale is sinfully consummated, seemingly with no consequences.
3. Professor Tolkien dates *Sir Gawain* to c. 1400. Although we do not know the author's name, Tolkien believed his language placed him in the West Midlands. Tolkien, *Sir Gawain and the Green Knight*, p. 1.
4. See p. 42, the story of Bricrui's feast.
5. Translated from Morris, *Sir Gawayne and The Green Knight, Lines 2189-2192.*

Merlin and Morgen Le Fay

1. Bromwich, *Trioedd Ynys Prydein*, p. 458.
2. Monmouth, *The History of the Kings of Britain*, pp. 166-167.
3. Malory, *Le Morte D'Arthur*, vol. 1, pp. 58-59.
4. Monmouth, G, *The Life of Merlin,* pp. 26-27.

5. Lindahl, McNamara, and Lindow, *Medieval Folklore*, p. 280.
6. Lindahl, McNamara, and Lindow, *Medieval Folklore*, p. 280.
7. Malory, *Le Morte D'Arthur*, vol. 1, p. 12.

The Holy Grail

1. De Voragine, *The Golden Legend*, p. 276.
2. Freeman, *Holy Bones*, p. 87.
3. De Troyes, *Arthurian Romances*, p. 5.
4. De Troyes, *Arthurian Romances*, p. 425.
5. De Troyes, *Arthurian Romances*, p. 457.
6. Lindahl, McNamara, and Lindow, *Medieval Folklore*, p. 184.
7. Lindahl, McNamara, and Lindow, *Medieval Folklore*, p. 22.
8. Malory, *Le Morte D'Arthur*, vol. 2, p. 361.

The Matter of England

1. Drake, Salisbury, and Herzman, *Four Romances of England.*
2. In 1362, Edward III introduced the statute of pleading which allowed cases to be admitted in court in the English language for the first time. It reflected the fact that French, by this time, was losing its preeminent position in Plantagenet culture. Jones, *The Plantagenets*, pp. 600-601.
3. Mortimer, *The Time Travellers Guide to Medieval England*, p. 39.
4. The real Faulk was one of many barons who rebelled against King John and forced the signing of the Magna Carta. His career seems to have trodden a very thin line between rebellion and outright banditry. Keen, *The Outlaws of Medieval Legend*, p. 40.
5. In addition to at least five different Middle English versions of Sir Bevis, there were at least three French/Anglo-Norman versions as well as versions in Dutch, Celtic, Russia, Old Norse, Italian, Romanian, and Yiddish.
6. Drake, Salisbury, and Herzman, *Four Romances of England*, Introduction.
7. Medieval dragons came in a variety of types. Whilst some were fire breathing, many are described as poisonous – breathing poisonous or plague bearing fumes or having a poisonous sting. In the case of Bevis' dragon, it spits venom caustic enough to dissolve armour and induce leprous sores. See discussion of dragons on p. 207.
8. Keen, *The Outlaws of Medieval Legend*, p. 79.
9. Keen, *The Outlaws of Medieval Legend*, p. 80.

Folklore, Storytelling, and Community

1. Southworth, *The English Medieval Minstrel*, p. 8.
2. The York Corpus Christi Pageants were first staged in the fourteenth century. The earliest attested Pageant was in 1376. The York Pageant ran throughout the later Middle Ages and into early modern times. The tradition was suppressed by the Tudors in the late 1560s, but later revived during the twentieth century. Beadle, *Medieval English Theatre*, p. 85.

3. Beadle, *Medieval English Theatre*, p. 219.
4. Beadle, *Medieval English Theatre*, p. 15.
5. Beadle, *Medieval English Theatre*, p. 14.
6. Southworth, *The English Medieval Minstrel*, p. 17.
7. Southworth, *The English Medieval Minstrel*, pp. 18-19.
8. Bower, quoted in Holt, *Robin Hood*, p. 40.
9. Barton, *The Shakespearean Forest*, p. 70.
10. Langland, *Piers the Ploughman*, vol. 1., lines 3275-3278.

Robin Hood and the Greenwood

1. Keen, *The Outlaws of Medieval Legend*, p. 97.
2. King Edward I became king in 1272. He was succeeded by his son Edward II and then by his grandson Edward III. As a result, a King Edward was on the throne of England from 1272 until the death of Edward III in 1377. *Geste* was, therefore, set at some time during this period.
3. Holt, *Robin Hood*, pp. 15-16.
4. Holt, *Robin Hood*, p. 33.
5. Keen, *The Outlaws of Medieval Legend*, pp. 162-163.
6. Holt, *Robin Hood*, p. 145-146. The staff is mentioned in early Robin Hood tales but not as a weapon of choice for Robin. In 'Robin Hood and the Potter', the Potter is armed with a quarterstaff, but Robin fights with a sword and buckler.
7. Holt, *Robin Hood*, pp. 160-166.
8. The early fifteenth-century outlaw 'Friar Tuck' appears to have been active from at least 1417 until at least 1429. His real name was Robert Stafford, a chaplain from Lindfield in Sussex. Holt, *Robin Hood*, pp. 58-59.
9. Keen, *The Outlaws of Medieval Legend*, pp. 176-177.
10. Keen, *The Outlaws of Medieval Legend*, p. 177.
11. Holt, *Robin Hood*, p. 162.
12. Holt, *Robin Hood*, p. 45.
13. Holt, *Robin Hood*, pp. 49-50.
14. Holt, *Robin Hood*, p. 52.

Of Earl Randolph and other Folktales

1. Alexander, 'Ranulf III', p. 153.
2. Barker *Agincourt*, p. 294.
3. Beadle, *Medieval English Theatre,* p. 14.
4. There was no concept of Father Christmas as we would recognise him during medieval times. The earliest English manifestation of an embryonic Santa can be found in a carol written by the Reverend Richard Smart during the 1460s. It features a character called 'Sir Christmas' who announces Christ's birth and encourages those who heard the good news to make merry. Ricket, *Ancient English Christmas Carols*, p. 218.

5. Keen, *The Outlaws of Medieval Legend*, p. 124.
6. Bouwman and Besamusca, *Of Reynaert the Fox*, pp. 42-43.

Festivals, Rituals and Folk Traditions

1. Hutton, *The Stations of the Sun*, p. 151.
2. Hutton, *The Stations of the Sun*, p. 180.
3. Orme, *Going to Church in Medieval England*, p. 288.
4. Orme, *Going to Church in Medieval England*, p. 140.
5. Cosman, *Medieval Holidays and Festivals*, p. 43.
6. Hutton, *The Stations of the Sun*, p. 264.
7. Hutton, *The Stations of the Sun*, p. 207.
8. Hutton, *The Stations of the Sun*, p. 214.
9. Hutton, *The Stations of the Sun*, p. 218.
10. Hutton, *The Stations of the Sun*, pp. 220-223.
11. Hutton, *The Stations of the Sun*, p. 225.
12. Malory, *Le Morte D'Arthur*, vol. 2, pp. 427-428.
13. Hutton, *The Stations of the Sun*, p. 242.
14. Mithen, *After the Ice*, p. 195.
15. Orme, *Going to Church in Medieval England*, pp. 294-295.
16. Robert Brunne, quoted in Hutton, *The Stations of the Sun*, p. 245.
17. See discussion of the York pageant plays on pp.166-167.
18. De Voragine, *The Golden Legend*, p. 336.
19. De Voragine, *The Golden Legend*, p. 336.
20. Hutton, *The Stations of the Sun*, p. 314.
21. Gantz, *Early Irish Myths and Sagas*, p. 155.
22. Hutton, *The Stations of the Sun*, pp. 367-369.
23. Modern Gaulish, *The Coligny Calendar and Celtic New Year.*
24. Hutton, *The Stations of the Sun*, p. 362.
25. De Voragine, *The Golden Legend*, p. 666.
26. Hutton, *The Stations of the Sun*, p. 13.
27. Mortimer, *The Time Travellers Guide to Medieval England*, p. 250.
28. Hutton, *The Stations of the Sun*, pp. 12-13.
29. Hutton, *The Stations of the Sun*, p. 92.
30. Hutton, *The Stations of the Sun*, p. 100.

Woodwose, Giants, and Beast-men of the Wild

1. Husband, *The Wild Man*, p. 1-3.
2. Husband, *The Wild Man*, p. 23.
3. Tolkien elects to translate the woodwose as a 'forest troll' in his version of *Sir Gawain and the Green Knight*. In doing so he sought to portray this creature in a language he felt the modern readers could more easily relate to. Tolkien, *Sir Gawain and the Green Knight*, p. 33.

4. de Troyes' description of the giant herdsman draws on medieval racist stereotyping. He presents his herdsman as resembling a Moor (among other things). This reflects that fact that white medieval Europeans associated sub-Saharan Africans with savagery. De Troyes, *Arthurian Romances*, pp. 298-299.
5. Monmouth, *The History of the Kings of Britain*, p. 239.
6. Wood, *Fantastic Creatures in Mythology and Folklore*, p. 45.
7. Wood, *Fantastic Creatures in Mythology and Folklore*, pp. 45-46.
8. De Voragine, *The Golden Legend*, p. 85.
9. De Voragine, *The Golden Legend*, p. 85.

The Perilous Fairy

1. See reference to elves in Anglo-Saxon magical remedies on p. 81.
2. Storms, *Anglo-Saxon Magic*, p. 247.
3. Hutton, *The Making of the Early Modern British Fairy Tradition*, p. 7.
4. Kieckhefer, *Magic in the Middle Ages*, p. 73.
5. Hutton, *The Making of the Early Modern British Fairy Tradition*, p. 14.
6. Hefty, *The Supernatural in the Ethnographic Writings of Giraldus Cambrensis*, pp. 26-27.
7. Schwieterman, *Fairies, Kingship, and the British Past*, pp. 16-17.
8. Schmitt, *Ghosts in the Middle Ages*, p. 111.
9. Walter Map, quoted in Schwieterman, *Fairies, Kingship, and the British Past*, p. 16.
10. Kieckhefer, *Magic in the Middle Ages* p. 53.
11. Bromwich, *Trioedd Ynys Prydein*, p. 91.
12. Bromwich, *Trioedd Ynys Prydein*, p. 92.
13. Westwood, and Simpson, *The Lore of the Land*, pp. 846-847.
14. Shaijan, *Goblin Mythology*, p. 7.
15. Storms, *Anglo-Saxon Magic*, p. 50.
16. Kieckhefer, *Magic in the Middle Ages*, p. 107.
17. Hutton, *The Making of the Early Modern British Fairy Tradition*, p. 17.
18. Tolkien, *Sir Gawain and the Green Knight*, p. 124.
19. Tolkien, *Sir Gawain and the Green Knight,* p. 124.
20. Hutton, *The Making of the Early Modern British Fairy Tradition,* p. 12.
21. See earlier discussion of the nature of demons on pp. 93-94.

The Medieval Bestiary

1. Wood, *Fantastic Creatures in Mythology and Folklore*, p. 6-7.
2. Isidore, *The Etymologies*, pp. 73-74.
3. Wood, *Fantastic Creatures in Mythology and Folklore*, p. 13.
4. Wood, *Fantastic Creatures in Mythology and Folklore*, pp. 14-15.
5. Wood, *Fantastic Creatures in Mythology and Folklore*, p. 18.
6. Wood, *Fantastic Creatures in Mythology and Folklore*, pp. 24-25.

7. Wood, *Fantastic Creatures in Mythology and Folklore*, p. 26
8. Wood, *Fantastic Creatures in Mythology and Folklore*, p. 26
9. Wood, *Fantastic Creatures in Mythology and Folklore*, p. 27.
10. Isidore, *The Etymologies*, p. 257.
11. Wood, *Fantastic Creatures in Mythology and Folklore*, p. 199.
12. Wood, *Fantastic Creatures in Mythology and Folklore*, p. 119.
13. Herodotus, *The Histories*, p. 124.
14. Herodotus, *The Histories*, p. 124.
15. Ovid, *Metamorphoses*, p. 345.
16. Isidore, *The Etymologies,* p. 265.
17. Wood, *Fantastic Creatures in Mythology and Folklore*, p. 116.
18. Wood, *Fantastic Creatures in Mythology and Folklore*, p. 100.
19. Willetts, *The Civilisation of Ancient Crete,* p. 111.
20. Herodotus, (trans. Sélincourt, de A), *The Histories*, p. 219.
21. Isidore, *The Etymologies*, p. 252.
22. Wood, *Fantastic Creatures in Mythology and Folklore*, pp. 101-102.
23. Hesiod, 'Theogony', p. 31.
24. Westwood and Simpson, *The Lore of the Land*, p. 120.
25. Wood, *Fantastic Creatures in Mythology and Folklore*, pp. 50-52.
26. Isidore, *The Etymologies*, p. 245.
27. Westwood and Simpson, *The Lore of the Land*, p. 120.
28. Wood, *Fantastic Creatures in Mythology and Folklore*, p. 53.
29. Wood, *Fantastic Creatures in Mythology and Folklore*, p. 68.
30. Wood, *Fantastic Creatures in Mythology and Folklore*, p. 65.
31. Wood, *Fantastic Creatures in Mythology and Folklore*, p. 66.
32. Cooper, *Brewer's Book of Myth and Legend*, p. 106.

The Great Dragon

1. Ovid, *Metamorphoses*, p. 75.
2. De Voragine, *The Golden Legend*, pp. 239-240.
3. Orme, *Going to Church in Medieval England*, pp. 290-292.
4. Sturluson, *The Prose Edda*, p. 76.
5. Sturluson, *The Prose Edda*, pp. 96-97.
6. De Troyes, *Arthurian Romances*, p. 337.
7. Garmonsway, *The Anglo-Saxon Chronicle*, p. 55.
8. Monmouth, *The History of the Kings of Britain*, p. 171.
9. Monmouth, *The History of the Kings of Britain*, p. 201.
10. Jones and Jones, *The Mabinogion*, pp. 91-93.
11. Stead, *Celtic Dragons from the River Thames*, p. 10.
12. Westwood and Simpson, *The Lore of the Land*, p. 732.

Mysteries in the Landscape

1. Westwood and Simpson, *The Lore of the Land*, p. 20.
2. Westwood and Simpson, *The Lore of the Land*, p. 26.
3. Westwood and Simpson, *The Lore of the Land*, p. 28.
4. Westwood and Simpson, *The Lore of the Land*, p. 796.
5. Monmouth, *The History of the Kings of Britain*, pp. 196-197.
6. Westwood and Simpson, *The Lore of the Land*, pp. 42-43.
7. See earlier discussion of May-Eve bonfires on p. 174.
8. Crawford, *The Poetic Edda*, p. 60-71.
9. Hutton, *The Stations of the Sun*, p. 220.
10. Binding and Wilson, *Ritual Protection Marks in Wookey Hole and Long Hole*, p. 47.
11. Binding and Wilson, *Ritual Protection Marks in Wookey Hole and Long Hole*, p. 60.
12. Westwood and Simpson, *The Lore of the Land*, p. 656.
13. Westwood and Simpson, *The Lore of the Land*, p. 114.

Bibliography

Alexander, J.W. '*Ranulf III of Chester: An Outlaw of Legend?* ' *Neuphilologische Mitteilungen* 83, No. 2 (1982): 152-157

Alexander, M. (trans.). *Beowulf: A Verse Translation*. (London: Penguin Classics, 1973)

'Apocalypse of John, Chapter 12'. *The Latin Vulgate New Testament Translation.* Vulgate.org, https://vulgate.org/nt/epistle/revelation_12.htm, accessed 3/10/2023.

Barber, M. *The Trial of the Templars* (Cambridge: Cambridge University Press, 1978)

Barker, J. *Agincourt: The King, The Campaign, The Battle* (London: Abacus, 2015)

Barton, A. *The Shakespearean Forest* (Cambridge: Cambridge University Press, 2017)

Beadle, R. *Medieval English Theatre* (Cambridge: Cambridge University Press, 1994)

Beard, M., J. North, and S. Price. *Religions of Rome, Volume 2: A Sourcebook* (Cambridge: Cambridge University Press, 2001)

Bede. *Ecclesiastical History of the English People*. Translated by L. Sherley-Price, R.E. Latham, and D.H. Farmer (London: Penguin Classics, 1990)

Bennett, M. *Richard II and the Revolution of 1399* (Stroud: Sutton Publishing, 1999)

Binding, C.J., and L.J. Wilson. 'Ritual Protection Marks in Wookey Hole and Long Hole, Somerset'. *Proceedings of the University of Bristol Speleological Society* 25, no. 1 (2010): 47-73

Bogin, M. *The Women Troubadours* (New York: Norton, 2013)

Bouwman, A., and B. Besamusca. *Of Reynaert the Fox: Text and Facing Translation of the Middle Dutch Beast Epic Van Den Vos Reynaerde* (Amsterdam: Amsterdam University Press, 2009)

Broedel, H.P. *The Malleus Maleficarum and the Construction of Witchcraft: Theology and Popular Belief.* Studies in Early Modern European History. (Manchester: Manchester University Press, 2004)

Bromwich, R. (ed. and trans.). *Trioedd Ynys Prydein, the Triads of the Island of Britain* (Cardiff: University of Wales Press, 2014)

Brondsted, J. *The Vikings* (Harmondsworth: Pelican, 1980)

Cawley, A.C. (ed.). *Everyman and Medieval Miracle Plays* (London: J.M. Dent & Sons, 1986)

Constant, E.A. *Concepts of Prophecy in the Middle Ages: Inspired Exegesis, Visions from God, and the Interactions of Theory and Practice* (PhD Thesis, University of Michigan, 2016)

Cooper, J.J. *Brewer's Book of Myth & Legend* (Oxford: Helicon, 1993)
Copeland, R. (ed.) *Classical Reception in English Literature, Volume I: 800–1558* (Oxford: Oxford University Press, 2020)
Cosman, M.P. *Medieval Holidays and Festivals,* (Piatkus Books, London, 1984)
Costen, M. *The Cathars and the Albigensian Crusade* (Manchester: Manchester University Press, 1997)
Coulton, G.G. *Medieval Panorama, Vol. 2: The Horizons of Thought* (Glasgow: The Fontana Library, 1961)
Crawford, J. (ed.). *The Poetic Edda* (Indianapolis: Hackett Publishing, 2015)
Davis, N. (ed.). *The Paston Letters* (Oxford: Oxford World's Classics, 2008)
De Troyes, C. *Arthurian Romances*. Translated by W.W. Kibler and C.W. Caroll (London: Penguin Classics, 2004)
De Voragine, J. *The Golden Legend*. Translated by W.G. Ryan (Princeton: Princeton University Press, 2012)
Drake, G., E. Salisbury, and R.B. Herzman. *Four Romances of England: King Horn, Havelok the Dane, Bevis of Hampton, Athelston* (Kalamazoo: Medieval Institute Publications, 1997)
Englander, D., D. Norman, R. O'Day, and W.R. Owens. *Culture and Belief in Europe 1450–1600* (Oxford: Blackwell, 1998)
Feros Ruys, J. *Demons in the Middle Ages* (Leeds: ARC Humanities Press, 2017)
Freeman, C. *Holy Bones, Holy Dust* (New Haven: Yale University Press, 2012)
Gantz, J. (trans). *Early Irish Myths and Sagas* (Harmondsworth: Penguin Classics, 1981)
Garmonsway, G.N. (trans.). *The Anglo-Saxon Chronicle* (Londo: J.M. Dent & Sons, 1972)
Giles J.A. and J. Ingram. *The Anglo-Saxon Chronicle*. Project Gutenberg, 1996. https://www.gutenberg.org/cache/epub/657/pg657-images.html
Gilson, E., and A.H.C. Downes (trans.). *The Mystical Theology of Saint Bernard* (New York: Sheed & Ward, 1940)
Gordon, S.R. *The Walking Dead in Medieval England: Literary and Archaeological Perspectives* (Phd Thesis, University of Manchester, 2013)
Gray, E. *Cath Maige Tuired: The Second Battle of Mag Tuired.* CELT: Corpus of Electronic Texts: A Project of University College, Cork (2003). https://celt.ucc.ie/published/T300010.html, accessed on 9/10/2023.
Gummer, B. *The Scourging Angel: The Black Death in the British Isles* (London: Vintage, 2010)
Haas, R. 'Trojan Sodomy and the Politics of Marriage in the Roman d'Enéas'. *Exemplaria* 20, no. 1 (2008): 46-69
Heather, P. *The Restoration of Rome* (London: Macmillan, 2013)
Hefty, E. *The Supernatural in the Ethnographic Writings of Giraldus Cambrensis* (MA diss., University of Wales, Cardiff, 2010)
Herodotus. *The Histories*. Translated by A. de Sélincourt (London: Penguin Classics, 2003)
Hesiod. 'Theogony'. In *Hesiod and Theognis: Theogony, Works and Days, and Elegies*. Edited by D. Wender (London: Penguin Classics, 1973)

Holt, J.C. *Robin Hood.* (London: Thames and Hudson, 1982)
Husband, T. *The Wild Man, Medieval Myth and Symbolism* (New York: Metropolitan Museum of Art, 1980)
Hutton, R. 'The Making of the Early Modern British Fairy Tradition'. *The Historical Journal* 57, no. 4 (2014): 1135-1156
Hutton, R. *The Stations of the Sun* (Oxford: Oxford University Press, 2001)
Isidore of Saville. *The Etymologies*. Translated by S.A. Barney, W.J. Lewis, J.A. Beach, and O. Berghof (Cambridge: Cambridge University Press, 2006)
Johnson, L. *The Shadow King* (London: Head of Zeus, 2020)
Jones, D. *The Plantagenets* (London: William Collins, 2013)
Jones, G., and T. Jones (trans.) *The Mabinogion* (London: J.M Dent & Sons, 1989)
Keen, M. *Chivalry* (New Haven: Yale University Press, 1984)
Keen, M. *The Outlaws of Medieval Legend* (London: Routledge, 2000)
Kieckhefer, R. *Magic in the Middle Ages* (Cambridge: Cambridge University Press, 1990)
Kinsella, T. (trans.) *The Táin: From the Irish Epic Tain Bó Cuailnge* (Oxford: Oxford University Press, 2002)
Knight, S., and T.H. Ohlgren (ed.). *Robin Hood and Other Outlaw Tales*. (Kalamazoo: Medieval Institute, 1997)
Langland, W. *Piers the Ploughman*. Translated by J.F. Goodridge (London: Penguin Classics, 1966)
Langland, W. *The Vision and Creed of Piers Ploughman, Volume I of II* (Project Gutenberg, ebook, release date 2013) https://www.gutenberg.org/files/43660/43660-h/43660-h.htm#vs3277
Levak, B.P. *The Witch-Hunt in Early Modern Europe* (London: Pearson Education, 1995)
Lewis, G., and R. Williams (trans.). *The Book of Taliesin* (London: Penguin Classics, 2019)
Lindahl, C., J. McNamara, J. Lindow. *Medieval Folklore: A Guide to Myths, Legends, Tales, Beliefs, and Customs* (New York: Oxford University Press, 2002)
Lupak, A. *An Oxford Guide to Arthurian Legend and Literature* (Oxford: Oxford Quick Reference, 2007)
Maddocks, F. *Hildegard of Bingen.* (London: Headline Book Publishing, 2002)
Malory, T. *Le Morte DArthur*. Edited by E. Strachey (Project Gutenberg ebook, 2014) https://www.gutenberg.org/cache/epub/46853/pg46853-images.html#Page_488
Malory, T. *Le Morte D'Arthur, Vol. 1* (London: Penguin Classics, 2004)
Malory, T. *Le Morte D'Arthur, Vol. 2* (London: Penguin Classics, 2004)
Mithen, S. *After the Ice* (London: Phoenix, 2004)
Matthews, J., and C. Matthews. *British and Irish Mythology* (London: Diamond Books, 1995)
'The Coligny Calendar and Celtic New Year: An Analysis'. *Modern Gaulish.* (Academia.edu (2021). , accessed 3/10/2023) https://www.academia.edu/45673247/The_Coligny_Calendar_and_Celtic_New_Year_An_Analysis

Monmouth, G. *The History of the Kings of Britain*. Translated by L. Thorpe (London: Penguin Classics, 1966)

Monmouth, G. *The Life of Merlin* (CreateSpace Independent Publishing Platform, 2014)

Moore, R.I. *The Formation of a Persecuting Society* (Oxford: Blackwell, 1990)

Morris, R. (ed.). *Sir Gawayne and The Green Knight* (London: John Childs & Sons, 1869); accessed via Project Guttenberg https://www.gutenberg.org/files/14568/14568-h/14568-h.htm

Mortimer, I. *The Fears of Henry IV* (London: Vintage, 2008)

Mortimer, I. *The Perfect King* (London: Vintage, 2008)

Mortimer, I. *The Time Travellers Guide to Medieval England,* (Vintage, London, 2021)

Nennius. *Historia Brittonum: A Student Translation*. Translated by A. Wolf and J. Morris (Chichester, 1980; accessed from academia.edu, 08/11/2022)

Newton, I. Keynes MS 28, Kings College Library, Cambridge University.

Orme, N. *Going to Church in Medieval England* (New Haven: Yale University Press, 2022)

Ovid. *Metamorphoses*. Translated by M.M. Innes (London: Penguin Classics, 1955)

Pálsson, H., and P. Edwards (trans.). *Eyrbyggja Saga* (London: Penguin Classics, 1989)

Revell, L. 'Religious and Ritual Practices in the Western Provinces'. Greece & Rome 54, no. 2 (2007): 210-228

Ricket, E. *Ancient English Christmas Carols: 1400-1700* (London: Chatto & Windus, 1914)

Rollo, David. 'Benoît de Sainte-Maure's Roman de Troie: Historiography, Forgery, and Fiction'. *Comparative Literature Studies* 32, no. 2 (1995): 191-225

Runciman, S. *A History of the Crusades, 1: The First Crusade* (London: Penguin, 1991)

Runciman, S. *A History of the Crusades, 2 :The Kingdom of Jerusalem,* (London: Penguin, 1990)

Schmitt, Jean-Claude. *Ghosts in the Middle Ages* (Chicago: University of Chicago Press, 1998)

Schwieterman, P.J. *Fairies, Kingship, and the British Past in Walter Map's De Nugis Curialium and Sir Orfeo* (Berkely: University of California, 2010)

Shaijan, A. 'Goblin Mythology: A Brief Study of the Archetype, Tracing the Explications in English Literature'. Global Journal of Human Social Science 19, no. 4 (2019): 7-9

Skene, W.F. *The Four Ancient Books of Wales* (Edinburgh: Edmonston and Douglas, 1868)

Southworth, J. *The English Medieval Minstrel*. (Woodbridge: Boydell Press, 1989)

Stead, I. 'Celtic Dragons from the River Thames'. Antiquaries Journal 64 (1984): 269-279

Storms, G. *Anglo-Saxon Magic* (Gravenhage: Martinus Nijhoff, 1948)

Sturluson, S. *The Prose Edda*. Translated by J. Byock (London: Penguin Classics, 2005)

Tolkien, J.R.R. *Sir Gawain & the Green Knight, Pearl & Sir Orfeo*. (London: Unwin Paperbacks, 1979)

Tomaryn Brucker, M. 'Remembering the Trojan War: Violence Past, Present, and Future in Benoît de Sainte-Maure's "Roman de Troie"'. *Speculum* 90, no. 2 (April 2015): 366-390

Weir, A. *Lancaster and York: The Wars of the Roses* (London: Pimlico, 1998)

Westwood, J., and J. Simpson. *The Lore of the Land* (London: Penguin Books, 2006)

Willetts, R.F. *The Civilisation of Ancient Crete* (New York: Phoenix, 2004)

Wood, J. *Fantastic Creatures in Mythology and Folklore* (London: Bloomsbury Academic, 2018)

Wood, M. *In Search of the Dark Ages* (London: BBC, 1982)

Index